Blackpool Council
BUILDING A BETTER COMMUNITY FOR ALL

D1612853

Cov
majc
a firr
discip
preser

- Wh
- Hov
- How
- How
- How
- How
- What
- How d

Drawing
engaging
book gives the reader a sense of what it is to study archaeology and
be an archaeologist. An essential text for students studying A-Level
archaeology,   n
degree in arch   g
or becoming ir

3 4114 00628 0183

Don Henson is Honorary Lecturer at University College London and was Head of Education for 17 years at the Council for British Archaeology. He is currently Chair of the World Archaeological Congress Public Education Committee, Director of the Centre for Audio-Visual Study and Practice in Archaeology at University College London and member of the National Trust Learning and Engagement Panel. He has written numerous articles and books about archaeology in education, public archaeology and the media's representations of archaeology. He is also a Trustee of the Yorkshire Dales Landscape Research Trust and helps carry out excavation and survey in the Dales every summer.

Also available from Routledge

Archaeology: The Basics, 2nd Edition
Clive Gamble
978-0-415-35975-7

Archaeology: The Key Concepts
Edited by Colin Renfrew and Paul Bahn
978-0-415-31758-0

Doing Archaeology

A Subject Guide for Students

Don Henson

Routledge
Taylor & Francis Group

LONDON AND NEW YORK

First published 2012
by Routledge
2 Park Square, Milton Park, Abingdon, Oxon OX14 4RN

Simultaneously published in the USA and Canada
by Routledge
711 Third Avenue, New York, NY 10017

*Routledge is an imprint of the Taylor & Francis Group,
an informa business*

British Library Cataloguing in Publication Data
A catalogue record for this book is available from the British Library

Library of Congress Cataloging in Publication Data
Henson, Donald.
Doing archaeology : a subject guide for students / Don Henson.
p. cm. — (Doing series)
1.   Archaeology. 2.   Archaeology—Textbooks.   I. Title.
CC75.H46 2012
930.1—dc23
2012000367

ISBN: 978-0-415-60211-2 (hbk)
ISBN: 978-0-415-60212-9 (pbk)
ISBN: 978-0-203-10987-8 (ebk)

Typeset in Times
by RefineCatch Limited, Bungay, Suffolk

Printed and bound in Great Britain by
CPI Group (UK) Ltd, Croydon, CR0 4YY

Contents

List of figures

Acknowledgements

Writing this book has been a very personal exploration of what archaeology is and what it means. I am acutely conscious of how little I know about many aspects of my own subject. This book would not have been possible without the work of numerous archaeologists thinking and writing about their own relationships with the past and their own practice as archaeologists. Who these people are will be evident from Selected reading at the end of the book.

My thoughts about archaeology have been developing and maturing ever since I began to study it as an undergraduate student at Sheffield University in 1975, in what seems like a different age. My days and evenings were spent in many conversations with fellow students and staff. Since then conversations have continued with colleagues at work and at conferences. Thirty-six years of talking and thinking have gone into making this book. Those who have contributed to my vision of archaeology over that time are too many to list completely. If any of you are missing from this all too short list then I apologise and blame my faltering memory.

From my days at Sheffield University: Graeme Barker, Dave Barrett, Keith Branigan, Helen Bush, Judy Cartledge, Neil Carver, Chris Cumberpatch, Robin Dennell, Dave Fine, Andrew Fleming, Chris Gosden, Stan Green, Pete Herring, Val Higgins, Linda Hurcombe, Chris Judge, Clay Mathers, Nigel Mills, Andy Myers, Pat Phillips, Nick Ralph, Linda Smith, Sue Stallibrass, Sheila Sutherland, Bob Sydes, Robin Torrence, Marek Zvelebil and many, many others.

From my professional days: Yozo Akayama, Margaret Beaumont, Tony Blackman, Steve Collier, Tim Copeland, Mike Corbishley, Paloma Gonzalez Marcen, Mark Hall, Pippa Henry, Matthew Johnson, Pam Judkins, Richard Lee, Jenny Lintern, Graham McElearney, Roger Martlew, Wendy North, Katsuyuki Okamura, Vikki Pearson, Tim Schadla-Hall, Harvey Sheldon, Anthony Sinclair, Peter Stone, Ray Sutcliffe, Nino Vella, Gerry Wait, Gordon Watson, Graham Wilkinson, and all my former colleagues at the Council for British Archaeology (too many to mention by name).

Special thanks go to Sophie Thomson who asked me to write the book in the first place, and her colleagues Andy Humphries and Rebecca Shillabeer for being the faces of Routledge for me. The reviewers of my first draft appointed by Routledge made many useful and helpful comments. Thanks also to Mark Hall for commenting on the final draft. My biggest thanks go to Helen McKinlay for being kind enough to be my cover artist after suffering my supervision on field surveys in the Yorkshire Dales.

Introduction

This book is aimed at anyone interested in pursuing archaeology at university. It is for sixth-form students wondering what to do at university, or for adults in employment or retired who fancy doing a subject they've always had an interest in. It is for those who may be wanting to follow a career in archaeology or to do a degree purely out of interest. The book will also be useful for first-year university students to help map their future studies, or who may be wondering about switching their degree from their original choice to archaeology. The main focus will be on archaeology as practised in the United Kingdom.

Archaeology is a popular subject. Programmes about archaeology on television will reach at least 3 million viewers. Around 200,000 people do archaeology or some kind of activity related to the remains of the past in their spare time as volunteers. It is popular because it deals with fascinating other worlds, because it deals with interesting human behaviour and because it is fun. There are many opportunities to study archaeology through many kinds of course at a wide range of universities. Even if you do not want to become a professional archaeologist, an archaeology degree will give you skills that most employers value highly, and it will give you an interest you can follow for life. It will also give you an all-round view of human life and behaviour that will help you make sense of an increasingly bewildering present.

This book is not an account of the past 2.5 million years of human development, nor about the rise of ancient civilisations or the archaeological remains of Britain or anywhere else. It is an account of archaeology as a discipline and area of work. It shows you what archaeology is and why it is worth studying. This book will help to orient you, help you to understand what archaeology is and its place in relation to other subjects. It will also show you why archaeology is more important than simply a curiosity about the past.

Part I provides an overview of archaeology as an academic discipline, and as a practice in the field. It begins by defining archaeology; something that is surprisingly hard to pin down and is often misunderstood, even by archaeologists. The history of archaeology is explored to show how archaeology has become what it is today. Archaeologists think deeply about many aspects of human behaviour and their work is governed by various theoretical approaches to the subject. These approaches are covered as part of the chapters dealing with the different dimensions of archaeology: time, place and people. It also covers the main areas in which archaeologists work, both professionally and as volunteers, and the kinds of archaeology practised. Although archaeology is one subject, it makes more sense to talk about different archaeologies. The kind of archaeology practised by prehistorians is very different to that of industrial archaeologists. Likewise, field archaeology is very different to heritage management.

Part II sets archaeology into its wider context as a discipline related to others that deal with cultural heritage and as a practice within today's world. The value of what archaeologists do is explored, along with major debates in the subject and the international context of archaeology. How it can be used for the benefit of people today is an important aspect of archaeology and this is treated in its own chapter.

Part III includes an introduction to archaeological methods, and where to study and find out more about archaeology. Archaeology magazines, organisations and websites are key places for finding out more about archaeology. The final chapter provides an anecdotal illustration of archaeology as practised to show just how fulfilling and how much fun it can be.

This is a guide to archaeology, not a detailed textbook on how to do it. It covers many areas of modern archaeology, often in a ridiculously short space. This book could easily be twice the size and still not cover everything in the detail it deserves. In part, it is also a personal view of what archaeology could and should be. This is inevitable. Archaeology is deeply personal. Archaeologists are highly committed people, with a very emotive response to the past. Archaeology is more a way of life than a profession or hobby. Words spoken in a 1944 feature film sum up well the deep connection we have with the past and its emotive power:

Isn't the house you were born in the most interesting house in the world for you? Don't you want to know how your father lived, and his father? . . . Well, there are more ways than one of getting close to your ancestors. Follow the old road, and as you walk, think of them and the old England. They climbed Chillingbourne Hill, just as you did. They sweated and paused for breath, just as you did today, and when you see the bluebells in the spring, and the wild thyme, and the broom, and the heather, you're only seeing what their eyes saw. You ford the same rivers, the same birds are singing. When you lie flat on your back and rest, and watch the clouds sailing, as I often do, you're so close to those other people, that you can hear the thrumming of the hooves of the horses, and the sound of the wheels on the road, and their laughter and talk, and the music of the instruments they carried. And when I turn the bend of the road, where they too saw the towers of Canterbury, I feel I've only to turn my head to see them on the road behind me.

Thomas Colpeper in *A Canterbury Tale*, film written, produced and
directed by Michael Powell and Emeric Pressburger, 1944

We all have different opinions about what archaeology means to each of us, but for all of us it brings us closer to people from the past. I hope this book will inspire you to do archaeology, and follow the path that I took way back in time, in 1975. It is a journey I have greatly enjoyed, and still do. I hope you will too.

PART I

AN OVERVIEW OF ARCHAEOLOGY

What is archaeology?

'Archaeology is the discipline concerned with the recovery, syste-matic description and study of material culture in the past'

'The undisciplined and questionless accumulation of data has in itself no more value than the collection of engine numbers or cheese labels'

David Clarke (1968), *Analytical archaeology*, pp. 12, 21

Basic definitions

What is archaeology? This is a simple question with a complex answer. The word can be used in different ways by different people and in different countries. Let me give a simple definition before I go on to look at the complexities that lie behind it:

Archaeology is the study of how people in different places in the past have behaved through the physical evidence that they have left behind.

It is, the study of people in places in the past: the three dimensions of people, space (place) and time (past). These will be explored further in Chapters 3 to 5.

The word 'archaeology' is of Greek origin, αρχαιολογια (arkhaiologia), meaning 'what we can say about ancient times'. As a word, it was useful to help the Greeks distinguish archaeology from the accounts of the past gathered from people who had witnessed recent events, which was considered as history. This is still a fundamental distinction. Archaeology deals with events and activities directly through physical evidence rather than relying on what people have said or written about these things.

Spelling: archaeology or archeology?

The original Greek spelling αρχαιολογια (arkhaiologia) was borrowed by Latin as *archaeologia*. In English this becomes 'archaeology'. In the USA, both 'archaeology' and 'archeology' are used.

Archeology is sometimes said to refer to a scientific or anthropological approach to the subject, and archaeology to a classical or historical approach. On the other hand, Barbara Little has pointed out that 'archeology' was adopted to save money in printing by the US Government Printing Office in 1891 when they replaced all 'a+e' letters with a plain 'e'. This then spread as an alternative spelling used in government controlled or connected work.

Let us have a look at how people called archaeologists describe what they do. Most professional archaeologists begin their careers through studying at university. The Quality Assurance Agency (QAA) issues guidance, called benchmarks, for the teaching of undergraduate honours degrees in British universities. The benchmark for archaeology was written by archaeologists themselves and defines archaeology as:

> the study of the human past through material remains (the latter is an extremely broad concept and includes: evidence in the current landscape, from buildings and monuments to ephemeral traces of activity; buried material, such as artefacts, biological remains, and structures; and written sources).
>
> http://www.qaa.ac.uk/academicinfrastructure/
> benchmark/statements/drafts/archaeologydraft06.asp

However, most archaeologists work outside universities. Their employers have come together in the Archaeology Forum. The Forum defines itself as 'a group of organisations in the United Kingdom concerned with the archaeological investigation, management and interpretation of the historic environment – both buried remains and standing structures' (http://www.britarch.ac.uk/archforum/). Archaeology as actually practised, then, is more than simply the study of the past. It is also concerned with managing and interpreting the remains of the past. Interpreting is used here in the sense of communicating the evidence of the past to the public. We will look at where archaeologists work and the different kinds of archaeology being practised in Chapter 6.

A few words about terminology

In the United Kingdom, the objects of study of the archaeologist are sometimes referred to as the 'built environment'. Many archaeologists care for the remains of the past by working alongside planners, architects and others as part of the planning system in local government. All built environments are of course also historic in that they contain old as well as new buildings and other traces of human activity in the past. These old traces are usually called the 'historic environment'. How old does the environment have to be before it is protected by planners and others? Not as old as you might think; about a generation, or roughly 30 years in the UK, where buildings from the 1960s and 1970s are now being listed as worth conserving.

In the USA, the term used for the care and conservation of the historic environment is 'cultural resource management'. Properly, the term also covers the care and conservation of all historical aspects of culture, such as documents, folk traditions, performing arts and religious practices.

Other terms you will come across include 'archaeological heritage' and 'cultural heritage'. The UNESCO *Convention concerning the protection of the world cultural and natural heritage* (adopted 16 November 1972 in Paris) makes a distinction between culture and nature. Cultural heritage is defined in Article 1 (http://whc.unesco.org/en/convention text) as:

- monuments: architectural works, works of monumental sculpture and painting, elements or structures of an archaeological nature, inscriptions, cave dwellings and combinations of features, which are of outstanding universal value from the point of view of history, art or science;
- groups of buildings: groups of separate or connected buildings which, because of their architecture, their homogeneity or their place in the landscape, are of outstanding universal value from the point of view of history, art or science;
- sites: works of man or the combined works of nature and man, and areas including archaeological sites which are of outstanding universal value from the historical, aesthetic, ethnological or anthropological point of view.

Cultural heritage then covers a wide range of objects and sites of a historical, artistic or scientific nature. Anything made by human hand is part of that cultural heritage. In the UNESCO definition, 'elements or structures of an archaeological nature' are treated separately to other parts of cultural heritage. On the other hand, most archaeologists will say that they study all aspects of culture. The Council of Europe in *The European Convention on the protection of the archaeological heritage* (revised at Valletta in January 1992) defines archaeological heritage in Article 1 as:

> all remains and objects and any other traces of humankind from past times. The notion of archaeological heritage includes structures, constructions, groups of buildings, developed sites, moveable objects, monuments of other kinds as well as their context, whether situated on land or under water.
>
> (http://conventions.coe.int/treaty/en/treaties/html/143.htm)

It is easiest to think of all these terms as defining increasingly more specific objects of study and management. The widest term is 'heritage', covering every aspect of the world handed down from the past. Within this is cultural heritage, the works of humankind, and within this is archaeological heritage, in turn treated as the historic environment in the UK (Figure 1.1).

To confuse things further, the term 'culture' is also used with two specific meanings in archaeology, not always clearly distinguished. One meaning of culture is a generic term for all human behaviour, as in 'material culture' (the physical evidence left behind by human behaviour) or 'cultural evolution' where human society is deemed to develop through stages of development from 'simpler' to 'more complex'. However, culture is also used to refer to different associations of remains, each of which is a specific, named culture. These named cultures are assumed to reflect the existence of ethnic or political groups. Changes in how we think about archaeology mean we no longer see cultures in quite the same way and the idea of a culture is seldom used now in the UK. It is still commonly used in the rest of Europe, where culture history is a favoured type of archaeology tracing the history of particular cultures over time. The notion of cultural evolution is still common in the USA where it has moved a long way from its original version, and been shorn of its nineteenth-century racist overtones. Both the global/general notion of human culture and the local/specific notion of particular cultures are still therefore very much part of archaeology.

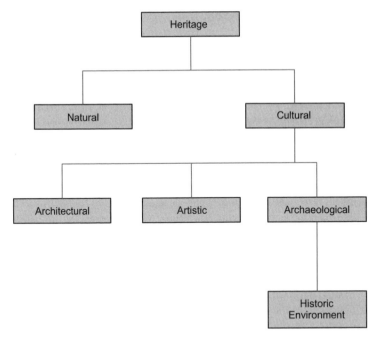

Figure 1.1 **Archaeology's place within heritage**

Culture

An archaeological culture is a recurring pattern of types of artefact or structure that occurs in one geographical area during a particular period of time. Here are summaries of representative definitions of culture by two influential twentieth-century archaeologists:

- Gordon Childe (1956) *A short introduction to archaeology*: 'culture is patterns of behaviour common to a group of persons, many of which are expressed in visible differences in material objects. A specific culture is formed of types of artefact associated together within a definite area or province.'
- James Deetz (1967) *Invitation to archaeology*: 'culture is learned human behaviour, and the habits and customs of any human group are integrated in a systematic manner such that politics, society, art, religion and technology all affect one another, and help that society adapt to its environment. The archaeological record reflects the culture that produced it.'

Archaeology's friends and neighbours

Archaeology is a well-defined subject in university research and teaching. In the USA, it forms part of anthropology, which is seen as having four main fields: social (cultural) anthropology, linguistic anthropology, physical (biological) anthropology, archaeology. These are separate subjects in the United Kingdom and the rest of Europe. Archaeology is often linked with history and classics, in that both subjects deal with the past and the passage of events over time. Many ideas about how to look at ancient societies have been brought into archaeology from geography, as both share a concern with how people make a living in the landscape and how different societies in different places interact. Many early societies, especially prehistoric ones, had similar ways of life to modern groups of hunter-gatherers or farmers studied by social anthropologists, and ideas about how people organise themselves in society are shared with sociology. If archaeology is concerned with studying people in places over time then we can see it shares the study of time with history, the study of places with geography and the study of people with sociology and anthropology (Figure 1.2).

In the United Kingdom, academic subjects are classified by the Joint Academic Coding System (JACS) for purposes of applying to university and compiling statistics. In this, archaeology is split in two. Archaeological science is placed in group F with chemistry, physics, forensic science, astronomy, geography and geology, while non-science archaeology is placed in group

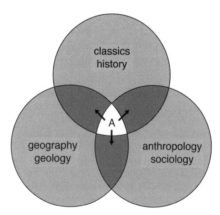

Figure 1.2 **Archaeology at the centre of other academic fields**

V with history, philosophy and theology. Anthropology and sociology are in group L with economics, politics and human geography. Archaeology finds a better home alongside geography for some purposes. In the UK Research Assessment Exercise for universities in 2008, archaeology was placed as part of main panel H with architecture and the built environment, planning and geography. All this is fairly confusing, but reflects the fact that archaeology encompasses an incredibly wide area of study and many aspects of human behaviour.

The UCAS university admissions service lists 78 per cent of archaeology undergraduate courses as BA (or MA in Scotland) arts courses and 22 per cent as BSc science courses. Archaeology can be studied on its own, or as a joint degree with other subjects. A wide range of other subjects can be studied with archaeology, but the commonest are: ancient history or classics, history, geography or ecology, anthropology or sociology, and forensics. Archaeology degrees are taught within a variety of different kinds of department in universities. Most of these are departments of archaeology, or archaeology with history or classics.

There are other subjects than archaeology that study cultural heritage. British universities offer various degrees in 'heritage studies'. A small number of courses are available in heritage studies itself, but there are more in various specialist areas, such as museums, heritage management, conservation, planning, tourism, public heritage. All of these deal with management and treatment of the physical traces of cultural and natural heritage. Archaeological heritage management is clearly part of this area of study and a few universities offer courses jointly covering archaeology and heritage.

Different archaeologies

What is not often appreciated, even by archaeologists, is that there is not one but several archaeologies. What I mean by this is that archaeology has within it various specialist areas of research. Archaeologists working in these areas tend to form separate sub-groups, publishing in different journals and often meeting in separate conferences. For example, university researchers in the UK will tend to attend the yearly TAG (Theoretical Archaeology Group) conference, while professional field archaeologists will tend to attend the Institute for Archaeologists annual conference. Some of the sub-groups use different techniques or theoretical approaches to the others. Classical archaeology and Egyptology are two immediately recognisable sub-groups, while others would include prehistoric archaeology, medieval archaeology, post-medieval and modern archaeology, industrial archaeology and maritime archaeology. In North America, there would be a distinction between anthropological archaeologists studying indigenous American (mainly prehistoric) societies and historical archaeologists studying the European settlers to North America. These are only a few of the divisions that are based on period or place of study. Other divisions are based on the application of particular archaeological techniques, such as forensic archaeology, geophysics or dendrochronology (dating wood by counting tree rings). Many archaeologists working in heritage management cover all periods and kinds of subjects.

The various sub-groups have national and international associations or societies to promote their interests and allow members to communicate with each other. A classical archaeologist might belong to the Society for the Promotion of Roman Studies in the UK and the International Association for Classical Archaeology, while a prehistorian might instead belong to the Prehistoric Society and the International Union of Pre- and Proto-Historic Sciences. Egyptologists could belong to the Egypt Exploration Society and the International Association of Egyptologists. There are some associations that cater for a wide range of different types of archaeologist. In the UK, these would include the Council for British Archaeology and, internationally, the World Archaeological Congress. For Europe, there is the European Association of Archaeologists. Key associations in the USA would be the Society for American Archaeology, the Society for Historical Archaeology and the Archaeological Institute of America.

What archaeology is, and is not

Let us return to our definition of archaeology as the study of how different people in the past have behaved through the physical evidence that they have left behind. The key characteristic that makes archaeology different to other subjects is that it studies the physical remains of the past. These remains can be large-scale landscapes, such as evidence of ancient field boundaries and settlements over 3,000 years old. They could be individual sites such as a burial mound or a cemetery, or the buried foundations of a Roman villa. Some archaeologists will study artefacts, such as flint tools. Others will study the canals, factories and other remains of eighteenth- and nineteenth-century industry. Yet others will study buildings still standing and in use since the medieval period. As we will see, there are also archaeologists who study the very recent past, of the last 100 years, or even last year. The past begins literally yesterday, and all physical evidence left behind by people can be studied by archaeologists. The evidence does not have to be ruins or buried remains.

It is important to know what archaeology is not. It is not the study of dinosaurs and other prehistoric animals or plants. The study of such fossils is palaeontology, which is part of the subject of geology. Where palaeontology and archaeology do overlap is in the study of ancient human fossils and the evolution of humans since they diverged from their ape cousins in Africa around 6 million years ago. Other subjects also study physical objects created by people but from a particular perspective. For example, art historians study art objects from ancient times to the present, and seek to place these works in their historical and contemporary context. Archaeology and art history therefore share some approaches and subject matter. A quick look through any directory of university courses for the public will reveal some interesting crossovers between such subjects as these. For example, the York University directory for 2010–11 included a course entitled *Anglo-Saxon treasure: Sutton Hoo and the Staffordshire hoard* placed not under archaeology but history of art. In the same directory, the course *An introduction to human evolution* is placed under science and social science, as representing palaeontology rather than archaeology. There are strong overlaps between archaeology and historical geography. A pioneer of this was a historian, W G Hoskins, who taught local history in adult education from the 1930s. He published his ground-breaking *The making of the English landscape* in 1955; Hoskins is accepted as a pioneer by historical geographers, local historians and landscape archaeologists.

Archaeology is not the pursuit of treasure. Forget images of Indiana Jones or Lara Croft battling through jungles and fighting off opponents to seize priceless antiquities. Looting of sites is not archaeology; it is unethical and illegal. Forget also the search for ancient civilisations and curses left behind to protect remains from being robbed. The reality is far more interesting and fun!

Archaeologists spend a great deal of their time recovering, conserving, classifying and analysing artefacts and monuments. They can be so focussed on the physical material that you would be forgiven for thinking that this is what they are studying. Is archaeology merely a technical exercise in how to classify and compare objects? The word is sometimes used in this way, and many people (even some archaeologists) assume that this is what archaeology is. The French intellectual historian, Michel Foucault, wrote a famous book, *The archaeology of knowledge*. This has nothing to do with archaeology. Foucault was using the word to describe a method of analysis.

11

Yet archaeology is so much more than a set of techniques. Archaeology is a search for what makes us human. The objects and sites are only important for what they tell us about the people who made and used them. The British archaeologist Sir Mortimer Wheeler repeatedly made this point in his book *Archaeology from the earth*:

> Year after year, individual after individual, learned society after learned society, we are prosaically revealing and cataloguing our discoveries. Too often we dig up mere things, unrepentantly forgetful that our proper aim is to dig up people.
>
> I envy the new generation its great opportunity, as never before, to dig up people rather than mere things, and to enable us, in the fullness of time, to view the past and the present as a single, continuous and not always unsuccessful battle between Man and his Environment and, above all, between Man and himself.
>
> (Wheeler, 1954)

Why archaeology matters

Archaeology covers every aspect of human existence, from birth to death. It takes in, along the way, how we feed ourselves, how we make a living, our artistic creativity, our spiritual beliefs and religious behaviours, the way we organise our society, our wars, our health and diseases, and many other things. It connects with a wide range of other subjects, and provides them with a time depth they do not themselves have. It offers to historians information about aspects of life not recorded in the documents handed down from the past, which in some periods only reflect the lives of wealthy and powerful adults (often males to the exclusion of women, children and the poor). For most of human existence (about 97 per cent of the time that our species has existed), archaeology is the only way to recover the human story as writing had not yet been invented.

David Lowenthal has suggested there are three ways in which we know the past: through memory, history and relics. Memory is very personal. No one else can share your own memories. Even two people who experience the same event will have different memories of it. These memories cannot be conserved. They are lost at death. They are also unreliable and can mislead us as to what happened and when. We may forget and revise our memories to suit how we want the past to have been. History is what was written down in the past and survives for us to read. People had to do the writing and wrote for a purpose. They were not necessarily full and accurate records of events. They may have been subjective and biased. Documents of early times often represent religious life and views, or the records of the rich and powerful. Relics on the other hand are widespread, and can represent all aspects of life in the past. They are the physical remains of the past. Through them, we can touch what people in the past also touched. But, relics are mute, needing interpretation to give up their information about past lives. It is the job of the archaeologists to bring life back to the relics.

There are other reasons why archaeology is important, which we will cover in Chapter 9. For now, I can say that archaeology is important for learning about ourselves. It is also fascinating as a voyage of exploration and discovery into our past. Importantly, it is also great fun.

2

How did archaeology begin?

> In that deluge of history, the account of the British monuments utterly perished: the discovery whereof I do here endeavour (for want of a written record) to work-out and restore after a kind of algebraical method, by comparing them . . . to make the stones give evidence for themselves.
>
> John Aubrey (1980) *Monumenta Britannica,* 1665–1693, p. 32

Archaeology has a long history and we can understand much about modern archaeology by understanding how it has developed. This chapter will outline how an interest in the physical remains of the past turned into a discipline called archaeology. Most archaeologists have a poor sense of their subject's history and have created an artificial difference between 'proper' modern archaeologists and early (somehow not 'proper') antiquarians. As we shall see, this is far too simplistic.

Ancient interest in the past

Today, we all know the past is different from the present and that the future will also be different. This has not always been so. In ancient Egypt, the past was an unchanging source of stability, a constant reference point to anchor the present. Ancient monuments were a part of everyday life. Crown Prince Khaemwaset (*c.*1283–1225 BC) restored many earlier temples and burial sites, and has been called, perhaps too eagerly, the first Egyptologist.

In ancient Babylon, kings looted the past to link themselves to past glories. King Nebuchadnezzar II (605–562 BC) excavated a 700-year-old temple in Larsa and had a school for boys with 1,600-year-old artefacts labelled 'for the marvel of the beholders'.

The idea that the past was different and worth being studied rather than looted or copied was developed by the ancient Greeks. Hekataios of Miletus (c.555–c.490/475 BC) wrote a chronological history of ancient Greek heroes, as well as a description of other places and peoples. To the modern eye, he was combining history with geography and anthropology, though these subjects did not then exist. Instead, the Greeks developed four themes that form the basis of all archaeology: the study of people (1) and places (2) in the past (3) through relics (4).

The word 'archaeology', as we have seen, is Greek in origin and two early writers were described by the Greeks as archaeologists: Hellanikos of Lesbos (496–411 BC) and Hippias of Elis (c.460–c.400 BC). This did not mean they were archaeologists in our sense of the word. What the Greeks meant was that they were interested in distant chronology, origins and ways of life by using the evidence of folklore, documents and genealogies (historians studied the recent past by interviewing people who had witnessed events).

Archaeology

αρχαιολογια (arkhaiologia, Greek), archaeologia (Latin) had the basic meaning of 'to speak of ancient times', or 'of how things began'. It covered the ancient, not the recent past. Dionysos of Halicarnassus (60–5 BC) defined archaeologia as the study of events without documentary evidence, which comes close to modern ideas about what archaeology is.

History

ίστορια (historia, Greek), historia (Latin) meant enquiry or research, what we might now call simply 'science' as in 'natural history' as the study of nature.

Antiquities

antiquitates (Latin) meant those things which are old, surviving from past times.

Greece later became part of the Roman Empire and its scholars continued to write about peoples and places. Pausanias (writing *c.* AD 160) produced a cultural geography of Greece detailing its ancient remains as they existed in his day. An important Roman writer was Marcus Terentius Varro (116–27 BC) who wrote a 41-volume work called *Antiquitates* (Antiquities) recording all the monuments of the ancient world. Varro introduced the idea of antiquities as relics which could tell us who did what, where and when in the past. He also thought that human society had passed through stages (hunting leading to pastoral nomadism and on to farming) giving us a possible way of sequencing the past. Sadly, most of Varro's work was lost and is known only through accounts by other writers.

Classical Greek and Roman writers were concerned with three things: different peoples, past times and different places. They had all the elements of modern archaeology but were writing very descriptive accounts with no application of an archaeological method. They were not yet archaeologists in our sense of the word.

The medieval interlude

The later Roman Empire gradually became Christian, and Christianity supplied a ready-made history and chronology in the Bible. The ancient past was pagan and so deemed by some as not worthy of being recorded. The past was either plundered for building materials or reused and reinterpreted in new Christian contexts. Emperor Charlemagne (800–814) excavated in Rome for remains to take back to his capital at Aachen and so claim the glory of ancient Rome for himself. Others hunted for religious relics or treasure. The English King Henry III licensed his brother the Earl of Cornwall in 1237 to dig for treasure. Scholars did write histories of the recently created Christian nations, but anything before the time when documents could be used as evidence was left to myth and legend. England produced two of the most famous works of history of the medieval period. The *Historia Ecclesiastica Gentis Anglorum* (Ecclesiastical History of the English People), written in 731 by Bede of Jarrow (673–735) was a true history in the modern sense of the word. It set new standards for historical writing. The *Historia Regum Britanniae* (History of the Kings of Britain) written in 1136 by Geoffrey of Monmouth (*c.*1100–*c.*1155) was a tissue of make-believe and myth that introduced the legends of Arthur to Western literature. One of the few historians to publicly attack the use of make-believe and myth was William of Malmesbury (*c.*1095–1143);

17

he was also one of the few who made notes of ancient monuments in his
writings.

Renaissance rebirth

New ideas about the world and how to study it began to develop in the
fourteenth century in what later became known as the Renaissance. This
was a conscious looking back to pre-Christian, Classical traditions in art
and scholarship. The poets Francesco Petrarca (1304–74) and Giovanni
Boccaccio (1313–75) visited Rome in 1337 and urged people to study its
classical remains, and themselves collected ancient artefacts. Flavio Biondo
(1392–1463) and Ciriaco of Ancona (1391–1452) made systematic surveys
of the ancient remains of Rome and the eastern Mediterranean. The artist
Raphael (Raffaello Sanzio, 1483–1520) was made Prefect of Antiquities of
Rome by the Pope and wrote a memorandum in 1515 calling for the accurate
surveying of monuments in Rome using plans (drawings as seen from above)
and elevations (drawings as seen from the side), which is now modern
practice. The Popes had already created the first public museum of antiquities
in 1471, the Palazzo dei Conservatori, and had legislated in 1462 to stop
people pillaging ancient remains for building materials. Rome also had one
of the very earliest societies of scholars interested in ancient remains, the
Academia Romana (1478–1527).

While modern attitudes to the remains of the past were developing in
Italy, in Britain the study of antiquities was slower to take off. William of
Malmesbury had incidentally recorded monuments, and Gerald of Wales
(1146–1223) had published itineraries of sites as part of his tours of Ireland
and Wales in 1188 and 1191. The first person in England to record local
monuments, landscapes and artefacts was William of Worcester (1415–82) in
his *Itinerarium* (itineraries or journeys). The next important figure was John
Leland (1503–52), appointed as King's Antiquary by Henry VIII in 1533.
His task was to record all the antiquities of England, but this included
manuscripts as well as monuments. He never published his work, prevented
by mental illness towards the end of his life. His *Itinerary* was eventually
published in 1710.

English antiquarians continued Leland's work from the 1560s onwards.
The antiquarians of this period knew each other and formed networks of
scholars. Many were heralds in the College of Arms, such as William Camden
(1551–1623), who was the most influential of these early scholars, publishing
his *Britannia* in 1586. This completed the *Itinerary* of William of Worcester

and was a comprehensive account of the antiquities of Britain. The first public museum, the Ark, was set up in Lambeth between 1610 and 1634 by John Tradescant (*c*.1575–1638) and later moved to Oxford to become the still existing Ashmolean Museum. In 1656, Sir William Dugdale (1605–86) was the first in Britain to accept that stone tools were made by ancient humans (first suggested in 1570 in Italy).

Antiquarian

Antiquarians are interested in all aspects of the past, such as genealogy and documents as well as monuments. They are observers and recorders of what survives.

Archaeologist

Someone who studies the physical remains of the past for information about past life and how the past has changed over time. They do not only describe remains but try to understand the people who left the remains.

Archaeology established

The early antiquarians became archaeologists in the late seventeenth and early eighteenth centuries in Scandinavia, Germany, France and England. A university professorship in antiquities was established at Uppsala in Sweden as early as 1662 (the first professorship in archaeology came in 1818 at Leiden University in the Netherlands). The early archaeologists developed five key methods for studying physical remains as sources of information for the past.

1 *Recognising that physical remains can be evidence for past events and peoples*: In England, John Aubrey (1626–97) realised that ancient monuments could be studied on their own as evidence for the past, collecting his studies of ancient landscapes in his unpublished *Monumenta Britannica*.
2 *Understanding the past by analogy with the present*: The next step is to understand past remains as similar to things we already know (identification by analogy). Robert Plott (1649–96) used analogy to explain the functions of artefacts at the Ashmolean Museum in Oxford where he was the first curator from 1683 (and could claim to be Britain's first professional archaeologist).

3 *Dating remains by their stratigraphic position*: The third step was the idea that monuments or other evidence could be dated by their physical position against each other (the idea of stratigraphy). This was included in a manual of excavation methods issued by Gotthilf Treuer in Germany in 1688. The first section (vertical slice) drawing of a monument showing the layers of its structure was by the Swede Olof Rudbeck in 1697.

4 *Establishing a chronology for the prehistoric past*: The fourth key method was to be able to produce a basic chronology for the past before written records. The Swiss Jacques Iselin had written a letter in 1719 outlining his idea of a stone age, followed by a bronze age, and in turn followed by an iron age. The idea was published in 1743 by Nicholas Mahudel (1704–47) in France in *Three Successive Ages of Stone, Bronze and Iron*.

5 *Creating sequences of sites and artefacts from younger to older*: To be able to place artefacts and monuments in such a sequence depends on being able to classify them into categories and place these in a series from earlier to later. This is the fifth stage: taxonomy (classifying things) and typology (placing them in a series). One of the first people to attempt both of these was the French Comte de Caylus (1692–1765) in his *Recueil d'Antiquités* written between 1752 and 1768. William Stukeley attempted to do the same for prehistoric monuments in his books on Stonehenge in 1740 and Avebury in 1743. The German Johann Winckelmann (1717–68) used the idea of styles changing over time in his *History of Ancient Art* in 1764, which became the basis for the whole field of classical archaeology.

Some of these early archaeologists were surprisingly modern in their views. William Stukeley was very firm about the need for conservation of ancient remains. He wrote against 'improvers' seeking to modernise medieval churches, and against farmers raiding prehistoric sites for building stone.

Archaeology now had a way of doing things. It also had societies of practitioners. The Royal Society of Antiquaries of Sweden was founded in 1630 and the Society of Antiquaries of London in 1717 (Figure 2.1). The Society of Dilettanti was also formed in England in 1734 to study classical art and archaeology (and still exists as a society of artists). Archaeology also had its journals. *Archaeologia* was founded in London in 1770, and is still published today. Finally, archaeology had its showcase museum. The Ashmolean Museum was founded in 1683, but the grand and imposing national museum, the British Museum, was opened in 1759.

Figure 2.1 The Society of Antiquaries is alive and well

Antiquarians or archaeologists?

All the key building blocks of archaeology were created by the early pioneers, and yet they are often dismissed today as mere antiquarians rather than archaeologists. In part this is an attitude of modern archaeologists seeking to differentiate themselves from early amateur pioneers with less developed techniques and ideas. We see ourselves as the professionals, understanding archaeological theory, using scientific techniques and being proper archaeologists, and those early folk were mere antiquarians!

Archaeology matures

The period between the mid-eighteenth century and the later nineteenth century was the heroic age of archaeology, when the big sites and early civilisations were first explored. Our major ideas about the past were put in place and archaeology became a recognised academic subject and a profession.

Widespread, systematic excavation as the main activity of archaeologists began in the early eighteenth century, with William Stukeley actively excavating from the 1720s. In Italy, the Roman city of Herculaneum was discovered in 1738 and Pompeii in 1743, and in Britain the great period of digging the barrows (burial mounds) began in the 1750s. William Borlase in Cornwall, Bryan Faussett and James Douglas in Kent, and Sir Richard Colt-Hoare and William Cunnington in Wiltshire excavated hundreds of barrows in the search for ancient artefacts between the 1750s and 1810s. While the German Karl Weber was beginning to develop modern methods of excavation at Pompeii after 1750, as yet the methods of the early British excavators were crude and they missed as much as they found. The peak period of barrow digging was the 1840s to the 1870s, under people such as Charles Warne, John Thurnham and William Greenwell. The last of the great amateur barrow diggers was the highly respected John Mortimer (1825–1911).

Great advances were made in the search for ancient civilisations. Napoleon had taken scholars with him when he invaded Egypt in 1798, revealing the ancient Egyptian civilisation to Europe. The ruins of the Ancient Maya were first explored in 1839. Excavations began in Mesopotamia (modern Iraq) in the 1840s. The ruins of Troy and Mycenae opened a window into the world of the Homeric Greek epics in the 1870s. Many of the early explorers of these civilisations were themselves larger than life characters and archaeology's association with the exotic and a reputation for adventure was set during this period.

Meanwhile, some people were at last becoming dissatisfied with the chronology provided by the Christian Bible. This told of a creation of the Earth only 6,000 years ago and a great flood that marked the beginning of serious history. Archaeologists began finding evidence of human tools with extinct animals, and geologists were finding evidence that the earth must have existed for far longer than 6,000 years. Sir Charles Lyell published his *Principles of Geology* in 1833, which demolished the belief in the great flood and established the true age of the earth as much older than the Bible allowed. Sir John Evans gave a talk at the Society of Antiquaries in 1859 establishing that humans had existed far back in prehistory, alongside extinct animals. This was the same year that Charles Darwin and Alfred Wallace announced their understanding of the evolution of life, effectively overturning the Christian belief in an unchanging divine creation. In spite of determined opposition from many at the time, archaeology was then free to develop ideas about how humans had evolved over many millions of years. Already, in 1857, the first remains of a separate human species in Europe had been found, the Neanderthals.

Danish and Swedish archaeologists made some of the most important breakthroughs in archaeological methods. The National Museum in Denmark had opened in 1819 with displays based on the three age system. Its curator, Christian Thomsen (1788–1865), developed the use of seriation and association for dating artefacts. Jens Worsaae (1821–85) emphasised the importance of meticulous excavation and recording (rather than simply digging for treasure) and of studying assemblages of artefacts in his *Danmarks Oldtid* in 1843. Hans Hildebrand (1842–1913) and Oscar Montelius (1843–1921) made great advances in the use of typology in the 1860s. Others were developing excavation methods, such as the proper understanding of stratigraphy by the Italian Giuseppi Fiorelli (1820–96) at Pompeii from 1860, and by the German Ernst Curtius (1814–96) at Olympia in Greece from 1875. In Britain, the key figures were Augustus Pitt-Rivers (1827–1900) working on Cranborne Chase from 1880, and Sir Flinders Petrie (1853–1942) who worked in Egypt from 1883. These two introduced typology, meticulous excavation and recording, and detailed publishing of excavations to British archaeology.

Association

Noting which artefacts occur together. An artefact of known date can be used to date other artefacts it is found with, or a structure it is found within.

Assemblage

A group of artefacts deposited at the same time as part of the same piece of human behaviour. It is the whole assemblage that helps us understand that behaviour, not a single artefact on its own.

Section

A vertical slice through a site or monument.

Seriation

The ordering of artefacts in time such that each period of time has its own characteristic types of artefact.

Stratigraphy

The layering of sediments and structure one above the other. Later strata (layers) overlie earlier ones, although some layers can be dug through lower layers. Good excavation depends on accurately identifying layers and how they lie in relation to each other.

Typology

A classification of artefacts showing how they change over time. All artefacts show changes in form over time depending on technological improvements and changes in fashion.

Having more accurately recorded data is all very well. But how do we interpret the data? The past is very different from today, and all places have seen successions of different cultures, one after the other. Why do cultures change? Why did the Stone Age develop into the Bronze Age? Why do styles of pottery change over time? Why did people begin cremating their dead instead of burying them? For Jens Worsaae, it was natural in 1843 to explain change by the movement of people. New cultures arose by invasion of one culture by another. After Darwin had made evolution respectable, it was more natural for Louis de Mortillet (1821–98) to propose in 1869 that cultures could evolve by themselves. Adam Ferguson (1723–1816) in 1792 proposed an early prehistoric stage of savagery leading to barbarism and leading in turn to civilisation. This was taken up by the American Lewis Henry Morgan (1818–81) and linked with archaeological and ethnographic evidence. Savagery was equated with hunting and gathering in the Palaeolithic (Old Stone Age) and Mesolithic (Middle Stone Age). Barbarism was equated with farming and the Neolithic (New Stone Age). Civilisation was broadly equated with the Bronze Age onwards. We no longer accept Morgan's scheme but we still find it hard not to create hierarchies of culture in our minds where we see cities as more advanced than farming and that in turn more advanced than hunting. These two big ideas, invasion/migration and independent evolution, crop up again and again in archaeology.

A key figure in British archaeology of this period was Sir John Lubbock (1834–1913). His book, *Prehistoric Times*, was published in 1865 and remained the standard textbook for archaeology well into the twentieth century. Lubbock was a politician as well as an archaeologist. He was responsible for the Ancient Monuments Protection Act in 1882. This selected a list of

68 ancient sites to be protected and properly recorded. Augustus Pitt-Rivers became the first Inspector of Ancient Monuments and the first professional field archaeologist in the United Kingdom. Until then, the only professional archaeologists in Britain were either museum curators or university professors. There has been a Professor of Archaeology at Cambridge University since 1851, of Classical Archaeology at Oxford from 1885 and of Egyptology at London from 1892. Most archaeologists were amateurs. Sir John Evans was a paper manufacturer, Lubbock a banker and MP, and Mortimer a corn merchant, while Stukeley had been a doctor and a clergyman. The most important organisations where archaeologists could meet were the national and local societies. The Society of Antiquaries remained the most important, but from the 1840s onwards the local county archaeology societies were founded and were the main organisations for archaeology for the next 100 years.

The astute reader will notice that all the names mentioned so far have been men. Sadly, the contribution of women to early archaeology has been neglected. Women did occupy key positions and made great contributions to archaeology. Johanna Mestorf (1829–1909) was an early pioneer who became a curator at the German National Museum in Kiel in 1873. One of the earliest British women archaeologists was Amelia Edwards (1831–92), working in Egypt from 1873 onwards, a key founder of the Egypt Exploration Society in 1882. The Italian Contessa Ersilia Lovatelli (1840–1925) was a highly respected expert in the archaeology of ancient Rome. Many Victorian women found an outlet for their talents abroad where attitudes were usually more accepting of women working alone, such as Lucy Mitchell (an American, 1845–88) and Gertrude Bell (1868–1926) in the Near East, Jane Harrison (1850–1928) and Eugenie Sellers Strong (1860–1943) in Greece and Italy, Margaret Murray (1863–1963), Janet Gourlay (1863–1912) and Margaret Benson (1865–1916) in Egypt. One of the few to work in Britain was Ella Armitage (1841–1931), in medieval archaeology. Only as late as 1938 did Oxford or Cambridge appoint a woman as a Professor of Archaeology: Dorothy Garrod (1892–1968) at Cambridge.

Modern archaeology

The main task of archaeology in the early twentieth century was to describe and define the different cultures of the past. The dominant idea for how cultures changed was still through invasion or migration, or perhaps by adopting new ideas through trade. Many archaeologists worked in the new nation states of Europe and it was natural for them to see competing nations

25

in prehistoric Europe migrating and conquering others. Some archaeologists saw one particular culture as more advanced than others, spreading the benefits of civilisation to other lesser cultures. For many this original home of civilisation was ancient Egypt, and all advances elsewhere such as building in stone or the beginnings of metallurgy were all due to borrowing from, or invasion by, more advanced cultures. One reason it was possible to make such claims was that there were very few ways to accurately date the ancient past in the absence of written records. Archaeologists used cross-dating, which relied on making links between cultures. An artefact from a civilisation with written records can be dated exactly. The same artefact, say a type of pottery or brooch, can be found exported to other cultures. A site from that culture with the foreign dated artefact can then itself be dated. A chain of links can be built from one culture to another, all ultimately leading back to the civilisation with written records. It is natural therefore to see a culture such as ancient Egypt or Sumeria as the origin of all things. This point of view is called diffusionism. Archaeology during the twentieth century developed a greater understanding of the internal processes at work in a culture that can lead to different kinds of change over time, often in an interaction with the environment, but also as a result of individual choices and the demands of social structures. The key figure in developing a more modern conception of culture and change was Gordon Childe (1892–1957), the great archaeologist who stood at the boundary between early and modern archaeology. More will be said about Childe in later chapters, but one of his legacies is that migration and diffusion must now take their place alongside other reasons for changes in culture. It is the debate between archaeologists advocating different mechanisms for change and for cultural differences that makes the subject so interesting to many.

Many different ways of doing archaeology and of approaches to the past have arisen since the early twentieth century. We now have better understandings of how human cultures have changed by looking at natural developments in society or changes in climate and environment, of how people use their environments, and of how people behave. We are more aware of our own biases, of the role of politics and how the peculiarities of our own society affect how we practise our archaeology. These will be explored in more detail in the chapters that follow. The next three chapters will explore the three fundamental dimensions of archaeology: time, places and people. Each has been the focus of developing different approaches and methodologies during the middle and later twentieth century. All three are essential aspects of archaeology.

3

Understanding time

Wrætlic is þes wealstan wyrde gebræcon	Curious is this stone wall by fate broken,
burgstede burston brosnað enta geweorc	dwellings fell, crumbles the work of giants,
hrofas sind gehrorene hreorge torras	rooves are fallen down, ruined peaks,
hrim geat torras berofen hrim on lime	frost overwhelmed peaks, despoiled of mortar by frost,
scearde scurbeorge scorene gedrorene	shaped rooves in pieces fallen,
ældo undereotene . . .	undone by age and time . . .

Old English poem, *The Ruin* (10th century)

Examining time forces us to look into the origins and development of human behaviour and ask some of the biggest of questions. Nowadays, we can easily say what human behaviour is like. But what is it to be human? We understand that humans are a distinct species of animal, related closely to other apes. Chimps, bonobos, gorillas and humans share a common ancestor. Although chimps and bonobos use and make simple tools (as do some other animals), they have not developed complex technologies and the use of raw materials in the same way that humans have. No chimp or bonobo has yet invented the electric toothbrush! But, when we pass farther back in time, we reach a point where our own species had yet to evolve. Instead, we have to deal with the remains of our ancestral species, and other early human relatives that later became extinct. The farther back in time we go, the less technologically developed is the material culture of these other species. At some point, we reach a time when our ancestors had yet to develop complex material culture. Archaeology is then left to study the biological development of our ancestors in the same way that geologists study the evolution of other animals. The excitement for the archaeologist lies in understanding what makes these early species human rather than ape. This is one of the most important questions that archaeology can address, which strikes at the very root of our identity and self-image as a species.

We can only ask questions such as 'what makes us human?' because we deal with the dimension of time. This dimension allows us to trace the development of human anatomy, technology and behaviour to see how these have changed in different ways in various parts of the world over the long span of the last 2.5 million years. Many archaeologists study only one period in the past, finding this easier and more satisfying than trying to gather and analyse evidence from millions of years of material culture. In this chapter, we will explore some of the kinds of archaeology that deal with time and human development. We will also look at how archaeologists organise their evidence into something called culture, and how the history of culture (how cultures change over time) is a fundamental part of archaeology.

The properties of time

Time is a fundamental dimension of archaeology. It has four properties: linearity, experience, resolution, scale. When observed, we see time passing in a line; things happen after each other and do not recur. Events cannot be rewound, replayed or fast-forwarded. This property – linearity – can be measured by a dating system and recorded as a narrative of events. On the other hand, time as subjectively experienced by people is more changeable. We all know that some days or activities pass quickly while others seem to drag. A younger person's memories operate differently to those of an older person who may remember in detail events from 50 years ago but have problems remembering what happened yesterday. Our ability to see time passing varies from the coarse resolution of overall outline to the fine resolution of detailed events. As time passes, less and less of the material culture of a society survives and it is usually only in the more recent past that we can see time with the fine resolution of daily or monthly events. The remains of the past that we find are the results of human actions in short timescales of one human lifetime, yet many of the important questions we seek to answer are about large-scale processes operating over hundreds or thousands of years. Historians and archaeologists see three different timescales. The longest timescales are those operating over thousands of years and cover broad patterns of human activity, such as the evolution and development of species and changes to climate and environment. Medium timescales cover hundreds of years and involve changes in the organisation of groups and societies, or in the economy. The shortest timescale is that of the human lifetime where events happen in single years or over decades. It is here we see the actions of individual human beings. Archaeology is odd in that all our evidence comes from the actions of individuals (the act of throwing away a broken pot, the building of a house, the burial of a relative etc.), yet we can seldom identify these individuals and can rarely plot individual life histories for them. We are far more able to plot changes in society and economy, and see the unfolding of long-term process of evolution and change. Our evidence comes from the shortest timescale, yet our understanding of the past is best at the medium and longer scales.

Palimpsest

All human activity is superimposed on the traces left behind by earlier activity, and partially destroys or reworks those traces. The result is a palimpsest, where traces of activity from different periods occur in the same archaeological record. This is easily seen in any town where a whole series of buildings from the Roman and medieval periods survive into the present (Figure 3.1), and in upland areas of Britain where modern farms and villages exist in eighteenth- and nineteenth-century field systems built over the traces of medieval trackways and boundaries, and contain remains of Roman and earlier farmsteads and prehistoric burial mounds. On a smaller scale, a single pot is a palimpsest of activities where it may be thrown away and broken but still have traces of its various uses such as cooking or storage and also show evidence of the techniques used to make it in the first place.

Changes in material culture

The passage of time sees many changes in material culture. Cultures develop over time, expand or contract their territory, move from one place to another, appear and disappear. Archaeologists spend a lot of their time tracing changes in the form and nature of artefacts and monuments. A particular form of an artefact is called a type of the artefact, and the creation of a series of types, each one newer or younger than the last, is called typology. We are all familiar with

Figure 3.1 **Roman, medieval and
Victorian co-existing in Bath**

typology. Take the mobile phone. We can recognise a simple typology from the Motorola DynaTAC 'brick' type phone (33 cm long and 900 gm in weight) in 1983, through the Motorola MicroTAC with its flip out mouthpiece in 1989 (18 cm and 340 gm), the Motorola StarTAC clam-shell type in 1996, the Nokia 8110 with sliding mouthpiece in 1998, to the Nokia 7110 in 1999 and its integrated Internet browser, the BlackBerry smart-phone in 2002 and the iPhone in 2007. Showing off the latest model of phone to your friends depends on them being able to recognise a typology of development and knowing what are the newest design features. Archaeologists arrange artefacts in a chronological series in a typology, and then use this to interpret human behaviour. This is seldom straightforward and often subjective. How would an archaeologist interpret the extendable 'aerial' in the Motorola MicroTAC phone? The phone had an invisible internal aerial and the extendable one was fake and only for show.

Archaeologists have devised elaborate typologies for all kinds of artefacts such as stone tools, pottery, metal brooches, coins and weapons. Pottery is especially prone to being divided into types, as are early metal tools such as axe heads. The earliest copper and bronze axe heads were made in shape very like the stone axe heads that people were familiar with. To stop these new axe heads splitting their hafts, a ridge was added across the width of the axe head. To fix the axe head so that it didn't move from side to side in its haft, ridges were added to the sides of it. The side ridges and cross ridge were then deepened. The side ridges could then be curved over to grip the haft. Later still someone had the idea of casting the bronze in a mould so that the axe head was hollow, with the haft then inserted into the axe head. A clear series of axe head types in copper and bronze has been established covering a period of 1,500 years. One of the key benefits of typology is that the types can help to date other finds made with them, so the type of bronze axe head can be used to say whether other artefacts from the same deposit are early or late in the Bronze Age. The reasons for changes in the type can be functional, as with the axe heads, but can also be due to other factors that may be social, religious, personal, political, etc.

Artefacts or artifacts?

An artefact is a humanly made or altered object. A motor car is an artefact, so is a carving knife. Artefacts are usually movable or can be carried. Buildings or structures are technically artefacts but are not usually described as such. Finds of animal bones or plant seeds on archaeological sites are not always artefacts in that they can be still in their natural state. A term sometimes used to cover finds like these is *ecofact*, although this is not a common term.

Artefact and artifact are both acceptable alternative spellings; artefact is the accepted UK spelling, while artifact is normally used in the USA.

Explaining change

One key question that we seek to answer is 'why do cultures change?'. If artefacts have histories, and cultures are made up of types of artefact, then cultures also have histories. Culture history is an important part of archaeology, tracing the descent and movement of cultures over time. It was the dominant kind of archaeology in the first half of the twentieth century and is still the main type of archaeology in many parts of the world.

In the modern world, people are divided into different ethnic groups (whether by nation, language, religion or whatever else). It was natural for archaeologists to assume that cultures represented ethnic groups in the past (usually identified with specific languages). This is now accepted as too simplistic. Many prehistorians, especially in the UK, have a deep distrust of ethnic explanations of culture. On the other hand, we know that ethnic groups have always existed and it is entirely right to explore the possibility that some cultural change can be explained by how these groups interacted. But we have to remember that a named culture is an archaeological category not an ethnic group, and we need to account for how cultures change through a wide variety of possible processes. We will explore the geographical spread of culture in the next chapter. For now, we will concentrate on how cultures change over time.

Culture and ethnicity

It is simple to make an equation of 'a culture = a people', and base this on an assumption that a people exists as a group united by common descent from ancestors. This can be dangerous. The most infamous example comes from Nazi Germany between 1933 and 1945. The Nazis employed archaeologists to search for and construct a clear ancestry for the Germanic peoples tied to past cultures, and used this to establish their claim of superiority over others. Since 1945, it has been difficult for archaeologists to use a simple link between cultures and people as a reaction against the misuse of this idea by the Nazi regime.

Changes in culture could have been the result of migration, invasion, trade between peoples, etc. But some archaeologists try to explain how culture changes without these external factors. We can instead focus on the capacities, capabilities, needs and desires of individuals. Although there are cultural norms, the 'right' way of doing things or making things for our culture, we all interpret these in slightly different ways. Personal preferences or different abilities in making things will mean each generation is slightly different to the one that came before. For example, the traditional British way of eating with a fork in the left hand and knife in the right is slowly making way among some people for the American way of only using a fork in the right hand. There can also be room for the individually creative inventor. Someone must have been the first person to have had the idea of cutting an impression of a stone axe head in a rock, smelting copper ore and pouring the molten copper into the rock, letting it cool and solidify and prising out the resulting copper axe head. A process like this does not happen by accident. In some societies, change may be driven by competition between people for resources or wealth, finding new ways of acquiring wealth or of showing off their wealth to others in ever more elaborate fashions or types of artefact. Is showing your friends that you have the latest type of mobile phone or iPad any different to showing off the latest type of knife or sword in the Bronze Age?

Culture history

Culture historians devise successions of cultures, named after a key archaeological site or type of artefact, one after the other in a particular region. Each culture is defined by what are thought to be characteristic artefacts, made and used by the people themselves for everyday purposes. It would make little sense to define the culture by goods that it imported from elsewhere, or that had a social significance that was likely to change according to the latest fashions. What we end up with in any particular region is a layer cake, with each layer being a different culture. For example, a generalised culture history for the prehistory of part of north-central Europe is given in Figure 3.2. The

Age	Culture	Date BP
Iron Age	La Tene	2400
	Hallstatt (Iron)	2650
Bronze Age	Hallstatt (Bronze)	3150
	Urnfield	3300
	Tumulus	3700
	Unetice	4100
	Bell Beaker	4350
Neolithic	Corded Ware	4750
	Globular Amphora	5050
	Michelsberg	5950
	Roessen	6550
	Linearbandkeramik (LBK)	7350
Mesolithic	Limburgian	11450
	Ahrensburgian	14000
Palaeolithic	Hamburgian	15000
	Magdalenian	18000
	Gravettian	30000
	Aurignacian	42000

Figure 3.2 **Culture history in north-central Europe**

danger of a table like this is that it gives the impression that each culture is uniform from beginning to end, that there are sharp boundaries between the cultures and that change must happen only at specific times and be very sudden. In reality, cultures are often messier than this. There will be changes within a culture so the later part is somewhat different to the earlier part, and one culture may gradually transform into a later culture, with no sharp break between them.

The most prominent early culture historian in the English-speaking world was Gordon Childe. His great contribution was to pull together a whole series of studies done by others into one coherent whole and see the patterns in cultures over long periods of time. He developed the idea that there had been two great changes in human culture since the end of the Ice Age. The first was the development of farming in the Near East, with the cultivation of wheat, barley and other crops, and the keeping of domestic animals such as cattle, sheep, goats and pigs. Farming involved, among other things, settling down in one place (rather than moving to follow wild game with the seasons), building permanent houses, being able to make and use fragile pottery, and establishing ownership of plots of land. Farming and its associated changes were summed up by Childe as the 'Neolithic Revolution'. His second change was the coming together of large numbers of people in cities, where specialists lived who did not farm directly themselves, but relied on rents, taxes or the work of others to provide them with food and clothing. These specialists might include priests, kings, bureaucrats, artists, physicians, etc. There would have been a hierarchical society with wealthy and poor. There would have been crafts that only specialists had the time to master, such as metalworking, painting, writing, literature. Childe called this the 'Urban Revolution' producing distinct civilisations. Childe only looked at Europe and the Near East. Other parts of the world such as America, east Asia and Africa had their own patterns of culture history, with their own farming and urban developments.

Many culture historians still tend to see changes as due to the migration of peoples and the diffusion of ideas and technology from one people to another. It can be an archaeology ideally suited to nationalists and racists (although Childe was neither of these).

Cultural evolution

Childe was not the only archaeologist to see human behaviour as passing through stages of development. Terms were used in the nineteenth century to describe these levels of development that we would not use today because the words are loaded with assumptions of superiority: savagery, barbarism and civilisation. Different terms were developed in the 1960s, based on social anthropology. The commonest scheme was a distinction between bands, tribes, chiefdoms and states. Each level would be less egalitarian than the one below, have a more complex economy and technology, a greater role for political leadership, greater numbers of specialists such as warriors or priests etc. For example, in Figure 3.2 the Aurignacian culture would be at the band level, while the LBK would be a tribal level culture, and the Hallstatt would be a culture of chiefdoms.

Social anthropology

Social anthropology, one of the branches of anthropology, studies the social organisation of societies. Social anthropologists often look at economic and political organisation, religious beliefs, kinship, gender roles, conflict and symbolism. It is often known as cultural anthropology in the USA and elsewhere. Other branches of anthropology are biological or physical anthropology, and linguistic anthropology.

Each level has certain characteristics, although these are an idealised set that may not be present in all cultures. The boundaries between them can also be somewhat blurred in practice with some societies that are an advanced example of one level being similar to less-well-developed examples of the next level.

- Bands: family groups of less than 100 people, no formal leadership structures, temporary or seasonal camps, lightly built houses, religion based on shamans (guides to the spirit world), mostly a hunter-gatherer or pastoral economy.
- Tribes: social groups of up to 5,000 people, specialist war parties, leadership vested in elders or priests, permanent villages, religion based on seasonal rituals and gatherings, well-built houses, burial structures, mostly farming or pastoral economies.
- Chiefdoms: large ethnic groups of up to 20,000 people based on kinship, ranked societies with hereditary chiefs having priestly functions and specialist warriors, craft specialists, forts, ritual centres, large-scale monuments, the economy involves redistribution of goods.

- States: groups of more than 20,000 people, a class hierarchy under a king, assembly or other authority, issuing laws and levying taxes, a specialist bureaucracy, an organised religion with a priesthood, towns, roads, large-scale defences, monumental architecture, based on common residence in a territory instead of links through kinship.

It is hard not to assume that the more complex levels were superior, more progressive and civilised than those that came before it. The dangers of this are obvious. In the nineteenth century, it allowed nations such as Britain and France to justify their imperial conquest of 'lesser' nations at 'less evolved' levels of culture in Africa and Asia. Cultural evolution assumes that a society will inevitably evolve into another level unless there is something to prevent it, such as a harsh environment that made farming impossible. It also assumes that change is inevitable. It is not a way of explaining why or exactly how one level of society develops into another. As a way of describing prehistoric cultures, such a scheme is a useful approximation but not without problems when applied in detail.

It is fair to say that culture history is still common in much of Europe and cultural evolution is common in America, whereas in the UK neither has been particularly common over the past 40 years. Both are approaches well suited to prehistory, and Britain has a long historical period and an extremely varied landscape in a small island that makes a geographical approach to prehistory more attractive, as we shall see in Chapter 4.

Marxism

As well as being a culture historian, Childe was one of the earliest Marxist archaeologists. Marxism has been attractive to many archaeologists, not as a political idea, but as a way of analysing the past. One of its attractions for Childe was that it offers a way of explaining why societies change. Marx derived his political views from an analysis of history. He saw the most important aspect of human life as being the struggle to find food, shelter and other material goods that make life worth living (what he called the infrastructure of life). The basic problem is that very few people make what they themselves use. We do not grow all our own food, or make all our own clothes or other goods. We have to rely on the work of others, which has to be organised, and the exchange of food and goods must be controlled in some way. Different stages of human development are characterised by different ways of getting food and goods from producers to consumers. Marx called these 'modes of production' and identified five main modes. The modern world is characterised by the capitalist mode where people work for wages. The medieval world was characterised by the feudal mode where food and other goods were produced by serfs, tied to the land. Societies such as ancient Greece or Rome relied on the ancient mode, where slaves did most of the work. Earlier civilisations used the Asiatic mode where religious sanctions allowed semi-divine rulers to force people to work on massive projects for their own benefit. Much of later prehistoric Europe was characterised by a tribal Germanic mode, where land was owned by extended families and power was dispersed among the heads of these families. Later writers added to or modified these modes. Whether these modes accurately describe the realities of the past is something to argue about. Past societies, when looked at across all continents and times, are likely to be far more complex than can be summed up in a few simple modes.

For a Marxist, the infrastructure is the basis for all other aspects of society such as politics, religion, art, etc. (what Marx called the superstructure, although modern Marxists will often use different definitions of infrastructure, structure and superstructure). Change the mode of production and all else also changes. Every system of production contained its own contradictions between the people who did the work and those who owned the resources and controlled the distribution of what they produced. Contradiction leads to conflict, which can only be overcome by repressive laws, violence or ideologies such as religion until the pressure from below becomes too great and a revolution occurs which moves society from one stage of production to another. So the ancient world gave way to feudalism, which in turn gave way to capitalism. This is now seen as too simplistic and Marxist ideas in archaeology have had to change a great deal. For example, Marvin Harris in the USA developed cultural materialism as a science of material culture by including social organisation alongside the modes of production (as a mode of reproduction, producing the next generation of children through marriage rules, etc.). These determine the structure (the economy, social organisation and politics), which in turn determine the superstructure of art, ritual, sport, science, beliefs, ideas (Figure 3.3). Change in the environment or in the levels of population will lead to changes in the structure and superstructure. Harris is only one example, and there are now many different forms of Marxist archaeology, and some would be hardly recognised as Marxist by Marx himself!

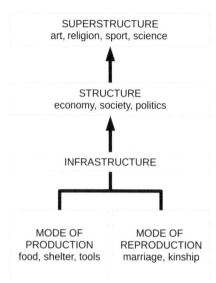

Figure 3.3 **Marxist structures of society**

Other approaches

The nature of the changes we can see in the archaeological record varies from the very slow and gradual, to the very sudden, even catastrophic. It would seem likely that the reasons for sudden and widespread changes would be different from the reasons for the many gradual and local changes that occur from one generation to the next. Culture history, cultural evolution and Marxist archaeologies all seek to provide explanations for change. They are the instinctive, default settings for many archaeologists in North America and continental Europe. Grand, over-arching theories of change are less favoured in the UK. Many British archaeologists are period specialists, and there has been more of a focus on continuity, on understanding the ways of life of the past and the characteristics of particular periods. Explanations of change tend to look towards particular and specific processes, such as the influence of changing climate, environmental degradation or individual motivations, for example the desire for wealth and status ('agency' in archaeological jargon), while change over the past 2,000 years can be adequately explained by known historical events.

Explaining change can be highly controversial with archaeologists holding many different views. Was the change from a hunting and gathering Mesolithic to a farming Neolithic brought about by the migration of farmers replacing native hunter-gatherers? Was it due to the gleeful adoption of farming by native peoples who saw all its advantages in their neighbours? Was it forced on hunter-gatherers due to changes in climate making hunting and gathering harder to sustain? Was it a natural evolution of advanced hunting and gathering practices? All these explanations for change have been put forward and all can be supported by various theories for change. The problem is that a change from hunting and gathering to farming is not only a change in how a people get their food. It also involves changes in the nature of society, types of settlement, the technology used, religious belief and practices, and most other aspects of human existence. Archaeologists are only now beginning to understand the full complexity of change, and its unpredictability. There are so many factors to be taken into account: the size of past societies, for example, or how individuals work together and compete, the role of networks of social and economic interaction, the scale over which change happens, how information flows between people, the role of individual agency, or the different degrees of heterogeneity (whether societies are conformist or thrive on differences between people).

Past (and present) human societies are immensely complex, and understanding this complexity is very hard. Simple explanations for change simply will not do. Archaeology has long had a tendency to want simple explanations (such as migration or the desire for social status). More recently, a range of theories from social and physical sciences has been used by archaeologists to help them explain change, for example catastrophe theory, chaos theory and complexity theory. None of these has all the answers, and it is one of the attractions of archaeology that it allows the use of different, and often competing, theories. A lot of the intellectual excitement of archaeology comes from the rival claims of different theories to have 'found the explanation' for a particular change.

Conclusion

There is a tendency to see change as either a collapse or as progress. Only rarely do we see change as neutral. Civilisations collapse. The Bronze Age was undoubtedly an advance over the Neolithic. Statements like these involve us making value judgements about the past, some periods or cultures being seen as better or worse than what came before. We evaluate the past with our own preconceived notions of what is right and wrong, good or bad. We also often forget the nature of the archaeological evidence that can seriously mislead us. Stone mosaic floors may seem to us more 'civilised' or more technologically advanced than wooden floors, but a skilled carpenter would probably disagree, and people at the time might have preferred woven woollen tapestries on the wall to show off their artistic taste instead of walking on mosaic floors. A stone-built Roman villa survives better to be found by the archaeologists than a wooden early medieval hall. We have excavated many villas, but few wooden halls. We have to ask ourselves, are we being misled into seeing the end of Roman Britain as a collapse of civilisation, or was it really a change in fashion and taste?

Time is all about change. Archaeologists need to take into account that societies are made up of individuals, and each item of material culture represents the actions and choices of these individuals. Changes in a culture over time are the result of individuals changing their choices, or their sons or daughters making different choices to their parents. These changes may be the result of the differences in tastes and behaviours between generations or in people as they progress from childhood to old age, either through 'natural' ageing or through having different life experiences. They may also be forced on individuals through changes in their external circumstances, such as war, famine, disease, climate change, new technology, etc. The task for the archaeologist is to try to understand what changes the human behaviour that results in a change in culture.

Time is only one dimension of archaeology. On its own, it allies us with other subjects that study the past such as history. Yet archaeology is more than simply about the past and the passage of time. The second dimension of archaeology, space, turns us towards geography and makes the subject a more powerful exploration of human behaviour, as we shall see in the next chapter.

4

Understanding place

monað modes lust mæla gehwylce   my heart's yearning complains
                                   every time
ferð to feran, þæt ic feor heonan as a companion to my spirit,
                                   that I far from hence
elþeodigra eard gesece.   a strange land should seek.
                         Old English poem, *The Seafarer* (ninth century)

The second dimension of archaeology is space. Spaces are not blank canvases; they are places used by people. Today, we are used to a fragmented patchwork of specialist spaces. We live (sleep, eat, look after our families) in a house. We travel to a separate location to work. Our travel may take us in a hermetically sealed box (car, bus or train) or we may walk or cycle and so make use of spaces as travelling corridors. We may worship our gods in other, separate locations. We will bury our dead in further separate locations. Our social life is also carried out in separate spaces, often at some distance from where we live. We will even deliberately go to a different space removed from any of these to escape our normal life for a time; that is, we go on holiday. In other words, we carry out all the activities of our life in separate spaces in separate locations. This is not necessarily how people in the past lived. Most people in the past lived in spatially separate communities where life, work and worship need not be separate activities.

4

Spatial scales

A fundamental property of space is scale. Archaeologists study human behaviour at different scales, from large regions down to sites and buildings within a site.

Over large regions, we may have many cultures, each having boundaries that mark it off from the others. These may not be hard and fast, and there may be zones in which two cultures meet and mingle or overlap. Nevertheless, there are boundaries across which people move into strange lands among foreigners with different ways of life. Sometimes a whole people may move, taking their culture from one area to another. Sometimes they may expand into new areas and take over, dominate or merge with other cultures. Interaction between peoples is an important part of understanding the role of place in the past.

Within any culture, there will be spatial relationships between its settlements. Individuals and families are not isolated. They are integrated with others by ties of marriage, political structures, religious activity, etc. Settled political entities (whether we call them tribes, chiefdoms, states or whatever) will have networks of power and control. Some settlements may be of greater size and wealth than others. There will be flows of goods in the form of rents or taxes, or redistribution from a lord to his followers. There will be flows of people as families intermarry. People from different settlements may gather together at central sites for seasonal religious or political gatherings. Bands of hunter-gatherers will move around large regions in search of plants and game.

Particular settlements will have their own territories where different activities are carried out at different locations. Hunting depends on finding the right animals, gathering on finding the right plants in the right places. Herding animals depends on knowing where the good grazing is. Growing crops depends on knowing where the right soils are. Raw materials occur at specific places to be mined or quarried. Settlements need supplies of water close by. There may be special sites where people worship gods, supernatural powers, ancestors or the forces of nature. There may be special areas reserved for burying the dead. People will also have set routes as they move through their territory. A term used to describe the relationship people have with their surrounding space is the taskscape. This is the overall set of activities carried out by a person or a community within the landscape. It is a way of thinking about places as sites of actively lived spaces rather than simply as an environment laid out for people to use or not.

Spatial relationships within a settlement can tell us much about past ways of life. There may be communal spaces for social, political or religious gatherings. There may be specific spaces for religious observances. There will be spaces for storage of goods, tools, animals, etc., as well as spaces for carrying out tasks such as tool making, smithing or weaving. There will also be the spaces where people actually lived, their domestic spaces. In these there will also be spatial relationships: the hearth for heating or cooking, spaces for sleeping, spaces for eating and so on. Some sites or buildings may have significantly segregated spaces allocated to only part of the community: male and female, rich and poor, adult and child. Knowing what artefacts have been found in which contexts is the main way in which we can assess the different uses of these spaces. Careful recording of where things were found, and what other artefacts they were found with is essential in archaeology.

Context

Context is one of the most important words in archaeology. Context is what gives artefacts their power to tell us about people's lives in the past. At its simplest, context is the exact place in which an artefact was found, what that place consisted of and what else was found in that same place. In the technical process of excavation, context has a precise meaning. Each human action that leaves a trace in the ground leaves some kind of deposit or feature that we can recognise. This may be a round patch of darker and looser soil where a wooden post once stood, a trodden surface of clay that was once the floor of a house, or a pile of slate where a roof has fallen in. On an excavation, each trace of human activity is treated as a context and given its own separate context number. For example, a simple post hole will have three contexts:

1   the ground surface into which it was cut;
2   the hole cut into the ground;
3   the filling of the hole with the rotted wooden post or soil backfill after a post has been removed.

Archaeological approaches need to be appropriate for the scale being investigated: region, polity, territory, site or structure. Underlying all archaeological examination of space is an understanding of the environment, what it provides for people, how the environment has shaped the archaeological evidence we find and how human behaviour alters the environment.

Understanding past environments

The Earth is enormously varied, from icy Arctic wastes to dry, sandy deserts, tropical forests, grasslands, marshy wetlands and high mountains. Britain has its flat plains, marshes, estuaries, rolling downland, rugged upland, high mountains and areas of vastly different geology and soils enabling very different ways of life. Climate and environment may have changed greatly but the need for human groups to find food, resources and shelter has not. All societies in the past faced the same issues of having to deal with the environments in which they found themselves.

We rely on basic physical needs to maintain our existence: water, food, materials to make tools, shelter and fire. These we get from the land in which we live, or by trading with others who have them in their own lands. But the land on which we live is more important than just a quarry for food and materials. It is also a place in which we experience our lives, where we give names to significant features and associate them with pleasurable or disturbing events. Places have meaning for us. They can be somewhere that makes us feel comfortable, or somewhere we wish to flee from.

Archaeologists analyse how resources are obtained from the environment and how they move between communities. This means that archaeology has a large area of overlap with geography and economics. We study similar themes, and have some similar methods. This is an important feature of archaeology in the United Kingdom with its wide variety of landscapes in a small area. The use of geographical methods in archaeology is sometimes called geoarchaeology, and helps us to understand processes of landscape formation, the formation of sites, and the distribution and interaction of settlements across large regions.

We cannot simply apply geographical methods to archaeological evidence. Geographers try to understand the world as it is today. Is today the same as the past? Understanding how settlements are placed in the landscape and how they work together politically and economically in the modern, urbanised, highly technological and highly connected world may not be the same as how they were placed and worked together in an earlier, more rural, less technological and less connected world. Even if there are enough similarities to allow us to apply a geographical method, we have a major problem. Archaeologists seldom recover enough evidence to completely reconstruct a place in the past. We also do not always know that all settlements and places in a region were in use at the same time.

Another major problem is that the very shape of the landscape has changed greatly over thousands of years. One very good example of this is the lost land of Doggerland. This is the name given to the North Sea between Britain and northern Germany and Denmark. This was once dry land after the end of the last Ice Age until it was drowned by rising sea levels around 8,500 years ago. Recent archaeological work has been able to reconstruct the lost land in some detail.

Environmental archaeology

Many people working in environmental archaeology are trained as geographers, biologists or zoologists and have become interested in the historical development of the landscape, its plants and animals. These other subjects can help us to know how soils form and why past human settlements become buried underground. Knowing about the physical, chemical and biological characteristics of soils is essential for understanding what archaeological remains survive, in what condition and where they will be found. For example, sandy soils are highly acidic and will destroy human and animal bone, leaving at best only dark stains in the soil. Knowing how hill slopes erode and change shape over time helps to understand why archaeological remains may be easier to find higher rather than lower on a slope. Understanding the role of earthworms in processing soil can help to explain why fragments of the same artefact can become separated in different levels in the soil. Chemical and structural analysis of soils can help to show whether they are entirely natural or wholly or partly humanly made. The accumulation of human rubbish and waste can produce thick soil deposits. Knowing how settlement sites decay and how artefacts are dispersed by natural processes is a key part of being able to interpret archaeological sites.

But, environmental archaeology is more than this. It can be an attempt to reconstruct the environment as it was at the time of the past culture we are investigating. Analysing pollen, or chemical traces in the soil, can reveal much about the vegetation and soils around the site. They can reveal direct traces of human activity such as burning off vegetation by hunters in the Mesolithic. Removal of woodlands by farmers to create grazing or open fields has dramatic effects on soil composition and fertility, as well as increasing flooding and deposition of soils elsewhere. Human actions can also leave obvious physical traces in the landscape, such as deliberately cut terraces to allow the growing of crops on hillsides, or the deliberate levelling of uneven ground to allow buildings to be put up. Knowing the make-up of the soils and vegetation around a site can help us see why some settlements prospered and why some remained poor, with different access to fertile soils or raw materials.

Once we have a good understanding of the environment and the raw materials it offers, we can begin to examine how people used that environment

45

and created spaces within it at different scales from the region down to the individual site or building.

Culture contact

It is important to understand that human cultures did not exist in isolation. Types of contact between cultures can include diplomatic alliances, warfare, trade and exploration. Some types of contact are more visible archaeologically than others, such as trade where we can study the flow of raw materials and goods. A scientific study of raw materials such as stone, obsidian, amber, pottery and bronze reveals the long-distance links between people living in different areas. One of the commonest rocks used to make Neolithic axe heads in Britain was a volcanic tuff (ash) from the Lake District. Axe heads made out of tuff are found in large numbers all over eastern and south-eastern Britain. Either people from a wide area were spending many days and weeks visiting the Lake District to quarry the stone, or, more likely, the people of the Lakes were trading their stone with others to the south and east.

There are limits, though, to how far archaeology can help us reconstruct patterns of contact between cultures. It is much harder to establish the flow of ideas than styles of decoration or fashions in clothing. We know from references and quotations in later Greek and Roman writers that in 320 BC a man called Pytheas sailed his ship on a voyage of exploration from the Greek colony of Marseilles in the western Mediterranean northwards to Britain and elsewhere, writing an account of what he saw. There is no archaeological evidence for this, but we have no reason to doubt that the voyage did happen.

Political ties are also hard to demonstrate by archaeology alone. There are finds of Roman pottery in western Britain from the fifth and sixth centuries, yet we know that Britain was no longer part of the Roman Empire after AD 410. We find information in historical documents that tell us that the Roman emperors were making diplomatic alliances with rulers in Britain at the time.

We can sometimes trace the movement of peoples between cultures. For example, the analysis of chemical elements in teeth can reveal where people grew up as children. A body in a wealthy burial (the Amesbury archer) near Stonehenge, dating from 2300 BC, was shown to have grown up in the Alpine region of central Europe. This person seems to have been an immigrant to Britain rather than an explorer or trader. Movement of people over long distances was clearly commoner than many archaeologists have been willing to admit.

Settlements in the landscape

Much of archaeology is concerned with finding past settlements. Finding such sites is only the first step though. We also seek to understand why the settlement is where it is, and how it relates to other settlements in the same area. We look for the patterns of sites in the landscape and how they form part of a regional system of settlement and economy. Geographical models of site locations have been widely used in archaeology, for example central place theory, which seeks to understand the hierarchies of sites in an area: which are central and which are subsidiary. It is exciting to find a Roman villa, but part of that excitement is asking questions such as what was the role of that villa in the region in Roman times. What relationship did the Romanised wealthy farmer of the villa have with smaller local farmers, cottagers and slaves? Was the villa owned by a wealthy outsider? Was the surplus grain and livestock of the villa sold in markets in the nearby town? Was grain or livestock paid in rent or taxes to the government or to the army in a nearby fort? Where did the craftsmen live who built the villa and its mosaics? Similar questions could be asked of any settlement site from any period in the past.

In the modern world we are used to thinking of settlements in terms of the numbers of people living in them, for example a single farm, a hamlet, a village, a town, a city or a conurbation. We also think of functions such as burial, work or worship as happening within settlements and that the most important places were the largest settlements. In earlier times, other factors might be more important in classifying settlements, and many activities happened elsewhere. For example, we might ask whether Neolithic long barrows were burial sites for an area of many settlements or for only one settlement, or how many different homesteads would come together to meet at Neolithic causewayed enclosures. The important regional sites in these cases appear not to have been settlements but burial sites or seasonal meeting places.

Use of space does not only involve settlements. We also want to understand large-scale patterns of hunting or farming. Features such as the pattern and shape of fields can tell us much about the history of the landscape. The use of the land over thousands of years has produced a complex pattern of fields with different layouts on top of each other, often over very large areas. Even simple methods such as counting and recording the number and types of tree species in hedgerows can help to date field systems. Landscape archaeology has a lot in common with geography and history. Most archaeologists of landscape look back to Professor W G Hoskins as the founder of landscape studies, although Hoskins himself was a local historian rather than an archaeologist.

Understanding single sites

Archaeologists focus on how people at specific sites found what they needed in their local area, using ideas from economics and geography. It was the insight of early archaeologists such as Sir Grahame Clark, who wrote *Prehistoric Europe: the economic basis* in 1952, which showed that we cannot study past cultures in isolation from their environments. In the past, we could not simply go down to the nearest ironmongers or hardware store for our tools. People had to make their tools from scratch. The stone knife can help to skin an animal. Stone scrapers can process the hide to make leather. Soft clay can be mixed with other things and shaped into pots to be hardened by fire. The right kind of plant stems can be used to make string and rope. The list of what nature can give is almost endless. But humans needed stone or metal tools for many of their most important activities. The most important stones for tools include flint, chert, quartz, quartzite and obsidian. Eventually, we worked out how to heat metal ores and produce copper, tin, lead and iron. We also learned how to mix ores to produce bronze and other alloys. Archaeology is often too dominated by studies of stone, metal and pottery, and we tend to forget the materials that rot away easily, such as plant and animal products used for tools, food, drink, flavourings, medicines, narcotics, fibres, fodder, dyes, perfumes, fuel, oils, etc. We especially forget the importance of wood and that specific types of wood are used for specific purposes. Understanding the properties of raw materials and where those materials can be found gives archaeology an area of overlap with subjects such as geology, chemistry and biology.

The raw materials we need for our tools are not found everywhere. They occur in specific locations. Few materials are distinctive enough that they can be easily tracked down to their source by eye. For those that can't, we must use scientific methods to characterise the materials and match them to their sources. This can include geological thin sections examined under a microscope, or it can be a chemical analysis of the material (looking for very small 'impurities' that differ in their amounts at different sources). In the case of stone and metals, we need a good geological understanding of their distribution.

Each site has its own catchment. Most people will seek to use their environment with least effort, and travelling out from home is a large part of the effort. Activities that need a lot of time and labour will happen closest to the home, within an easily walkable territory. Studies of present day peoples suggest that the home territory for most hunter-gatherers would be within a 6-mile radius of home (a 2-hour walk), and for farmers it would be within a 3-mile radius (a 1-hour walk). We can think of this as similar to modern commuting where there is a distance beyond which travelling to work is less and less attractive. The average commuting time to London is just under 1 hour, with only a few hardy souls commuting from York to London, a journey time of just under 2 hours. Distance rules like this offer us a rough rule of thumb for the extent of the land exploited from any one settlement. Site catchment offers a way of understanding why settlements were sited where they were, and what kind of work was being done at them. We look at the pattern of resources within the home territory of the site, such as the soils and what kinds of crops they could have supported in the case of a farming settlement. Sites are often on the edges between ecological zones. This allows both zones, such as mountain pasture and lowland arable, to be exploited from one site with the least effort.

Site catchment analysis has flaws of course. For it to work we need an accurate reconstruction of past environments, which is not always possible. The distances exploited from the settlement will be affected by the nature of the landscape and how close other settlements are, and so will not always be the idealised 1- or 2-hour walking journey. We also assume that the resources were obvious to people who did not have our sophisticated ability to analyse soil properties or knowledge of the local underground geology. We further assume that people were motivated only by economic considerations when it came to deciding where to live. Other matters such as religion or politics could have been just as important. But, overall, it is a useful way of trying to understand how people were living at a site, and their relationship to the environment around it.

On-site patterning

Understanding what people were doing at any one site depends on being able to interpret what artefacts are found on the site and the patterns of where artefacts were found. The American archaeologists Lewis and Sally Binford (*New perspectives in archaeology*, 1968) and Michael Schiffer (*Behavioural archaeology*, 1976) independently noted a problem with this. We have a static pattern of archaeological finds that we need to match with dynamic patterns of behaviour by people in the past. They suggested that the way to do this was to rely on ethnographic analogy. We have to assume that human behaviour remains broadly the same over time. If we can see patterns of behaviour that leave particular material evidence behind in modern or recently documented societies, then we can assume that if we see similar material evidence on an archaeological site it was produced by similar behaviour. Binford called this 'middle range theory': how to analyse the range in the middle between static evidence and dynamic behaviour. He was concerned that observation of ethnographic behaviour should be done by archaeologists, and done rigorously. We would see the spatial patterns in the material culture that result from activities such as processing crops. Archaeology here overlaps with anthropology and ethnography. The terms ethno-archaeology or living archaeology are sometimes used for the archaeological analysis of present day societies.

Naturally, there are problems with this. Can we assume that human behaviour does not change over time? This is a risky assumption when we go back into the Palaeolithic where we are dealing with other pre-modern humans. Can we assume that the range of behaviour we see at the present is the full range of possible behaviours that existed in the past? We must always allow for the possibility that some behaviour in the past is very different to anything we can see at the present.

The most constant behaviours are those that deal with economic processes or technology, where there are limited possibilities imposed by nature. There are only a few ways in which crops can be processed, based on the physical structure of wheat, barley, rice, maize, etc. Behaviours which deal with non-physical processes such as religious worship or expressing social status involve an almost infinite choice of possibilities and are far harder to predict or analyse.

Personal and family spaces

Living in buildings involves the use of spaces within them for different activities. The design of buildings can reflect or determine the nature of these activities, the relationships between the people who live or work in the building and how people move through the building. Buildings have rules about who does what where. In our modern Western houses, the rules are based on activity. We generally do not sleep in the same room that we sit in during the day (unless you live in a student flat), and we often cook in another separate area. The rules may be different in non-Western societies, based for example on gender, so that men and women will sleep and carry out their activities in different parts of the building, or even in separate buildings. In the historic past, we may have documents to help us reconstruct the rules, but, for prehistory, we must rely on the pattern of artefacts and other archaeological features to try and reconstruct the use of space.

One approach to understanding how spaces were used is to look at buildings as arenas for experiencing activities. The layout of the building and its position in relation to others on the same site can be revealing. For example, the change from open halls to houses divided into separate rooms in later medieval Britain was closely related to changes in the nature of society. The open hall allowed the whole household to eat and work in the same space as an integrated, yet hierarchical unit under the lord and lady. This idea of a communally inhabited arena that was also marked out to show people's social status and place within the community could be extended to other spaces within the medieval world. The traditional social order began to break down with the Reformation and other social, political and technological changes in the sixteenth century, and the result is a change in the use of space within houses and other buildings. The old open spaces were replaced by closed-off private spaces instead. Other ways of looking at space include the notion of private and public activities. Secluded medieval nunneries were private spaces, designed differently from the more publicly oriented spaces of monasteries for many, but not all, orders of monks. Spaces can also be controlled. The pattern of wooden upright posts or stones inside Late Neolithic henges has been interpreted as controlling the movement of people to particular routes as part of the ceremonial activities within the henge. The uprights, surrounding earthen banks and entrances, can be seen as ways of restricting sight of the ceremonies taking place inside. Henges were sites of performance where taking part and watching was controlled by the nature of the space. This approach also helps us to understand the design of medieval churches.

People have a highly personal relationship with their environment. Specific places in the landscape may have personal associations with happy or sad events. Religion and myth may give certain places a significance. People have emotional responses to places based on the physical feeling of a place or an appreciation for its beauty or lack of it. Of course, knowing how people in the past thought and felt about their environment is impossible without written documents or place-names to guide us. Even for most historical periods, written documents seldom help us. Some archaeologists have turned to philosophy to give them a framework for analysing past experience, for example phenomenology. This particular philosophy stresses the need to understand how people subjectively experience the world around them. For archaeologists, this means trying to place ourselves back in the past in particular places and use our senses of sight, hearing and smell (as well as thoughts and feelings) to try to reimagine the world through the eyes of our forebears. Empathising with past people is a worthwhile attempt but obviously carries the danger that we simply impose our own feelings and responses onto the past.

Conclusion

Our use of space permeates our lives and yet is something we are often unaware of. Archaeology enlarges our knowledge of how space has been used over thousands of years. We can investigate some big issues. Environmental archaeology gives us insights into long-term climate change and of our response to such change. It allows us to see how our over-exploitation of the landscape can bring ruin to our way of life. An appreciation of culture contact in the past does much to reduce ideas of cultural selfishness, isolation or superiority in the present. Understanding the importance of territories and the exploitation of resources helps us to make sense of the many, seemingly senseless, wars that plague our planet. The design of our towns and cities can be understood much more clearly with an archaeological understanding of taskscapes and the meaningful experience of places by individuals.

One of the key contributions of archaeology is to add the time dimension to our understanding of environment and landscape. This makes archaeology a form of historical geography, and there are many overlaps between the two. Yet archaeology is more than this, and it is its third dimension, to be explored in the next chapter, which gives archaeology its special place as a discipline.

5

Understanding people

Year after year, individual after individual, learned society after learned society, we are prosaically revealing and cataloguing our discoveries. Too often we dig up mere things, unrepentantly forgetful that our proper aim is to dig up people.

Sir Mortimer Wheeler (1954) *Archaeology from the earth*

Who are people?

Understanding how we change over time and how we use space gives us a much better understanding of ourselves. Yet, for a fuller understanding, we also need to turn the spotlight on the third dimension of archaeology, people. Strangely, people are sometimes forgotten by archaeologists, who get engrossed in describing, measuring and analysing artefacts and structures instead.

We need to be clear what we mean by 'people'. Of course, one meaning of people is individual human beings. Individuals are capable of feeling, of expressing themselves and acting in ways different to others according to their likes, dislikes and capacities. But who is the individual? There is the physical–biological human being and the abstract notion of the person (or persona). Personas are created and moulded by social activity. The same individual may have one persona and set of behaviours as a parent in the home, and another as 'one of the lads' on the rugby field or in the pub.

We also use the word 'people' to refer to several individuals at once. Individuals have always formed groups, in which they will have different roles and status. The groups themselves may have different roles and status within society. Groups are highly complex. Some groups act like communities, with explicitly recognised norms of behaviour constraining the individuals to behave in ways acceptable to the wider group. Behaving in the right way gains acceptance and a social persona is created, for example by adopting clothing, speech patterns and body adornments. That communities often express themselves in material culture is obviously useful for helping us to identify them through archaeology. There are many kinds of community we might identify. The easiest to see are residential groups. Others we have to work harder to identify, such as genetic groups (families and lineages), functional groups (e.g. warriors, miners), status groups (e.g. nobles, freemen, slaves), economic groups (e.g. landowners, craftsmen, workers).

Archaeologists need to ask various questions to understand people in the past. How do individuals express themselves? Do they follow or avoid the norms of group behaviour? How do groups maintain themselves? How do different groups interact? What role do individuals and groups play in society as a whole? There are clear overlaps here between archaeology and other subjects such as sociology, social anthropology and economics.

Mapping material culture onto human behaviour is not straightforward. A twentieth-century British archaeologist, Christopher Hawkes, came up with a 'ladder of inference' to explain the difficulties (Figure 5.1). The higher up the ladder, the harder it is to recover information by archaeology alone and the more we have to rely on ethnographic analogy and historical documents. Recovering ancient technology is easier than recovering ancient spiritual life.

As with space, we have to study people at different scales. We can study society as a whole, trying to understand human behaviour in general. We can also focus on particular cultures or communities. On the other hand, we can recover information about individuals. To simplify hugely, this coincides with three particular types of archaeology. Traditional archaeology focused on cultures and communities, as seen with culture history in Chapter 3. The New Archaeology of the 1960s and 1970s was aimed at understanding human behaviour in general. The post-processual archaeologies of the 1980s and 1990s were more concerned to explore individual human experience. Other types of archaeology study the complex interaction between both individual and group behaviours.

Rungs of the ladder	Examples	Kinds of evidence
spiritual life	afterlife beliefs, gods	grave goods, history, ethnography
religious institutions	priesthoods, ceremonies	'ritual' sites, ethnography, history
political institutions	tribes, chiefs, dispensing justice	cultures, status goods, ethnography, history
social institutions	family, marriage, inheritance	skeletal and DNA, ethnography, history
economics	trading materials and goods	sourcing of materials, history
subsistence	growing crops, cooking	cereal grains, animal bones, hearths, pottery
technology	making tools and buildings	artefacts and structures

Figure 5.1   **Hawkes's Ladder of Inference**

New Archaeology

New Archaeology is no longer new. It was a major form of archaeology in the United Kingdom and America from the 1960s to the 1980s, and is nowadays often referred to as processual archaeology. One of the aims of the New Archaeologists was to understand how a past society functioned, rather than how past cultures developed over time. It could be characterised as a kind of a sociology of the past, although in the UK it began by adapting ideas from the New Geography of the 1960s. The key aspect of the New Archaeology, as developed by David Clarke in the United Kingdom in his *Analytical archaeology* of 1968 and Kent Flannery in the USA in the late 1960s, was that society is an interaction of different aspects of human behaviour. Clarke used systems theory, where a change in behaviour in one part of the system would have a knock-on effect on other parts of the system. All parts of the system are ultimately interconnected with the others. For example, if population increases, then more land has to be cultivated or the methods of farming have to be intensified to produce more food. That in turn can change who owns the new lands being cultivated. Or those who manage

55

to be more efficient at producing food can become wealthy at the expense of others. This in turn could lead to a challenge to the traditional political leaders of society. A change in population therefore could lead to changes in farming, in society and in politics.

Clarke called the different aspects of society 'sub-systems', including the social (e.g. kinship, rank, status), the religious, the psychological (ideas), the economic and the material culture (technology). These were only devices to allow us to analyse behaviour and we can create whatever sub-systems we like. We can see that material culture reflects all other aspects of human behaviour.

The New Archaeology freed archaeologists to shed light on past cultures as living societies. It gave us concepts to help us think about the past, such as homeostasis, feedback, adaptation and variables. It gave us a way of analysing the past through models and using flow charts, statistics and computer simulations. It gave us the confidence to look at big issues such as the origins of states or of social stratification.

Impenetrable jargon?

New Archaeology developed a particular jargon, the specialised use of words that can make it hard to read and understand what New Archaeologists wrote. Here are a few examples of words used by New Archaeologists.

- Attribute: a basic characteristic that can be described or measured, e.g. the shape of the rim of a pot.
- Extra-somatic: beyond the body, extending the physical capability of a person, e.g. tools allow us to do things our hands on their own cannot.
- Feedback: an effect on one part of the system that causes changes elsewhere which feed back into and change the first part of the system.
- Homeostasis: system stability, where changes in all the parts of a system balance each other and cancel out.
- Models: an idealised description of how past societies might have been.
- Polythetic: the overlapping of attributes so that not all artefacts from the same culture will share all the same attributes and that some attributes may be shared with other cultures.
- Stochastic: something that is not certain but only probable.
- Variable: a quantity or value that can be measured and is not fixed.

New Archaeology has its flaws. Some American archaeologists, such as Lewis Binford, sought to develop general laws of human behaviour and saw material culture as mostly an adaptation to the environment. Change in a society was therefore imposed by changes in the environment. Other archaeologists felt that this reduced people to being pawns of external factors rather than having a choice of how to behave and respond. Human behaviour is based on individual differences and choices that make it very hard to find any universal laws of behaviour. Instead, we end up with statistical probabilities rather than scientific laws. New Archaeology aimed at being more rigorous and scientific than traditional archaeology, and therefore more objective. But this is impossible, as we all bring unconscious biases to our work based on our own culture, our social and educational background, our politics, our likes, dislikes and preconceived ideas, etc. Nevertheless, the New Archaeology brought human behaviour back to archaeology as one of our main objects of study. It also emphasised to us that we must study all aspects of past societies as they all interconnect and affect each other. These are no mean achievements.

Marxism again

At its heart, Marxism is a theory of human behaviour and appeals to many archaeologists as a way of looking at the dynamics of past societies. It sees human nature as conditioned by the economic necessities of life, and classifies people by their position within socio-economic groups. Marxist ideas offer a way of explaining how societies change over time, as seen in Chapter 3, but they also help us focus on how people behave and interact with others.

Marx's ideas were most developed in describing medieval and modern societies. Archaeologists have produced their own interpretations of earlier periods based on some of his ideas. For example, the American anthropologist Marshall Sahlins created a theoretical model about how prehistoric economies and societies worked. He described what he called the Domestic Mode of Production. The means of production (land, labour, tools, plants, animals) were owned or held by family households. They did the work themselves, and divided their tasks by gender and age. Technology would be small-scale, widely available and easily made. Production of food would be for the livelihood of the family, satisfying their needs rather than accumulating a surplus. Trade would be limited to obtaining items that were needed but could not be had in the immediate area. There would be only slight differences in wealth, which would depend on the size and abilities of families and their access to resources. Such a society is what we may see in the Palaeolithic and Mesolithic with small hunter-gatherer groups leaving behind little in the way of finds, structures or obvious signs of wealth and property.

Farming communities have larger populations, are usually less mobile and rely on trade with neighbours for more of their raw materials and goods. They also need to establish rules of ownership over land, where crops are grown and animals are pastured. They may need to mobilise labour for large projects such as irrigation. Conflicts between groups over resources lead to organised warfare and the need for people to act as warriors and provide some kind of political leadership. Households may quarrel over resources and there will need to be some way of judging disputes. Marxists would see all these needs as connected with the control of resources and means of production. The need to obtain and distribute food and raw materials would produce a ruling class with a vested interest in controlling the rest of the community.

It is one of the achievements of Marxism that we now see economics as deeply embedded within other aspects of society. For an archaeologist, the task is to understand how the relationship between economics and other areas of life can be seen in the material culture. This is not always as easy as some archaeologists think.

Ethnography in prehistory

Understanding ancient societies does not have to rely on Marxism. Ethnographers have studied different kinds of society using a wide range of ideas. This gives us a range of possibilities for understanding how past societies worked.

There are many questions we might be able to shed light on by using ethnography. For example, how can we explain the movement of goods in a tribal or chiefdom society of the kind that existed from the Neolithic to the Bronze Age in most of Europe, where there was no coinage or any form of money? We can begin with the notion of reciprocity. This is the simple idea that if I do something for you, then at some point in the future I will expect you to do something for me. Of course, if you happen to be a close friend or relative, I may be a bit more relaxed about that as I will be more generous towards people who are closest to me. The notion of reciprocity extends to the giving of things (we can say that economics is socially embedded). Ethnographers have observed that there is a generalised reciprocity within the household and among close kin, where people are expected to be altruistic, sharing and friendly, with little expectation of immediate return. Among the tribe, there may be balanced reciprocity where links are kept up through marriage and bonds of distant kinship, and there is an expectation of fair return for a gift. With outsiders, there will be negative reciprocity where people will haggle and barter or even see outright theft and warfare as perfectly legitimate. Any giving will need to be carefully staged to force an expectation of a return. Hence the importance of becoming a blood-brother with a stranger. It sets up a fictitious but accepted kinship that prevents negative reciprocity. Goods can then move between families and individuals as part of normal social relationships including the giving of gifts. Of course, people can manipulate the idea of reciprocity by deliberately giving away large gifts to others, putting them in their debt and so accumulating status.

We can begin to see how Neolithic stone axe heads might move between different groups from the Lake District to the Yorkshire Wolds in northern England. We can ask what the return was, the reciprocal gifts going from the Wolds to the Lakes. Was it goods that we cannot see archaeologically, such as wheat, or something intangible such as political alliance against enemies? A distribution map of stone axe head finds begins to become a model of human behaviour. The problem for archaeologists is to find ways of working out which behaviours underlie the patterns we see in the evidence. This is easier said than done.

Culture and ethnicity

We assume that cultures represent specific societies in the past, bound together perhaps by politics or ethnicity. There is no simple way of deciding what is used by any group or society to mark itself off from others. In the modern world, it can be one or more of several markers, for example:

- religion: e.g. Catholic Croats, Orthodox Serbs, Moslem Bosnians all speaking the Serbo-Croat language;
- language: e.g. Catalan, Castilian, Galician and Basque speakers in Spain;
- political separation: e.g. German-speaking Catholics divided among Germany, Austria and Switzerland;
- social or economic status: e.g. youth culture groups and gangs, working- and middle-class styles of dress;
- occupation: e.g. the different fieldwork and research practices of archaeologists and historians.

The idea of ethnicity and identity is hotly debated in sociology and social anthropology. There are several features common to ethnic groups: a group name, a myth of common descent/origin, a sense of shared history, a distinctive culture, a territorial homeland, solidarity (self-awareness of identity).

Ethnic groups can appear and disappear over time, but can also have very long histories. Even those with long histories may change their characteristics over time while keeping a sense of a name and identity.

Many aspects of culture are intangible (non-material), so archaeologists can only study part of a past culture (the tangible material culture). We also cannot fully recover a past culture, finding all the sites, artefacts, buildings and structures. David Clarke looked at carefully recorded North American peoples to try and see how far archaeological units could correspond to tribal units or languages. He suggested that only about 15 per cent of a tribe's culture would survive to be found by archaeologists in the future. He also showed that around 30 per cent of artefact types were shared between unrelated tribes. If two separate assemblages of artefacts shared around 65 per cent of types then they most likely came from the same tribe. But he also showed that there were exceptions to this and it is hard to simply equate a culture with a past people.

A common type of burial in the Early Bronze Age in Britain is a single person placed in a grave with a raised, round mound over the top. A small proportion of bodies were buried with artefacts such as a tall pottery beaker, necklaces and other ornaments made of jet, amber, glass or gold, archery wrist-guards, copper knives and awls, flint daggers and arrowheads, stone 'battle axes', boar tusks, whetstones, and other stone and bone tools. The pottery and other artefacts are very distinctive, and similar to items found in other parts of western Europe. The name Beaker culture was given to sites associated with this kind of pottery (dated 2400 to 1800 BC). There has been a lot of debate about what the Beaker culture represents, and whether we can even speak of a 'Beaker culture'. It was long seen as a marker of a new immigrant people into Britain, but more lately was thought to be adopted by the existing elite trading in copper and tin and importing new status items to show off their wealth. While the idea of a migrant people has largely been abandoned, new chemical analyses of skeletal materials is throwing up some surprises. The Amesbury Archer, a man buried near Stonehenge around 2300 BC with a very rich assemblage of Beaker artefacts, was shown to have grown up in the northern Alps, and so a migrant to Britain. Perhaps the Beaker culture may represent a people after all!

Gender and identity

Over the past 30 years, feminist ideas have come into archaeology, and helped us understand gender, sex and sexuality in the past. The differences between men and women have been discussed since at least the time of the ancient

Greeks. This usually sets two categories in opposition to each other: male and female. This may seem logical, but obscures the nature of gender which is only loosely based on biology. There are ethnographic accounts of societies which recognise many more than two genders, often with specific roles and characteristics that blend male and female in different ways.

What is gender?

It is easy to confuse gender with sex, and sexuality. Most archaeologists would use the following definitions:

- Gender: the cultural interpretation of sexual differences (e.g. how male, female and ambiguous sexual identities are characterised by behaviour and dress);
- Sex: the physical expression of genetic sexual identity (male, female and inter-sexed bodies);
- Sexuality: the expression of sexual preferences (heterosexual, gay, lesbian, bisexual).

A person may be quite effeminate and adopt female gender behaviour and roles, yet be physically male and heterosexual. Exploring gender, sex and sexuality is an interesting way of exploring how people construct their identities.

The feminist challenge made us recognise that we had unconsciously analysed the past from a restricted, male, perspective. Our studies focussed mostly on assumed male aspects of life such as hunting, warfare, political status while neglecting aspects such as child rearing, plant gathering, etc. We have also assumed that gender roles in the past were as we see them today. Some assume males are aggressive, territorial, competitive, promiscuous, risk taking, acquisitive and status conscious, while females are passive, altruistic, cooperative, loyal, risk averse, generous and nurturing. These are both caricatures, true only of the extremes and not of most men or women. This also need not be how earlier societies saw gender differences.

There are two main ways of looking at gender in archaeology. We can try to establish women's roles in ancient societies, and challenge assumptions about the male nature of certain tasks (Figure 5.2). Is it true that men hunt and make stone tools, while women gather plant foods and make baskets? Studies that challenge such assumptions are common in American archaeology. We can also look at how gender is consciously manipulated through material culture as part of the creation of identities. Studies like this are especially

Figure 5.2 **Female flint knapping in the Palaeolithic according to George Worthington Smith (thanks to Luton Culture)**

common in British and Scandinavian archaeology, influenced by philosophy and sociology.

Direct evidence for sexual activity is rare in archaeology, for example brothel tokens from Roman sites. Evidence for gender is commoner. Burials in the Early Bronze Age in Britain are usually of bodies laid in a crouching position on one side. Male skeletons are mostly buried with the face looking to the north-east, while female skeletons face the south-west. What this means we can only guess, most likely something related to religious belief. Differences allow us to see the deliberate bending of genders, for example male skeletons facing the 'wrong' way, or female skeletons with 'male' artefacts such as a dagger or arrows. In eastern Europe, some 20 per cent of Iron Age Sarmatian warrior burials are female, backing up the ancient Greek myths of fierce women warriors they called Amazons. How were these women warriors seen by their own society? Could they have been a third gender, or were they regarded socially as males? Modern Inuit hunters were normally male, and if the family had no sons then a daughter would be raised as a boy and be expected to act as a boy.

Agency and the individual

One of the central problems for an archaeology of behaviour is that the archaeological record was made by the acts of individual human beings. Why is this a problem? Because as archaeologists we deal instead with cultures and assemblages of artefacts. We analyse these into patterns. We create classes of artefact such as an arrowhead or types such as the cruciform brooch. These and the sites we analyse are examples of group behaviour, people following social norms and accepted ways of doing or making things. As a result, archaeology has borrowed the notion of agency from sociology to try and explore the role of individuals in the past.

Individual actions may be intended, such as deciding where to dig a rubbish pit and what rubbish to put in it. We have to understand the reasoning behind the intentions such as why the pit was dug where it was and not somewhere else. Actions may also be unintended, such as digging the pit through the unknown buried remains of a house from a previous settlement. Can we distinguish intended from unintended actions? Assuming that we know how individuals behave in the past depends on those individuals being like ourselves. Their own ideas and beliefs may be completely different from our own. This is an especially serious problem in the study of the Palaeolithic. Can we really say we understand how a Neanderthal individual thought?

Determining the individual actions that make up an artefact is easy. We can use the idea of a life history for an artefact to identify a whole set of choices made by individuals. These choices are affected by various factors such as tradition, social expectations, economics, technology and the environment. Seen in this way, agency differs little from Clarke's systems approach. In the Late Neolithic an individual tool-maker (flint knapper) had various choices. What type of flint did they use, and how did they get hold of it? Did they knap the flint the way they were taught or find their own method? Did they prefer to make an arrowhead with a pointed base or a rounded base? The idea of agency forces the archaeologist to ask why that choice and not others. Our ability to see individuals' choices depends on finding variations from the norm, for example finding reddish-brown flint artefacts on a site where most of the flint is brownish-black. But we still find it hard to explain why that individual made that particular choice.

63

Castles: a case study in gender and agency

Medieval castles are traditionally seen as male spaces, as fortifications for defence in war by armed knights. Yet, they yield non-military, non-masculine finds, for example finding a bone baby's dummy and metal thimbles at Sandal Castle in the north of England. In medieval times, aristocratic men and women were seen as very different and living almost in separate worlds. Men and women would have their separate households and living spaces, and this should be reflected in the design of the castle. The women's spaces would be the farthest away from the main entrance and most secluded from public affairs. At Chepstow Castle, the women's hall and private courtyard lay at the far end of the castle, invisible from the keep. Private courtyards or gardens were a common feature of women's spaces. In medieval literature, the private garden was often a symbol for chastity, a woman's space that was also available for romantic encounters. Does all this mean that women were passive and subordinate in medieval society, kept hidden away and protected? The idea of agency answers that by seeing women as active participants in medieval life, exploiting their elevated position both as desirable objects of chivalry and as the matriarch running the household with real power over household finances.

Thinking ourselves into the past

The importing of agency from sociology and anthropology was a revolt against some of the more extreme versions of New Archaeology that saw impersonal forces directing human behaviour from the outside. They seemed to deny a role for the individual (although a close reading of David Clarke shows that there was always a role for individuals in his version of New Archaeology). Critics of New Archaeology, especially as it was practised in the USA, thought that it was overly concerned with the processes that kept societies stable. Hence, 'processual archaeology' was coined to describe New Archaeology by its critics. These critics have been described as post-processualists, a name applied to various ideas in archaeology since the 1980s. These ideas were enthusiastically taken up in Britain and Scandinavia and by some American archaeologists. Leading figures in post-processual archaeology would be Ian Hodder (*Reading the past*, 1986), Michael Shanks and Chris Tilley (*Social theory and archaeology*, 1987), and Julian Thomas (*Time, culture and identity*, 1996).

Post-processualists believe that culture is made by individuals within the constraints imposed by their society. These constraints come from the traditional ways of doing things that are unique to each society. We have to understand the historical development of each society on its own, rather than spend our time chasing general laws of human behaviour that work across all societies. The idea of agency is a key post-processual idea and has two consequences. Archaeologists are themselves agents within archaeology; we consciously choose what we study and how we interpret the evidence, reflecting our own upbringing, temperament and beliefs. We cannot be objective and neutral. We also accept people in the past as agents. We should therefore try to understand how they thought and felt about the world they lived in and the choices they made. Material culture can be seen as symbolic of human thought and feeling, instead of merely a technical device to accomplish certain tasks.

How can we know the minds of past individuals? Can we ever know in the sense of feeling for ourselves the exact feelings of someone else? For most of archaeology, we are dealing with people who did not leave diaries behind. The best we can do is to think and feel ourselves inside the ancient house that they lived in, or walk the processional route that they walked, and use our knowledge and imagination to place ourselves in the shoes of the long dead person. Even then, the best we can say is that this is how we think the past person might have felt. This kind of archaeology is sometimes called cognitive archaeology, part of a wider field of interpretive archaeology.

The term 'cognitive archaeology' confusingly also refers to another kind of attempt to explore past minds. This is the addition of another rung at the top of Hawkes's ladder, trying to understand the development of human mental capacities such as speech, art, symbolism or writing. This is firmly part of a 'processual' approach, trying to determine the evidence for development of mental faculties. This is just as hard as the alternative 'post-processual' cognitive archaeology of empathy. How do we prove a link between material culture and the human mind?

Conclusion

Modern day archaeology has realised the full complexity of human societies and the evidence left behind for us to study. We try to understand the relationship between people and their societies, between different societies, between communities and their environment, and how all of these change and develop over time. The subject of archaeology is immensely complex, yet offers us the chance to understand ourselves in all our rich diversity. We try to study the whole of human behaviour, and this gives us an overlap with many other subjects. Archaeology is an exciting discipline which can unlock a better understanding of ourselves today, not just in the past.

We have to keep in mind that archaeology is a practice carried out today within particular societies, and that its role in those societies is varied, open to debate and at times highly political and controversial. This will form the basis for much of the rest of this book.

6

Where archaeologists work

> It is the remarkable and, on the whole, very happy mixture of amateurs and professionals which has given British archaeology its special value and character and which has enabled it to accomplish so much.
>
> Kenneth Hudson (1981) *A social history of archaeology*

In Chapter 1, I gave a simple definition of archaeology, that it 'is the study of how people in different places in the past have behaved through the physical evidence that they have left behind'. I went on to add that archaeology as practised 'is also concerned with managing and interpreting the remains of the past'. Managing the remains of the past is often described as a specialist area of work within archaeology, known as heritage management, and includes conserving sites, protecting archaeological remains, interpreting archaeology to the public, managing historic attractions and recording sites.

Who are archaeologists? In a profession such as medicine or law you have to belong to a professional body to be able to practise. You would not want to be operated on by an amateur surgeon with no qualifications! In most European countries, you must have an archaeology degree and be employed by an 'officially' recognised organisation to be able to carry out archaeology. Some archaeologists apply this same logic to the UK and call archaeologists only those who are employed as such. However, anyone can be an archaeologist in the UK. A lot of archaeology is done by local societies and individuals as a non-paid leisure activity. This voluntary sector of archaeology actually has more people practising archaeology than the professional sector.

Who employs archaeologists? There are five main kinds of employer:

- national organisations;
- archaeological field units and trusts (contractors);
- local authorities (curators);
- museums;
- universities and colleges.

National organisations

The national organisations that represent archaeology in the UK are the Council for British Archaeology (CBA) and Archaeology Scotland. These provide a bridge between amateur and professional archaeology of all kinds, acting to promote the subject to government and the public. Both are independent charities, not government organisations.

The UK national agencies managed or funded directly by government are English Heritage, Historic Scotland, Cadw (in Wales) and the Northern Ireland Environment Agency. They employ Inspectors of Ancient Monuments and Historic Buildings Inspectors who preserve and protect ancient sites and buildings, monitor fieldwork, and recommend grants. Much of their work is taken up with writing reports and giving advice. English Heritage also contains the Centre for Archaeology which forms a mobile fieldwork team, and has sections concerned with the conservation of finds, illustration and publication, and specialised scientific services provided through the Ancient Monuments Laboratory. Most of the national agencies have education services dealing with school visits to their sites.

Also funded by government are the two Royal Commissions on the Ancient and Historical Monuments of Wales and Scotland. These aim to compile and make available surveys of ancient monuments, buildings and other field remains. They make much use of aerial photographs of sites and landscapes. The equivalent body in England has been absorbed into English Heritage.

The National Trust is an independent organisation, founded in 1895, and promotes the permanent preservation for the nation of natural landscapes and historic buildings. There are estimated to be more than 40,000 sites of archaeological interest in the ownership of the National Trust, about 6 per cent of the UK total. The Trust employs Regional Archaeologists within its consultancy arm who record, survey and occasionally excavate sites in its care. The National Trust covers England, Wales and Northern Ireland. The equivalent body in Scotland is the National Trust for Scotland.

Many other national bodies, including the National Parks, the Environment Agency, the Highways Agency and the Forestry Commission, also employ archaeologists, to record, survey and sometimes excavate sites.

Archaeological field units and trusts

Most archaeological fieldwork is carried out by independent units. These vary a good deal in size and organisation, with a few attached to museums, local authorities or universities, but mostly existing as independent commercial companies, trusts or charities. They provide the bulk of jobs in the practical side of archaeology – such as surveying, excavation, photography, finds processing – together with special expertise such as the study of animal bones, human remains, artefacts, finds conservation, editorial and drawing skills.

Most of the work done by the field units is paid for by developers, as one of the conditions they must fulfil in return for getting planning permission from the local authority. This means a lot of archaeology is done, but also that the amount of archaeology depends on the health of the economy. When the economy is booming, there is a lot of new building work and more jobs for archaeologists. When the economy is doing badly, there is less work and less jobs. Units will compete with each other for the tenders to carry out the work, and will have a small team of permanent staff to manage their excavations and surveys. Most of the workforce will be hired on short-term contracts for particular projects or periods of a few months at a time.

The kind of work done by field units varies. It is not always excavation. Desktop surveys gather together all known information about a site and may reveal long-lost features or information about previous excavations. A watching brief is simply observing building work and making a simple record of anything that happens to turn up on sites where remains are not expected or are of low importance. Field survey is the accurate mapping and recording of features at the surface. Building survey is the accurate recording of a building and all its architectural features. Geophysical survey uses scientific instruments to reveal features buried below ground. Full-scale excavation may be the last stage of a project and can be as simple as a small trench open and shut within one day or a large open area taking many weeks (in rare cases, years) to excavate. A field archaeologist will be expected to develop expertise in most of these types of work.

Local authorities

Most county councils and some districts and unitary authorities employ archaeologists. An important role for many of them is to provide advice on the conservation or recording of archaeological remains when applications for planning permission are being determined, and to ensure that fieldwork is carried out to a high enough standard. Such curatorial work relies upon the Historic Environment Records (HER), databases of the historic environment, usually kept at county or regional level. An HER should have its own team to keep it updated, and to assist the local authority in monitoring planning applications.

Local authority archaeologists are often referred to informally as curators because their main concern is to care for the long-term sustainability of remains of the past. Once a site is excavated it cannot be put back together; it is effectively quarried away and destroyed. It is important to ask whether a site is better excavated now or conserved for the future. If conserved, it is not being investigated for information and cannot help us in understanding the past. If excavated, we may destroy valuable information that future archaeologists could recover with more sophisticated, yet-to-be-developed techniques.

Museums

Museums may be nationally funded, run by local authorities, independent trusts or based in universities. They offer a range of job opportunities. Only a few museum staff will be archaeologists. Other staff will be social historians, conservators, technicians, etc. Keepers of Archaeology may be involved in fieldwork, but are more often responsible for looking after and researching collections of artefacts, and making displays and exhibitions. An important part of the job of the museum archaeologist is to deal with enquiries from the public, often identifying finds that they have brought in. Many museums also offer opportunities for conservators working with artefacts and finds. Some museums have outreach or education services involving the public with education and archaeology. Heritage interpretation centres are becoming commoner, with emphasis on reconstruction and presentation to the public. Museums and other centres provide opportunities for archaeological consultants, especially those with experience in the fields of marketing and design.

It is in the museum that the archaeologists' work can be told to the public. The basic purpose of museums is to collect, store and research material culture. Based on their collections, the museum curator is able to tell the story of the past in creative, highly visual ways. The displays and exhibitions show only a small proportion of the collections, most of which are carefully held in stores. These collections are an important resource for external researchers. They are also important for schools. They give pupils the chance to handle real artefacts, and investigating the past through material remains gives many a thrill that they don't get from reading a book about it. They may get the chance to touch the child's doll that a Victorian girl once touched, or the leather shoe that was once worn on a Roman foot.

Universities and colleges

Over 50 universities and colleges of higher education offer careers as lecturers or technicians. Competition for lecturers' posts is fierce, and is not usually to be considered without a PhD, or an equivalent level of achievement. Universities are centres of archaeological research as well as teaching; some of the most interesting and progressive projects are based within them. A number of universities also foster specialised aspects of the discipline: for example maritime archaeology, archaeological science, aerial or industrial archaeology.

Archaeologists also teach outside of universities. There are colleges offering qualifications below the level of a degree. Some of these qualifications cover archaeology directly such as the AS and A Level in Archaeology in England, Wales and Northern Ireland. Others deal with archaeology indirectly through subjects such as classical civilisations or leisure and tourism. A few universities offer courses to the general public, and archaeology is a popular subject in these. Courses are also offered through adult education organisations such as the WEA (Workers' Educational Association) or the University of the Third Age.

Archaeology is not a subject in the school curriculum, but can be used to support history and other subjects. To become a teacher in schools you must have either a postgraduate PGCE qualification or an undergraduate degree with qualified teacher status. Through misinterpreting regulations, some universities and colleges will refuse to take archaeology graduates onto PGCE courses, but there are now alternative ways of teacher training (see the Training and Development Agency for Schools website, http://www.tda.gov. uk/get-into-teaching/teacher-training-options.aspx). Archaeology graduates will find it easier to get onto primary rather than secondary PGCE courses. Getting on secondary PGCE courses is easier with a joint undergraduate degree where archaeology is studied alongside a subject such as history or geography. The Council for British Archaeology has a leaflet explaining why teacher training courses should accept archaeology graduates which can be used to support your application.

Other employment

Some archaeologists make a living as freelance consultants with a particular specialist skill. This could be something like geophysical prospection, where remote sensing is used to reveal underground features. More often it will be finds analysis where the freelancer specialises in a particular kind of artefact or remains, for example human bone, pottery or flint. There are also a few forensic archaeologists who work with the police on crime scenes. They have even been involved in uncovering remains from scenes of international war-crimes in recent years.

Developers who hire their own archaeological contractors may turn to a consultant for advice. Consultants may also be called upon to advise local authorities on particular issues, and are sometimes engaged by national agencies or the private sector to undertake specialised research. Some consultants are based in engineering companies or in specialist archaeological service companies.

It is important to realise that archaeology is not well paid. In 2008, the average professional full-time archaeologist was paid only 78 per cent of the national UK average salary. The lowest quarter earned less than 55 per cent of the UK average, and the highest quarter more than 93 per cent of the average. On the other hand, the job satisfaction in archaeology is very high. Whether this is enough to compensate for the low salaries is up to each individual to decide.

Local societies and independents

A great deal of archaeology is done by amateurs, volunteers who do their archaeology in their spare time or in retirement. Many of these volunteers have long been active as archaeologists and have developed a high level of skill equal to, or greater than, that of many professionals (Figure 6.1). Most belong to a local archaeology society or heritage group. These can cover a whole county, but more often take in a smaller area. Some societies focus on a very local place, for example a particular village or piece of woodland. Many will carry out their own field surveys and excavations, as well as looking at historical documents. Some will be active in campaigning for the conservation

Figure 6.1 **Upper Wharfedale Heritage Group using GPS on site**

or maintenance of heritage sites. There are also a few independent amateurs, people who act on their own in researching the past out of their own interest. They are often people able to devote a lot of time to archaeology and who have developed considerable knowledge and expertise. The best of them are often invited to speak at professional conferences and their work can be highly respected. Local groups also include young people. The Young Archaeologists' Club caters for young people aged 8 to 16, and has local branches all over the UK led by professional or volunteer leaders. Some of these have carried out their own fieldwork and made genuinely new discoveries.

Metal-detecting clubs

There has been a big growth in metal detecting as a hobby since the 1970s. If they have the permission of the landowners then detectorists can scan their land for metal artefacts. They act individually or in clubs. Most of the time, they find modern iron and small everyday artefacts from the Roman period

Figure 6.2   Metal detecting the excavation spoil
heap

to the present. Very rarely do they find any 'treasure'. Some detectorists have
raided known and protected archaeological sites, and sought to make money
from selling the finds on the antiquities market. Many archaeologists were
very hostile towards metal detecting (and some still are). More recently,
archaeologists have made great efforts to talk to detectorists and improve
their understanding of the importance of careful and proper recording of finds,
and of acting within the law. There is even a mutually agreed national code
of practice for responsible metal detecting, developed largely by the Council
for British Archaeology, the Portable Antiquities Scheme and the National
Council for Metal Detecting. Most detectorists respect this and carry out their
hobby as a way of finding out about the past (Figure 6.2). Only a very few
still detect for treasure and even fewer seek to detect illegally and in secret.
The results of metal detecting have changed our interpretations of particular
sites, such as battlefields, and of some activities in the past, such as the extent
of early medieval rural markets in England.

Portable Antiquities Scheme

The Treasure Act of 1996 made it illegal not to report finds of gold, silver or prehistoric metalwork in England and Wales. The Portable Antiquities Scheme was set up in 1997 to work with members of the public, including metal-detecting clubs, to make sure that finds were recorded. A network of finds liaison officers are responsible for this, and for spreading good practice in how to recover and report finds. The Scheme has been highly successful in capturing the information from detecting and making it available to the local historic environment records and so able to be studied.

Community projects

Some archaeology is carried out as particular projects where professional archaeologists work with members of local communities. These may be local societies but can also be members of the general public. In the UK, much of the funding for these projects has come from the Heritage Lottery Fund (itself funded by sales of national lottery tickets). Some projects are top-down, in that they begin with professional archaeologists wishing to involve local people in their work. Others are bottom-up and start up with the local people who get the funding to employ any professional help they may need. Working with local groups is a growing specialism within archaeology, usually known in the UK as community archaeology.

Who are archaeologists?

Professional archaeology has grown greatly over the past 50 years. In the 1960s, there were only 200 archaeologists employed in the UK. By 2008, before the economic crisis and recession of 2008–9, this had grown to nearly 7,000. However, this is a small figure when compared to the number of people active in voluntary archaeology and heritage. A survey by the Council for British Archaeology in 2010 found 2,030 local groups actively involved with archaeological remains or physical heritage, with an estimated total membership of 215,000 people.

More than half of professional archaeologists in the UK work in field archaeology. Around 25 per cent work for national agencies or local authorities, with some 15 per cent in universities and 5 per cent in museums. Women account for around 40 per cent of archaeologists in the UK, and dominate work in museums where 60 per cent of the archaeologists are women. The older and more senior the archaeologist, the more likely they are to be men. Women are far less likely to be directors of field units, university lecturers, project managers and field supervisors. They are more likely to be conservators, editors, education officers, finds officers, photographers, records officers, buildings archaeologists, illustrators or archaeological scientists. The American archaeologist Joan Gero has pointed out how women tend to dominate particular areas of research in archaeology, such as pottery, textiles and ornaments. They also more often carry out fine detailed and practical studies of the past, especially focussing on artefacts, instead of general theoretical overviews.

Archaeology is a practical discipline, both intellectual and yet very physical. It appeals to people with a wide variety of capabilities. We know that people make sense of the world around them in different ways, and these ways are often called different intelligences, kinds of learning or learning styles. One scheme has three kinds of learning: cognitive learning through reasoning and intellectual capability, affective learning through emotion and intuition, and psycho-motor learning through physical manipulation. Archaeology suits all three kinds of learner. We analyse the evidence of sites and artefacts in logical and rational ways. We empathise with people in the past and enjoy the emotional thrill of discovery. We also enjoy the physicality of excavation and experimentation. Some 90 per cent of professional archaeologists in the UK have a university degree (and effectively 100 per cent of those under the age of 30). Conventional education, with its emphasis on writing essays and sitting written exams, favours people with high cognitive intelligence, rather than those who score highly on affective or psycho-motor intelligences. Yet many people who did not study for university degrees or who left school early have still gone into archaeology as volunteers.

People with disabilities also become archaeologists. A major category of people who often leave education early are those with dyslexia, who may not have been supported enough at school. The recent Inclusive Accessible Archaeology project, led by Reading University, highlighted dyslexia as a major disability among archaeology students, and work by the Council for British Archaeology (CBA) also found dyslexia to be commoner than average among some of the voluntary archaeologists surveyed. A recent survey by the CBA of its members revealed that 16 per cent categorise themselves as disabled, and the Young Archaeologists' Club (YAC) has significant numbers of members with special educational needs. Archaeology really is a subject for everyone.

A great variety of people become archaeologists, but archaeologists are often a particular kind of person. It is very hard to describe this person, yet archaeologists can find the company of other archaeologists easier, more satisfying and comfortable than the company of non-archaeologists. They not only have shared interests but shared outlooks and attitudes, ways of thinking and behaving. In part, this comes from a perspective on life that understands our lives today as short steps in a very long history of human activity. It also comes from being interested in the past as another world, different to the present, and carrying out activities that are somehow not quite normal (such as kneeling down and scraping away at the ground with a trowel). Taking part in field projects is to immerse yourself in another world, where the normal behaviours of society can be ignored. The field project is a bubble with its own rules of behaviour. It can be a form of tribal existence. For this reason, archaeology can be a retreat from the present day and 'normal' life, and can be more of an alternative lifestyle choice than a profession or vocation. Archaeologists in film and on television may come across as larger than life adventurers and eccentrics, or as serious, obsessive scientists. Some archaeologists really are like this, but many are not. All you need is an insatiable curiosity about the past, a love of ancient remains and a willingness to see the life you live today as not the only way people can live or behave. Archaeologists are comfortable with being nonconformists for whom present day behaviours and fashions are only temporary in the long time span of human existence. We can revel in the teamwork of excavations but also have an individual personal relationship with the past. We like detailed observation and recording, and may have an obsession with particular artefacts. We enjoy the detective work of uncovering the past and the puzzle of reconstructing human behaviour from artefacts and sites. We also often see the present through sceptical eyes. Only half jokingly, we may say that the Neolithic Revolution was a big mistake and civilisation has gone downhill ever since!

So far, we have covered archaeology in the singular, as one discipline. In practice, there are different kinds of archaeological research, each with its own characteristics. This will be explored in the next chapter.

7

Which pasts
do we study?

*Her mon mæg giet gesion hiora swæð, ac we him ne cunnon
æfterspyrigan, forðæm we habbað nu ægðer forlæten ge þone
welan ge þone wisdom forðamþe we noldon to ðæm spore mid ure
mode onlutan.*

(Here we may yet see their tracks, but we cannot follow them,
because we have now lost both the wealth and the wisdom as we
would not bend to those tracks with our minds.)

King Alfred the Great, Preface to the *Translation of Pope
Gregory's Regula Pastoralis,* c.887

Archaeology is such a broad subject that archaeologists will often specialise
in a particular aspect of it. One of the commonest ways of specialising is to
study one particular period. Each period has its own community of scholars,
conferences and journals. Other archaeologists specialise in particular kinds
of material, such as pottery, stone tools, industrial or maritime finds, while
others may specialise in particular techniques of investigation, such as
geophysical prospection. Here we will simply look at the different period
specialisms in archaeology.

Palaeoanthropology

The study of the fossil remains of human ancestors is often known as
palaeoanthropology, or as biological anthropology in the UK and physical

anthropology in the USA. The archaeological study of material culture begins with the first stone tools made by our ancestors around 2.5 million years ago.

There is a lot of disagreement about how to classify the relationships between human and other primates. Figure 7.1 presents one commonly used classification. So we have hominoids, hominids, hominines and hominins. Confused? So are some archaeologists and the words *hominine* and *hominin* are not always used in the right way. The term *hominines* should be used to refer to gorillas, chimps and humans; this is not to be confused with *hominins*, which refers only to humans and our direct ancestors. Using studies of DNA, we think that the common ancestor of all hominoids lived before 23 million years ago, while gorillas split off from other hominines around 9 million years ago, and chimps and humans split around 6 million years ago.

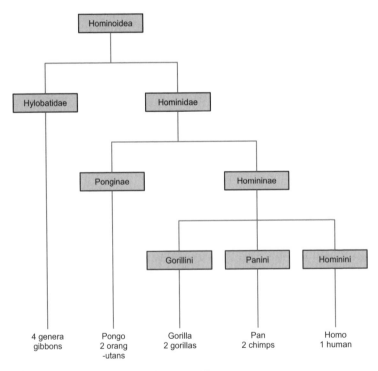

Figure 7.1 A classification of Hominoidea

Naming of species

Biological naming of animals is precise. Each separate kind of creature is given a species name and place within a particular genus of animals that are very closely related. When written, the genus should begin with an upper-case letter and the species always with a lower-case letter. So we have the Bornean orangutan, *Pongo pygmaeus,* and the Sumatran orangutan, *Pongo abelii*; the western gorilla, *Gorilla gorilla,* and the eastern gorilla, *Gorilla beringei;* the chimpanzee, *Pan troglodytes,* and the bonobo, *Pan paniscus;* and humans, *Homo sapiens.*

Hominin fossils are rare, there are many gaps in the data and there are endless disagreements about the story of human evolution with exaggerated claims and angry debates between rival scholars. Palaeoanthropologists are a lot like early explorers excitedly making and naming new finds and competing for fame and glory. It takes a strong mind not to treat their own spectacular discovery as a new species and proclaim that they have the crucial missing link in the story of human development.

The big issue in early hominin studies is the question 'what makes us human?'. Trying to find the earliest evidence of human behaviour is one of the important tasks facing palaeoanthropologists. While other hominines make and use tools, only hominins have deliberately shaped stone tools into pounding, cutting, scraping and boring tools. The earliest evidence for these tools comes from Africa (modern Ethiopia), at around 2.5 million years ago (although marks of cutting on the bones of animals dismembered for their meat have been found from around 3.3 million years ago). Apart from making tools, other things that mark us as human include walking upright on two legs, using complex verbal language and wearing clothes. Claims of the earliest evidence for the deliberate use of fire, the making of ornaments and clothing, the use of pigments for body painting and deliberate burial of the dead are frequently made and disputed.

Prehistory

Prehistorians deal with the past before written records (which appear at different times in different places). To make sense of prehistory, we have to use analogies with modern societies living lifestyles similar to those of prehistory. Prehistorians have to take a different approach to other archaeologists who can use written records to flesh out their picture of the past. They had to pioneer the use of scientific dating methods, and the use of sociology, anthropology or geography to explain their data.

Most prehistoric human culture has not left physical traces, and intangible culture such as language, dance or religious belief is almost impossible to reconstruct without written documents. Artefacts made of organic materials such as wood, leather, basketry, textiles, etc., will decay in the ground unless in very dry or constantly waterlogged conditions. We are left mostly with stone, metals, pottery and bone. The study of stone artefacts dominates our knowledge of human behaviour up to about 10,000 years ago.

Prehistory accounts for 97.5 per cent of the existence of our species *Homo sapiens*. For most of this time, people lived by hunting wild animals and gathering wild plant foods. A major change was the development of farming crops such as wheat, barley, lentils, beans and flax, and herding animals such as cattle, sheep, goats and pigs over 10,000 years ago in the Near East. Farming in other parts of the world involved plants such as rice, maize, squash, millet, sorghum, yam, taro, cotton, potatoes and animals such as the llama and alpaca. Farming allowed surplus food to be stored, communities to stay in one place permanently, the growth of large towns and the ability to support people who could specialise in activities not directly related to producing food, such as priests, warriors and kings. Farmers shape and exploit the land, and over-exploitation of the land has ruined many environments in the past. Prehistorians have long had an overlap with geographers and a strong focus on studying human interaction with environment and climate.

Early farmers built the first burial mounds in Europe and the first large-scale religious sites. Burials can reveal a lot of information about people and their position in society. Those who study later prehistory are often very interested in issues of identity, social organisation and religion alongside farming and land use. Making the first copper and bronze tools happened in prehistory, and were a big advance on stone tools. They allow finer woodworking, more effective weapons and armour. Copper and tin are not widely available and those who controlled the mining and trade of these could become wealthy. We can see the wealthy and the powerful for the first time through the use of gold and other precious materials. Many prehistorians are therefore interested in ideas about how society develops and the growth of social and political hierarchies.

The end of prehistory happened at different times. Many places remained prehistoric until conquest by the likes of Britain and France in the nineteenth century. Other places developed their own writing early and became historical societies, some of which brought others into the orbit of history by conquest. Societies that are known about and referred to by others in their writings but do not yet have writing themselves are sometimes known as proto-historic.

Ancient and classical archaeology

There is a tendency to equate 'prehistoric' with 'primitive'. This should be resisted. Prehistoric societies were capable of great sophistication in their architecture, ways of life, ability to live off and within nature, and their political and social systems, and could produce arts and crafts of great beauty. Some of these very complex societies are termed 'civilisations' by archaeologists. The archaeologist Gordon Childe listed the main characteristics of civilisation as very large settlements (towns rather than villages), surplus food production that could support specialist professions, craftsmen and an elite ruling class, monumental architecture, writing, the use of a calendar and mathematics, sophisticated art, long-distance trade and the organisation of societies into political states or empires. Not all civilisations will have had all of these. Most did, however, even if the writing systems have in some cases yet to be deciphered. As a result, we can name kings and ruling dynasties, the rise and fall of competing empires, note the occurrence of battles, read ancient literature and get to know the religious practices and gods of societies very different from our own. This is the excitement of studying ancient historical civilisations. They are at once both exotic and very familiar. They have material culture, language and religion very different from our own, and yet seem like our own selves in that they have politics, warfare, arts and literature and the names of real people we can relate to.

The great civilisations of Europe, Africa and Asia are found in the central and eastern Mediterranean, Egypt, Mesopotamia, Iran, the Indus Valley, China and South East Asia. In the Americas they occur in the Andes and Meso-America. Africa south of the Sahara also had its civilisations, for example Zimbabwe and Benin, most of them relatively ignored and little explored by archaeologists until very recently. Some of these societies attract only a handful of scholars in the UK, being more studied in other countries. Ancient Rome, classical Greece and ancient Egypt are perhaps the commonest of civilisations to be studied in Europe. The study of Rome and Greece together is known as classical archaeology, while the study of ancient Egypt is, rather logically, Egyptology.

The Renaissance treated Greek and Roman art and literature as the foundation of 'Western civilisation'. This attitude is hard to shake off. Still

83

today, Greece and Rome evoke notions of high culture, civilisation and progress even though these notions have long since been shown to be modern ideas imposed on the past.

Egypt has a place in the modern Western imagination far ahead of all other civilisations. It is one of the earliest of all civilisations, with remains of an epic scale that cannot fail to impress. It is an important land in the Old Testament of the Bible and central to Jewish and Christian religious tradition. Its pictorial art and hieroglyphic writing seem accessible and aesthetically pleasing to a Western mind. It is no surprise that to some excitable and untrained minds in the late nineteenth and early twentieth centuries it was seen as the origin of all later civilisations. This has long since been seen to be nonsense, yet Egypt still exerts a strong pull on the western imagination.

Other civilisations have less of a public profile, but are no less interesting or important. Mesopotamia is broadly the area we now know as Iraq, where the Sumerian civilisation arose and the later Babylonian and Assyrian empires. Other literate civilisations with their own independently developed writing systems were the Hittites in modern-day Turkey, the Minoans on Crete, the Harappa in modern-day Pakistan and India, and the Shang empire in China. The Aztec and Inca empires (in modern Mexico and Peru) that were encountered and destroyed by the Spanish in the sixteenth century were only very recent creations, and were the latest in a line of ancient civilisations. These included the Olmec, Zapotec, Teotihuacan and Toltec in Mexico, the Maya in modern Honduras and Yucatan, and the Moche, Wari and the Tiwanaku among others in the Andes.

The archaeology of ancient civilisations often includes the study of inscriptions and ancient languages. This is especially true of Egyptology, Assyriology and Mayan archaeology. One of the great challenges in archaeology is the decipherment of forgotten scripts, such as those of Minoan Linear A, the Indus Valley, the Olmec and Zapotec cultures, or the proper translation and understanding of extinct languages such as Etruscan or Iberian. For those who love languages, there can be no greater fun than trying to understand and resurrect a dead language.

The traditional approach of classical archaeologists has been to use the archaeology to shed light on historical events or ancient literature. The presence of documentary evidence enables archaeological material to be described and analysed in more detail and with more certainty than in prehistoric archaeology. In recent years, some classical archaeologists have developed an interest in explanation and theory, and understanding long-term processes of change. Most still focus on grand architecture, art history and artefacts to a much greater degree than in prehistory. This focus on the obvious and spectacular remains means that archaeologists have often neglected the less obvious, more mundane archaeology of the ordinary people, of the rural sites outside the cities, or the poorer workers who built the fine palaces and tombs. In Roman archaeology, we still know more about the army and the rich elite who lived in villas than we do about the majority of the contemporary population.

Medieval archaeology

The transition from the ancient Roman Empire into a Byzantine Empire in the eastern Mediterranean and a set of independent kingdoms in western and northern Europe marks the beginning of medieval Europe. A lot of scholarly ink has been spilt pointlessly trying to define the moment when the ancient world finally became medieval. It seems generally accepted now that the change happened in politics in the fifth century AD and in the economy by the seventh century. Unsurprisingly, there was no one morning when people woke up and said to themselves 'we're in the medieval period now!'.

Medieval archaeology deals with a world that is recognisably the foundation of the world we live in today. There is a great deal of continuity in Europe where modern villages and towns were often founded in medieval times. There are many medieval buildings still standing and in use. Two of the major religious traditions of the modern world, Christianity and Islam, began their role as organised, state-sponsored religions in the early medieval period, and many of their religious sites and structures have been in continuous use for over 1,000 years. Many European nations trace a continuous existence back into the medieval period, while for others key medieval battles or events are still part of their national identities. Medieval archaeology can be politically and religiously important, and can be bound up with modern identities and how we see ourselves as nations.

The earliest work in medieval archaeology focussed on ecclesiastical sites (churches, cathedrals, monasteries) and castles. Only later did attention shift to include villages, towns, industrial sites, landscapes, etc. Medieval archaeology produces large amounts of data with many hundreds of sites and thousands of finds. There has been a lot of work on the growth of towns, the development of villages, castles and churches, and styles of buildings. Links with local history and historical geography have improved our understanding of landscapes. Linking this with the history of place-names has been especially important. The large numbers of artefacts have stimulated

85

interest in medieval technology, craftsmanship and the location and methods of industrial production, such as pottery making, iron working and salt production. The growth of metal detecting has increased the number of metal finds, especially coins, and has changed our ideas about various aspects of the medieval economy.

Some people still have an image of the medieval period as one in which not much happened apart from endless wars, and that the period was one of stagnation rather than progress. This is of course nonsense. The medieval period was one of constant change and development, and complex social, political and economic organisation. There are big issues that medieval archaeology can engage with. These include the so-called clash of civilisations (e.g. West–East, Christian–Muslim), long-term climate change and its effects on settlement and population, the spread of epidemic diseases worldwide, the growth of political power and social hierarchies, the origins of urbanisation and the modern money-based international economy, and the importance of technological change and its effects on society and economy. More specific themes include the role of women and gender in shaping material culture, the relationship between material culture and ethnic identity (just how do we recognise an Anglo-Saxon, a Viking and a Briton from their artefacts, and what do these categories of ethnicity actually mean?), and the social and symbolic uses of space within buildings.

Some people also think that the medieval world was a drab and repressive world of plague, feudal oppression, great poverty for most people, superstition and cruelty. Yet we know that it could also be a very colourful world, expanding and inventive, with legal freedoms, more social mobility than we thought, superb craftsmanship and high art creating works of stunning beauty, and great and emotionally moving literature. Archaeology has been able to bring to life the everyday lives of ordinary people, and give new insight into the lives of the rich and powerful who are recorded in the historical documents.

The relationship between medieval archaeology and history has not always been easy. Until quite recently, most historians and archaeologists knew little about each other's work. They trained in different departments, published in different journals and went to different conferences. There were large areas of misunderstanding between them and they often had strong prejudices against each other. They have since had to acknowledge that they only study a part of the evidence for the period and that good understanding of medieval times depends on using all available sources, with archaeologists, historians and others working together and respecting each other's methods.

Archaeology of the modern era

When does the modern world begin? This is a big question without a clear answer. Different continents and nations could give different answers to this. In the colonised nations, the coming of European settlers marked a radical break with the native tradition of settlement. For North America this could be 1607 and the successful colonisation of Virginia, and for South America 1520 with the destruction of the Aztec Empire. In Australia, European settlement did not begin until 1788. For Britain, the modern era is sometimes taken as beginning with the English religious split from Rome in 1534 and the Scottish split in 1560, or in England with the beginnings of the Tudor dynasty in 1485. There is a further sharp break in material culture in the Industrial Revolution after 1760 (the period before this is sometimes known as the 'early modern' period). In colonised nations, the term 'historical archaeology' is used to describe the archaeological study of modern times. In the UK, the commoner term is post-medieval archaeology. In contrast, 'historical archaeology' in the UK covers all archaeology since the Roman conquest and includes classical and medieval archaeology.

The past 500 years have seen big changes in both the countryside and the towns. The archaeology of this period is concerned with recording these changes and understanding how they happened at different times, at different speeds in different parts of Britain. Excavation has played a smaller role than field survey and the analysis of buildings and structures. Much rescue archaeology in the cities has traditionally dug through recent layers without careful study in order to reach medieval or Roman remains. This is changing and even nineteenth-century layers now often receive proper investigation as much as the earlier layers. There is still much that archaeology can tell us about the growth of modern towns, the development of town planning and the building of overcrowded homes for the new urban working class. In more rural areas, the style and format of houses changed a great deal, as did the location of farms and the types of farm building. Even the modern pattern of fields had its origins in this period with the enclosure of medieval open fields or the drainage of wetlands to make new farmland. The wealthy replaced their castles and moated sites with fine country houses and mansions, often with elaborate parks and gardens. Garden archaeology is one of the newest specialisms of this period (now also being studied in the medieval period). New types of building occur, such as nonconformist chapels and meeting houses, theatres and cinemas and sports stadiums. Before the advent of the railways, long-distance transport could be by mail coach (with accommodation and refreshment provided by the new coaching inns), by pack-horse with stone-laid routes being created across northern uplands, or on foot by driving herds of cattle or sheep along upland drove roads. The past 500 years have also seen military conflict or threats of invasion, so archaeologists can also study Tudor coastal forts, Civil War defences and siege-works, Jacobite rebellion fortifications, nineteenth- and twentieth-century coastal defences, First World War practice trenches and Second World War airfields among other kinds of site.

Rescue archaeology

Growing development of the towns and countryside in the 1950s and 1960s was leading to increasing destruction of archaeological sites, as there was little public funding for archaeology and few laws to help archaeologists investigate vanishing remains. An organisation called Rescue was formed in 1971 to campaign against this destruction and for 'rescue archaeology'. Their call was for the excavation of sites that were being destroyed through the building of new shops, houses or roads, etc. The information in those sites was rescued from being lost forever. This contrasted with research archaeology where sites were not under threat of destruction. Most modern archaeology is now rescue archaeology, funded by developers under planning guidance and legislation from government.

The post-medieval period has abundant documentary evidence, including the first estate plans and maps, wills, parish records and censuses. Although documents can represent powerful individual voices and can be highly emotive as sources for people's lives in the past, there is also much that the documents do not record, or which they misrepresent. For example, the Defence of Britain archaeology project revealed how Second World War defences were often not built in the way described in the official records. Also, it is one thing to read about the conditions in the slums in the industrial towns, but excavating human remains showing physical traces of malnutrition and disease can reveal living conditions in a direct and powerful way.

Post-medieval archaeology has an uneasy relationship with industrial archaeology. Some archaeologists see them as distinct, with post-medieval studies concentrating on 1500–1750 and industrial archaeology on the era after 1750. Others would see industrial archaeology as studying the evidence of industry and technology from the whole post-medieval era, leaving post-medieval archaeology to study other non-industrial aspects of life. Industrial archaeology in the UK began in the 1960s with the study of canals and railways, and then spread to other areas of industry. It has been concerned with recording and conserving industrial sites and monuments, and is seen by some archaeologists as limited to heritage management, rather than trying to analyse the industrial past. It has suffered from a lack of academic acceptance and is seen by many as an amateur 'geek' pursuit. This is unfair.

The main focus of study for most industrial archaeologists has been the iron and steel industries, coal mining, canals, textiles, corn mills, steam engines, brick and tile kilns, and quarries. These are the classic industries of the Industrial Revolution of the late eighteenth and early nineteenth centuries. Industries of the twentieth century, such as light engineering, electronics, and the exploitation of more modern materials, such as plastics, are rarely studied but are just as legitimate objects of study. Modern industrial archaeologists are interested in the lives of people who worked in industry as much as the technology. Suggestions as to future directions for industrial archaeology include looking at the effects new technologies had on industrial production, how the products of industry were used by consumers, the use of space within factories to control workers, patterns of industrial landscapes, and how industrialisation affected social identities expressed through the class system.

Even the archaeology of the twentieth century can reveal new information or help us better understand what we think we know from even recent history. One major example is the Council for British Archaeology's Defence of Britain project from 1995 to 2002. Nearly 20,000 twentieth-century military sites in the United Kingdom were recorded by an army of some 600 volunteers. The project recorded details of anti-invasion defences such as stop lines, area defence, roadblocks, beach and bridge defences made up of pillboxes, anti-tank obstacles, infantry fieldworks, spigot mortars, barrel flame traps, etc. Whole new types of monument and a new terminology entered archaeology. Much of what was found provided the details to complement and correct the documentary record, for example showing that some documents did not accurately record what was actually built or created.

In the colonial English-speaking nations, Australia, Canada, New Zealand and the USA, there is a longer tradition of the recent historical past as a serious part of archaeology and often a better understanding of sequences of artefact types of the eighteenth and nineteenth centuries than in Britain. Particular themes of historical archaeology in these nations include the relationship between imported and locally made goods, the clearance and farming of new lands, building of new settlements and development of house types, the relationship of the settlers and their descendants with the

89

indigenous inhabitants, the role of women in colonial society, also the role of slaves, and issues of ethnicity and identity among immigrant groups. In other words, there is more concern for the human behaviour underlying the material culture of the modern period than in traditional British post-medieval archaeology.

PART II

ARCHAEOLOGY IN ITS WIDER CONTEXT

8

World archaeology

every person has a right to engage with the cultural heritage of their choice, while respecting the rights and freedoms of others, as an aspect of the right freely to participate in cultural life enshrined in the United Nations Universal Declaration of Human Rights (1948) and guaranteed by the International Covenant on Economic, Social and Cultural Rights (1966)

Preamble to the Council of Europe (2005) Framework Convention on the Value of Cultural Heritage for Society

Different parts of the world practise archaeology in different ways. The way in which the profession of archaeology is structured can be different, and also the methods used and the focus of research. On the other hand, the boundaries and existence of many modern countries go back only to the nineteenth or twentieth centuries. The heritage of the past may be claimed by them as part of their identities, but can also be seen as a common human heritage, existing from a time before modern nations existed. Archaeology is international in scope and increasingly international in practice.

International agreements

There are various international organisations and agreements which deal with archaeology on a world-wide basis. At the highest level is the United Nations Educational, Scientific and Cultural Organization (UNESCO), founded in

1946. This issues conventions which member states sign up to and adopt as legally binding, or recommendations which have no legal force. Several of these cover archaeology or the tangible cultural heritage.

The Hague Convention 1954

This is the Convention for the Protection of Cultural Property in the Event of Armed Conflict and is designed to prevent the destruction of significant cultural heritage during war. More than 90 countries have ratified the Convention and agreed to abide by it, but the United Kingdom is not yet included.

The New Delhi recommendations 1956

Recommendations on International Principles Applicable to Archaeological Excavations aim to regulate archaeological investigation in the public interest through state control of archaeology, suppression of trade in illegal antiquities and the adoption of proper storage, treatment and documentation of finds.

The Cultural Property Convention 1970

The Convention on the Means of Prohibiting and Preventing the Illicit Import, Export and Transfer of Ownership of Cultural Property was designed to prevent excavation and export of objects of cultural heritage (of importance for archaeology, prehistory, history, literature, art or science) without the permission of the government.

The World Heritage Convention 1972

The Convention concerning the Protection of the World Cultural and Natural Heritage has created a list of World Heritage Sites deemed to be of universal significance for mankind (Figure 8.1), and encourages proper conservation and management of these, although it does not give these sites any international legal protection.

The Underwater Heritage Convention 2001

Looting by treasure hunters of underwater wrecks has long been a problem and the Convention on the Protection of the Underwater Cultural Heritage is designed to strengthen national governments' attempts to prevent this.

Figure 8.1   The Kinkakuji (Golden Pavilion) World Heritage
Site in Kyoto, Japan

Important international associations for archaeology are the International
Council of Museums (ICOM) and the International Council on Monuments and Sites (ICOMOS), founded in 1964. These are non-governmental
associations and issue declarations (known as charters) aimed at persuading
governments to follow basic principles of good practice.

The Athens Charter 1931, and the Venice Charter 1964

The Athens Charter for the Restoration of Historic Monuments agreed in
1931 by an international conference of architects and archaeologists laid
down rules for the restoration of ancient buildings and monuments, and for
respecting the historic character of cities. This was extended and strengthened
by the Venice Charter for the Restoration and Conservation of Monuments
and Sites in 1964, which led to the founding of ICOMOS. Both charters
aimed to safeguard the historical authenticity of buildings and monuments
by preserving their physical structure. However, not all countries accept
the importance of physical remains as heritage. For example, in Japan the
ancient wooden Shinto shrines and Buddhist temples are regularly rebuilt.
The heritage of these sites lies in the religious practices and the craftsmanship
of the builders. As a result, the Nara Document on Authenticity was issued
in 1994, and accepted by UNESCO and ICOMOS, to allow for national
differences in attitudes to heritage conservation.

The Lausanne Charter 1990

The ICOMOS Charter for the Protection and Management of the Archaeo-logical Heritage aims to set out good practice in managing archaeological heritage and the training of professional archaeological heritage managers. It also recommends that sites should only be excavated where absolutely necessary since excavation also destroys sites by removing them.

The Ename Charter 2008

The ICOMOS Charter for the Interpretation and Presentation of Cultural Heritage Sites goes beyond simply conserving heritage remains and sets out good practice in presenting remains to the public. It calls for the right of people to have access to heritage and lays down the responsibilities of heritage managers to respect local communities and principles of authenticity as laid down in the Nara Document.

The Convention on Stolen or Illegally Exported Cultural Objects 1995

There is one international association aimed at harmonising commercial law, the International Institute for the Unification of Private Law, UNIDROIT (founded in 1926), which has issued an important convention for archaeology.

This Convention is aimed at restoring stolen antiquities to their original owners and preventing people from buying illegally obtained antiquities. This has not yet been ratified by the United Kingdom, but Parliament has made it a criminal offence to deal in any cultural object that has been illegally excavated or removed.

The London Convention 1969, and the Valletta Convention 1992

The Council of Europe was founded in 1949 to spread the principles of democracy and human rights within Europe. It is entirely separate from the European Union. The Council has issued various conventions covering archaeology.

The Convention for the Protection of the Archaeological Heritage was designed to give legal protection for archaeological heritage and ensure high standards of archaeological work. The Convention was updated and extended by the Valletta Convention which added clauses on how archaeology should be funded, and be included as part of planning controls on development (e.g. construction of new buildings and roads).

A convention on architecture (Granada) 1985

The Convention for the Protection of the Architectural Heritage was aimed at protecting historic buildings, industrial facilities and even contemporary architecture.

The Faro Convention 1995

This Framework Convention on the Value of Cultural Heritage for Society breaks new ground in setting out reasons why cultural heritage should be managed and conserving by outlining its values. It is a resource for human development, enhances cultural diversity, promotes mutual respect between different cultures and can support economic development.

Anti-colonial reactions in archaeology

Many of the leading organisations in archaeology have been dominated by Europe and North America. This could lead to differences of view with other countries with different traditions, as shown by the need to modify the Venice Charter with the Nara Document. As old imperial powers, many of the 'Western' nations had little knowledge or interest in the views of native peoples, and usually ignored native ideas of heritage. These attitudes came to a head in 1986, when a group of archaeologists in the United Kingdom called for a ban on inviting South African archaeologists to an international conference because of South Africa's apartheid policies. A bitter split took place in archaeology, and a new organisation was formed, the World Archaeological Congress (WAC), with a mission to respect all cultures and involve non-Western peoples in debates about archaeology.

Much of the ethos behind WAC came from Marxists and feminists who criticised traditional archaeologists as mostly white European upper-class men, unable to accept alternative interpretations of the past and unwilling to engage in partnership with local people. WAC dedicated itself to providing an arena for native voices and alternative non-Western perspectives on the past. It recognises that archaeology must be aware of the politics it operates within and must be relevant to the concerns of the people whose heritage it studies. It controversially accepts that native traditions about the past may be non-scientific, even religiously based, but that these are just as valid as Western scientific views.

Disagreements between archaeologists about the relationship between archaeology and native cultures have mostly occurred in the United States, Australia and South Africa, countries where white immigrant colonists came into contact with native peoples. The indigenous Australian aborigines had no written historical documents and so were prehistoric until 1788, dependent on European colonists for their voice. Only in recent years has the Aboriginal voice been heard and respected in its own right. We in Europe see the past as something separate from the present, something gone and no longer directly connected to now. The Aboriginal view of time is different, where the past is a living part of the present, not divorced from now. Archaeologists are not studying a long dead culture, but a culture with living descendants who feel a deep connection with their ancestors. For a long time, aborigines objected to archaeologists excavating their ancestors' remains, disturbing the spiritual relationship they have with them. The archaeological study of Aboriginal settlement in Australia has now taken into account modern Aboriginal sensitivities and views about their past. Archaeological work can even help Aboriginal groups establish their claims to land under the Land Rights Act of 1976.

There is a similar situation in North America where the indigenous peoples have long been battling with archaeologists to have their ancestors treated with appropriate respect. Some see archaeologists as agents of white oppression, 'stealing' their culture for display in museums for the entertainment of the 'whites', while others are willing to work with archaeologists to help establish their claims to land, resources or traditional ways of life. Under the Native American Graves Protection and Repatriation Act 1990 (NAGPRA), lineal descendants of the buried people or their tribe can demand the return of human remains, grave goods and other objects excavated in federal or tribal land. The case of human remains is highly emotive. Archaeologists naturally wish to study the remains, while for many native people this is spiritually insulting. Human remains found at Kennewick in 1996 proved to be over 9,000 years old and offered archaeologists the chance to study a rare example of early humans in North America. The remains were claimed by four different modern tribes under NAGPRA. The courts eventually decided it was impossible to establish whether Kennewick Man had any living descendants and the skeleton remained with the archaeologists.

In both Australia and the United States there is often a tension between two kinds of archaeology: the archaeology of the native inhabitants reaching back deep into prehistory, and the archaeology of the white settlers reaching back only 200–400 years. They adopt different approaches and often serve different purposes, one helping native groups to have a voice, the other establishing the white settlers as the dominant heritage of the nation. An extreme example of this would be in South Africa where the Apartheid regime was concerned to portray the white settlers as either taking over an empty land or taking land from inferior, uncivilised natives. Some archaeologists were happy to go along with this, others tried to ignore the politics and only research uncontroversial topics, while yet others actively used archaeological evidence to undermine Apartheid. Since the end of Apartheid in 1994, the South African government has supported archaeology to uncover a past that all South Africans can feel is theirs, and restores black African pride in their historical achievements.

One of the best examples of African achievement revealed by archaeology is the Zimbabwean culture in southern Africa, named after the site of Great Zimbabwe. The culture is represented by stone-built royal compounds and associated stone towns. Portuguese explorers in the sixteenth century were told about fabulous stone cities somewhere inland by the coastal African people they met. At a time when Europeans believed that the chronology of human history was fixed by the Bible, it was natural to think that these cities were the lost civilisation of Ophir, which traded gold with the Biblical figures of King Solomon or the Queen of Sheba. The King or Queen must therefore have built the stone towns to trade with the natives. The ruins of Great Zimbabwe were first explored by Europeans in 1871, and taken over as part of the British colony of Rhodesia in 1890. The colony was set up by a trading company, the British South Africa Company, which sponsored an archaeological excavation at the ruins. Other Zimbabwean sites were looted for gold over the next 10 years. These 'excavations' 'proved' the sites to have been built by Phoenician traders from the Middle East, rather than by native Africans. The white settlers refused to believe that the native Africans were capable of civilisation and used the Zimbabwean culture to prove the need for foreign rule to bring civilisation to the area. Excavations by properly qualified archaeologists in 1905 and 1929 showed that Great Zimbabwe was indeed built by native Africans. This was refuted by the white settlers, who continued to promote the idea that the sites had been founded by white peoples from the Middle East right up to 1980 when the colony of Rhodesia finally gained legal independence under a majority African government. When the Rhodesian government ordered that all official guidebooks and references to Great Zimbabwe must accept its Phoenician origins, only one archaeologist went along with this, and the government's own Inspector of Monuments, Peter Garlake, resigned in protest. Political use of the site did not end with independence though. The new nation immediately adopted Zimbabwe as its name. Although the site was built by ancestors of only one of the African peoples in modern Zimbabwe, it is promoted by the government as belonging to the whole modern population, many of whom do not belong to the people who built the site.

International archaeology

The World Archaeological Congress (WAC) is not the only international association for archaeologists. There have been international conferences on archaeology since the nineteenth century. One was organised by the Italian Society of Natural Science in 1865. This led to the formation of the International Palaeo-ethnological Congress in 1866, which quickly renamed itself as the International Congress of Archaeology and Anthropology in 1867 (known as the CIAAP after its name in French). This then merged into the International Institute of Anthropology (IIA) in 1921. Archaeologists in Europe are very prickly about being a separate discipline, and not being part of anthropology. A new organisation was formed to break away from the IIA in 1931, the International Congress of Prehistoric and Protohistoric Sciences, which changed its name in 1954 to the International Union of Prehistoric and Protohistoric Sciences (IUPPS). It was a proposed meeting of the IUPPS in 1986 that led to the break away of the WAC.

The IUPPS and its predecessors had a vision of archaeology as a science, revealing the past history of humankind as a story of progress from prehistory to the present, where Western democratic life and technology was the summit of human achievement. WAC, of course, has a very different view. The IUPPS has been dominated by a culture history approach to the past, while the WAC has a more post-processual view.

Archaeology of course deals with more than only prehistory or protohistory. With the collapse of Communism in Europe, a new association to bring archaeologists together from all over the continent was created in 1994, the European Association of Archaeologists (EAA). This explicitly covers prehistory, classical, medieval and modern archaeology. It holds conferences every year in a different country in Europe, and publishes the *European Journal of Archaeology*. It also has codes of practice for its members, committing them to following international and European charters and conventions and to work to a high technical and ethical standard.

The great benefit of international organisations and their conferences is that they bring together archaeologists who work in different countries with different ideas about how archaeology should be practised and how the past should be investigated and interpreted. It can be quite a shock to realise that your own way of working and thinking is not the only way of doing archaeology. It is refreshing to have your own assumptions about archaeology challenged by others with different ideas. The disadvantage of international conferences is that they simply allow people to show off their own national archaeologies without learning from others. Many archaeologists find it hard to think outside the boundaries of modern nations and cultures. Back in 1943, the British archaeologist Sir Grahame Clark urged archaeologists to study humanity in general and adopt a truly worldwide perspective. For Clark, archaeology offered us the chance to see that all people had behaviours and experiences in common, no matter what their nationality or ethnic origin. Archaeology could unite people in realising their common origins and humanity. This is sadly still a very rare perspective.

British archaeologists abroad

There is a long tradition of archaeologists working in other countries which continues today. The British urge to explore the Mediterranean and the Middle East began with the Grand Tours of largely upper-class young men from the late seventeenth century and the craze for collecting anti-quities. As archaeology became more organised and recognised as serious scholarship, research abroad was funded and organised through British Schools and Institutes, based either in the countries being studied or in London.

British Schools and Institutes abroad are funded through the British Academy and now are:

- the British Institute at Ankara (covering Turkey and the Black Sea);
- the British Institute in Eastern Africa (the east coast of Africa from Sudan to Zimbabwe);
- the British Institute of Persian Studies (modern Iran);
- the British School at Athens (Greece);
- the British School at Rome (Italy);
- the Council for British Research in the Levant (includes Institutes in Jordan and Israel).

Other groups that are based in the UK are:

- the African Studies Association;
- the Association for South East Asian Studies (from Burma to Indonesia);
- the British Association for South Asia Studies (covers Afghanistan southwards to Sri Lanka);
- the British Society for Middle Eastern Studies;
- the Institute for the Study of the Americas;
- the Society for Libyan Studies.

Two organisations that have been funded by the British Academy in the past are:

- the British Institute for the Study of Iraq (not based in Iraq since the Gulf War of 1990);
- the Egypt Exploration Society (based in London).

These organisations help to fund research overseas and do much to help British archaeologists avoid studying only Britain. But they have been criticised by some as relics of the Imperial era when many of the countries being studied had no archaeologists of their own. In the twentieth century, more of these countries developed their own archaeology services and began to manage their own monuments and sites. British archaeologists can be seen as white Westerners interfering in the archaeology of other countries, and sometimes they have had a poor record of not working closely with local archaeologists.

What makes British archaeology different?

Going to any international conference will soon reveal how different British archaeology is from that of most other countries. This is the result of a combination of the past history of these countries, their academic traditions and ways of working, and the different legal frameworks that govern the professional practice of archaeological research.

Britain is an island with a long and continuous history, most of it prehistoric. It has strong elements of continuity with very few successful invasions or conquests. It is an island, separate from the continent, and developed in a different way and with less influence from other cultures. It is a hugely varied land in a small area with many different landscapes, soils and ways of living. Modern Britain has large, built-up urban areas, an increasing demand for new housing and building, with intensive farming all adding to the pressures on the historic environment. There is a common feeling that we are an overcrowded island, increasingly destroying its historic environment. Yet we also recognise the value of that environment for tourism. We know that tourists come to Britain not for our gloriously warm climate and sunny beaches, but for our cultural heritage and history. This makes British archaeology very insular, not very aware of how its remains relate to the rest of Europe. It also makes us distrust explanations for the past that rely on invasions or movements of people. We instead have a keen awareness of how people's ways of life depend on their geographical environment, and see explaining continuity as important as explaining change. We are very protective of archaeological remains and heritage management is a big part of British archaeology.

The academic tradition in British universities is based on a type of education where students are expected to question and develop their own ideas. It is also highly competitive, where universities and colleges compete for students and funding, as well as prestige. This can lead to quarrelsome debates, a deliberate desire to question seemingly accepted ideas and the view that you have to come up with something new or different to be successful. This sometimes means that our views of the past are seldom agreed and often swing between wildly opposite explanations. Archaeology in Britain has a strongly defined identity as a separate subject. This promotes high professional and academic standards, and brings a lot of money into archaeology for research. However, it also divorces us from allied subjects such as anthropology, history or heritage studies and means we can be quite ignorant about ideas and methods that could help us investigate the past. We have also created different archaeological silos, sub-disciplines such as prehistory, classical, medieval, industrial, maritime archaeology whose members seldom talk to each other. The universities themselves are in a silo separate from professional field archaeology. Academics and field archaeologists will attend different conferences, publish in different journals and be interested in different topics of study. One of the few arenas for all kinds of archaeologists is the Council for British Archaeology.

The legal and professional framework of archaeology in Britain is dominated by the need for archaeology to prevent the historic environment being destroyed by building new houses, shops, roads, airports, pipelines, etc. Developers can appoint whom they wish to carry out archaeological work and so archaeology field units will compete with each other for contracts. This has the effect of keeping costs down, and so archaeological salaries are kept low. Doing an excavation on time and cheaply becomes more important than doing it well and contributing to research. There is also a large voluntary sector of local societies and individuals who do archaeology not as a job but for interest and fun. Anyone can legally excavate or do fieldwork. Making sure work is done to professional standards is a job done by archaeologists themselves. While there is some protection for archaeological remains by being placed on a schedule or list, the legal position in England and Wales is that all archaeological finds belong to the owner of the land who can do with them whatever they wish, unless they happen to be 'treasure', while in Scotland all finds belong to the crown. There is a low level of government interest in controlling or managing archaeology, and the main agent of heritage management is local councils. Archaeology is also hugely popular among the public through public events such as the Festival of British Archaeology and high profile television programmes.

Contact with archaeologists from elsewhere is unsettling. They do things differently abroad! Some of the key differences are in the nature of academic authority, the role of the state, control of who can do archaeology, the importance of culture history, dislike of archaeological theory, the relationship between archaeology and nationalism, and the hierarchy within archaeology.

Academic archaeology

In some countries, university education is based on the idea of respect for authority. Good students are those who follow their teachers and repeat what they have been taught. To disagree would be disrespectful. Earlier scholars are seen as people whose wisdom is to be built upon, not challenged or demolished. This produces a consensus style of academic debate, and an unwillingness to indulge in speculation, new ideas or theories. Academic archaeology has status and respect, and has a role in guiding the work of field archaeologists.

Role of the state

Many countries think of archaeology as contributing to national identity, and the state plays a role in managing and controlling archaeology. In France, only licensed archaeologists can legally be in charge of excavations, and most rescue archaeology is carried out by a state organisation, INRAP. In Greece, all excavations are carried out either by the state archaeology service or by other organisations given special permits by the service. The state ensures that archaeology is done to high standards, that archaeology has a voice in government, and can integrate excavations into national programmes of research. In Sweden, all excavations must contribute towards agreed research and help answer questions about the past.

Who can do archaeology?

Most countries abroad ensure that only professional archaeologists can be in charge of excavations. This is also true in Northern Ireland where only licensed archaeologists can excavate. The result is a small voluntary sector, where local societies may hold regular lectures and field trips but do not get involved in doing archaeology for themselves. Archaeologists are those who are qualified and licensed as archaeologists, whereas anyone in Britain can be an archaeologist.

Culture history

Most countries in the world are either new nations arising out of the break-up of the colonial empires in the twentieth century or have identifiable ethnic groups within them, for example Russia (with 20 per cent of the population being one of 160 different ethnic groups) or India (independent since 1949 and with nearly 2,000 separate languages). It is natural to see the past as a series of named cultures representing particular peoples, the national group or other ethnic groups. Archaeology consists of tracing the development and migration of cultures over time and culture history is the dominant type of archaeology in much of the world. Researchers seldom ask why cultures change, or why people behave in a particular way.

Dislike of theory

Culture history encourages a style of archaeology that focuses on recording the detailed differences between artefacts and buildings belonging to different cultures. Archaeology becomes a body of techniques rather than an investigative science. A retreat to being technicians and recorders of past cultures is also common where archaeology has had to be practised under military or ideological dictatorships, for example Imperial Japan or Nazi Germany. Dealing in ideas or understanding human behaviour can involve challenging the dictatorship's views of how society should be organised, or in going along with views of the past the archaeologist knows to be false. It is safer to retreat to being a technician recording the past.

105

Nationalism

It is hard for most archaeologists to place themselves outside their own nation and culture and avoid being influenced by the national ideologies of the country they live in. It is also common in newly independent nations for archaeology to be part of the attempt to provide a worthy and independent past, for example Ireland (independent of Britain in 1921) or Korea (independent of Japan since 1945). The remains of former colonial masters may be ignored, while sites associated with national identity may be given great prominence. Evidence may even be deliberately misrepresented or falsified in support of nationalism. The actions of some Hindu archaeologists at Ayodhya in India led to the deaths of over 2,000 people in riots between Hindus and Muslims over ownership of the site of a mosque that was supposed to have been built on top of a Hindu temple.

Hierarchy

It is common in countries where archaeologists are licensed to do fieldwork for there to be minimum qualifications for getting the licence (usually a Master's degree, sometimes a PhD). Only those with such qualifications may be called archaeologists. Much of the actual physical work on an excavation would be done by a class of people regarded as technicians or labourers. In Britain, all people working on an excavation would nowadays have a university degree and be thought of as an archaeologist. In a country like Germany, only the directors and supervisors would be archaeologists, the specialists would be vocationally trained technicians and the diggers would be casual labourers. Along with hierarchy comes authority. The archaeologist is in charge and has a monopoly on deciding what, where and how to excavate. Archaeologists also have a monopoly on how the past is interpreted.

British archaeology is most like archaeology in countries heavily influenced by Britain, such as Canada, Australia and New Zealand. The United States is also similar in being unregulated by the state and highly competitive between universities and field units. But the USA differs from Britain in that archaeology is seen as a branch of anthropology, and in having indigenous, native peoples whose history and attitudes to the past are different to that of incoming white settlers. US university degrees are also structured differently to those of the UK, making it hard to compare a BA, MA or PhD between the two countries.

No matter which country we work in, archaeologists have a common fascination with the physical remains of the past and a desire to know about the human story since our origins as a species. We can begin to create a more fruitful international archaeology by asking ourselves why we do archaeology. Does archaeology have a value for society today? This is what we will explore in the next chapter.

9

Archaeology's value

> It connects us to the then, the now and the what-is-yet-to-come.
> It tells us about who we are, what we've been and what we might
> become. It connects us to all the rest of humankind. It makes us both
> marvel and despair at what we're capable of.
>
> Nola Merckel (member of the public),
> contribution to the History Matters campaign 2006

Unlike archaeologists, historians have a long tradition of justifying themselves by finding reasons for studying the past. In ancient Greece, the historian Thucydides (455–400 BC) studied the past to try and better understand why people behaved in certain ways. The past was more than simply a rollicking good story of past events. By modern times, a whole set of reasons had been created for the study of the past. A good summary of these comes from the English philosopher and scientist, Joseph Priestley:

> History enabled students to understand change and cause and effect, to
> improve their judgement and understanding, to lose their prejudices,
> and to learn from the past how to improve affairs in the future and
> appreciate the wide variety of human nature.
>
> Joseph Priestley (1803) *Lectures on history and general policy*

In spite of this understanding of why we study the past, many people fail to see that it has any value. This is due to two problems shared by both history and archaeology. Firstly, although both subjects study the very recent past, most of the past they study is of events long since over and people long since dead. It may be interesting but, being the past, it is divorced from the present and seems to have little relevance to modern day problems. Secondly, the results of studying the past are often presented as chronological narratives of events. These are like stories, and as stories they can be taken as simply entertaining and nothing more. Unfortunately, the past is ignored at our peril (this will be explored in more detail in Chapter 12). The past can teach us lessons we can learn from. This is true of both history and archaeology. Archaeology is fun, but it is also important. Unlike historians, most archaeologists have only very recently tried to understand why we study the past through archaeology. Many archaeologists seem to have great difficulty in explaining why they do archaeology other than for enjoyment or out of interest in the stories of the long dead past:

> it seems to me that archaeology is still a widely misunderstood subject (not least by some of its friends, and even of its practitioners), and as a result of this it is still far from having achieved the place, either in formal education or in the general consciousness of society, to which its achievements, and its relevance to our human condition, entitle it.
>
> Professor John Evans (1975)
> *Archaeology as education and profession*

Not much has changed since then. There are still archaeologists who cannot explain why archaeology is important, and many who think that, because archaeology is enjoyable and interesting, the government should provide money to support it. In recent years, various organisations have realised that government will not give money or other support for archaeology for these reasons. Archaeologists have to show why government should support them, by explaining the value archaeology has for the rest of society.

Statements of value

There have been many international agreements on archaeology. But only recently have those agreements included statements about the value of archaeology or of heritage. The Faro Convention is a key document. It states that engaging with cultural heritage is a natural human right. In finding, recording and investigating the remains of the past, archaeologists create and manage cultural heritage. We do it on behalf of everyone, not only for ourselves. The Convention claims that people benefit from cultural heritage through sustainable economic development, enhancement of cultural diversity, promotion of dialogue between cultures, artistic creativity and human development in peaceful and democratic societies. These are big claims that can seem rather remote from the actual process of excavating a site or mapping earthworks in a field.

In recent years, various organisations in Britain have tried to define the value of archaeology more closely. In 2005, a group of archaeological organisations in the United Kingdom, the Archaeology Forum, listed the contributions archaeology made to society as:

- key to understanding human history without written records;
- a core contribution to local identity and sense of who we are;
- a sense of place and common cultural perspectives;
- links people with continuity and change in their surroundings and society;
- a major contribution to tourist income and heritage-led regeneration.

A major conference on the value of heritage in Britain was held in 2006. This included a wide variety of organisations involved in archaeology and heritage. A political think tank, Demos, presented a vision of how the value of heritage could be defined, distinguishing between 'intrinsic', 'instrumental' and 'institutional' values (Figure 9.1). Intrinsic values come

Figure 9.1 Intrinsic value of craftsmanship and association with Shakespeare, instrumental value of entertainment for the public, and institutional value for the status of theatre at The Globe, London

111

from the intellectual, emotional or spiritual importance of heritage for individuals, for example as sites to research, as places of beauty or as sites with religious meaning. Instrumental values come from the social and economic benefits of heritage, such as urban regeneration or reduction in crime. Institutional value is created by heritage organisations and is part of the use of heritage as cultural capital to give status to heritage and the organisations themselves.

Also in 2006, a group of historical, heritage and archaeological organisations ran a three-month public campaign called 'History matters: pass it on'. Some 46,000 people wrote public diaries or sent messages to the campaign and told us why they valued the past. The reasons they gave fell into four groups:

- People have a passion for finding out about past times. The past is mysterious, fascinating and fun. We can commemorate the lives of earlier people.
- We can understand ourselves by studying the past. We can answer the big questions about being human and human behaviour. The past puts our present world into perspective.
- The past creates our identities. It gives us a sense of roots and of belonging. We can understand what it means to be British and the origins of our particular way of life.
- The past can help us to choose the future. We can learn lessons from the mistakes of the past, or relearn wisdoms we have lost.

So, we know that the public value the past a great deal. But organisations which are responsible for managing the historic environment have to demonstrate that the money spent on heritage is not wasted. The idea of heritage having an economic or financial value is attractive, since we can measure this kind of value in numbers of pounds. A report of 2005 did exactly this for English Heritage, the Heritage Lottery Fund, and two government departments (Culture, Media and Sport, and Transport), by using economic techniques to value heritage as a way of justifying funding by the public purse. All other values, including people's non-material attitudes to heritage, were downgraded and seen as less important than the generation of financial income from visits to heritage sites, and the increase in property prices near those sites.

As archaeologists, we want not only to conserve the historic environment but also to study it. We feel that its economic value is less than its value as an object of research. The Institute for Archaeologists (IfA) issued standards and guidance for stewardship of the historic environment in 2008. These seek to balance the different kinds of value ascribed to physical heritage. The significance of what they called 'historic assets' lies in three sets of values:

- evidential values: evidence for the human past;
- conferred values: people's perceptions of the beauty of heritage, its associations with significant events and meaning for the community;
- instrumental values: including economic, educational, academic, recreational and social benefits people derive from heritage.

If all this seems confusing, it is because it is confusing! Nothing has value in itself. Values are given to things by people and organisations. They will have different reasons for this, and so the values they give will be different. It is clear though that the past has a lot of values given to it by people, and these values are more than simply as an object of research. As archaeologists we have to learn to share the past with others who value it for different reasons. We also have to learn that what we do is valued by others, and this helps us to argue our case for government support for archaeology.

Why people like the past

Knowing that what we do is valued by people is comforting. But, if we are going to use the idea of value then we also need to know *why* people give value to the past. Fortunately, an American geographer, David Lowenthal, explored this issue in great detail in an important book published in 1985, *The past is a foreign country*.

Lowenthal pointed out that the past has certain properties (he called these values, but this is confusing as they are not the same as the values discussed above). He identified four particular properties:

- Antiquity: the idea that being old gives status, that its remoteness gives it a mystique, that it helps to explain origins, and it can be seen as primitive and therefore pure and innocent.
- Continuity: we see the past as still part of our lives now. It is where we have come from. We feel connected to our ancestors.
- Termination: the past is dead and gone, and is completed. It is therefore unchanging and stable, and can provide a sense of permanence.

113

- Sequence: the past exists in a chronological framework which extends through the present into the future. We feel ourselves to be part of the march of time, of something bigger than ourselves.

When we study the past, we feel we are revisiting it in some way, placing ourselves back in time. Lowenthal notices that people do this for various reasons. For some it is the intellectual challenge of trying to understand and explain the past. This is the answer that most archaeologists would probably give for being archaeologists. For some, the past represents a golden age when life was simpler, purer, less corrupted and is an escape from the modern world with all its complexities, annoyances, problems and injustices. This may be a reason why some re-enactors recreate and act out periods of the past. It may also be a reason why some people do archaeology, as a retreat from 'real' life. Others enjoy the idea of being a modern person with the skills and knowledge to be lord and master of the past. They can feel superior over the past, and gain a sense of fulfilment through being able to write about their version of the past, which is of course the only correct version. This sense of omnipotence can be seen at various archaeological conferences among academics and field archaeologists. Closely linked to this is a desire to change and put right the wrongs of the past. For example, we can somehow make amends for slavery by studying it and admitting how awful it was in our publications and conference talks. One perfectly good reason for studying the past that is shared by most people is simply enjoyment. Archaeology is fun, exciting, challenging, emotionally stimulating and fulfilling. The past is an exotic other place where life was different, and therefore fascinating.

Getting to know the past has many benefits. It helps us make sense of the present and provides a sense of permanence and stability that reassures us in times of change. It can help us to validate the present by providing it with an origin or example to follow. But it can also be used to subvert the present by finding alternative ways of doing things from the past that might be better than what we do now. The past gives us our cultural identity and our sense of difference from other people. But it can also give us a strong sense of a common humanity. We all have pasts, and the further back in time we go the more of that past is shared between people today. The past gives us lessons about how to do things, and a lot of fun arguing over whether these are the right lessons or not. The past can enrich our lives through its beauty, the sense of wonder it provides or the thrill of touching something made hundreds or thousands of years ago. The past is also an escape from a troubled present and a source of comfort for many.

The past as physical object

While there are various ways of describing this instrumental value by archaeologists and heritage organisations, they have in common a view of the past as physical remains: as heritage sites or artefacts needing to be managed and conserved. The past exists in the present only as heritage objects.

Objects exist to be used. Tim Darvill (1993) has shown how they can be a resource to be consumed by different groups. Archaeologists use the remains of the past for research. Artists often find inspiration from ancient sites or remains. Teachers use artefacts and sites to unlock literacy, maths, historical skills, etc., among their pupils. The tourism industry makes huge amounts of money by promoting heritage as something to be visited and experienced on holiday. Film makers and novelists use heritage as a backdrop for entertainment. Nations use monuments and sites as symbols of identity. The list goes on and is potentially endless. One curious property of heritage is that it can also be valued by people who do not actually use it. Darvill calls these the option and existence values of heritage. Option value demands that heritage be preserved for possible future use, while existence value is an acceptance that a site or a monument is reassuring to people simply by existing. They may have no desire to see it or visit it themselves but are happy to support its existence for others to use.

Archaeologists share the use of remains of the past with others. The prehistoric site of Stonehenge, awe-inspiring, mysterious and one of the most well-known sites in Britain, has been studied by archaeologists for over 300 years. It has also been used to make money out of visitors, and images of the stones appeared on tourist souvenirs as early as the mid-nineteenth century. The site has been used by advertisers as an emblem either of Britishness or of solidity and dependability for everything from tea bags to the motor car. It has been drawn and painted by artists, and the colours and textures of the stones have inspired pottery makers. The site was used for music festivals in the 1970s and 1980s, and Stonehenge has been a name, an image and a theme used by many popular musicians and groups. It has become a ceremonial site again for modern Druids (in spite of there being no connection at all between Stonehenge and the ancient Druids), modern pagans and alternative healers. More to the liking of some archaeologists, Stonehenge is also now the name of a brewery making real ales!

There is one aspect of heritage as object that disturbs many archaeologists. This is the buying and selling of artefacts for money. There are two sources of this unease. One is the academic attitude towards archaeological remains as a source of knowledge about the past which finds it hard to accept that artefacts can also have a monetary value. The other is that many antiquities being bought and sold have been illegally taken from ancient sites. The robbing of artefacts removes them from a site without any proper recording of where they have come from and what other artefacts or features they were associated with. Without this information on their context, the artefacts are almost useless as a source of evidence for the past. The information they could have given us is lost forever. The trade in antiquities is not wrong in itself. What is wrong is the robbing of sites to feed an insatiable market among dealers who do not care about the research value of the artefacts. There are international conventions and national laws against the trade in illicitly obtained antiquities but they are hard to enforce. For many local people in poor countries, the looting of local sites to sell to Western dealers can raise more money than the people could normally earn in a year. Criminal gangs target sites to make large amounts of money, especially in times of war. The aftermath of the Iraq War, with the breakdown of government control, saw widespread looting of ancient sites and antiquities turning up in the Western antiquities markets.

Robbing of sites and treasure hunting are not only a problem in countries with weak or ill-funded archaeology services. It is also a problem in the United Kingdom and the Western world generally. The increasing use of metal detectors as a hobby from the 1970s onwards has led to widespread treasure hunting by thousands of detectorists. While most detectorists are responsible, there are still those who illegally raid sites and sell their finds. One notorious case that helped to change legal attitudes towards treasure hunting was the finding of Roman coins at a temple at Wanborough in Surrey in 1983. The finds were made by responsible detectorists who reported their finds properly. Other detectorists got to know the location, and eventually there were up to 40 detectorists working at night to loot the site. The result was that coins worth £2 million were sold on the antiquities markets. Five criminal trials were held in 1986, but only 3 people were found guilty and the heaviest sentence was a fine of £1,000. The law has since been changed, but the problem of looting of sites is hard to deal with.

The role of archaeologists

As professional archaeologists, we naturally see ourselves as guardians of past sites and artefacts, and see these as our cultural capital. We have the knowledge and the skills to make sure that precious evidence is conserved for study. Unfortunately, this means we can become elitist and see ourselves as the only proper people to be allowed access to the remains of the past. Others with different motives for engaging with remains such as spiritual or commercial reasons are treated with suspicion. We also act as the arbiters of heritage, deciding when something is worth conserving or not. Others may disagree with us on this but have no power to challenge us. There may be sites which are precious to people that archaeology does not recognise as worthy of study, for example twentieth-century football grounds. For many people, the remains of the past have a deeply religious significance, which is directly opposed to its significance for archaeology. One of the starkest examples of this in the United Kingdom has been the battles between archaeologists and others over the remains of the so-called Seahenge timber circle in Norfolk. A professional archaeological evaluation of a Bronze Age wooden circle came face to face with strong opposition from people with a non-archaeological and highly emotive approach to the same site which can only be described as spiritual. Archaeologists had the remains excavated and removed to save them from erosion by the sea, while many people felt that was sacrilege, disrespectful to the site, and wanted the circle to stay where it was.

Cultural capital

Capital is the name given to a resource that can be accumulated. We are all used to the idea of economic capital, the money and valued possessions we own. Cultural capital is the educated knowledge and skills that people have. Like all capital, it can be used to give them an advantage over others. Having an archaeology degree gives archaeologists an advantage over others. The degree is part of our cultural capital. The remains of the past can also be a form of capital if access to them is restricted so that only archaeologists have access to them, such as heritage sites that are only open to the public when we allow it.

We need to understand our role. It is all too easy to see ourselves as a kind of priesthood, with specialist knowledge and skills, safeguarding ancient remains on behalf of everyone else but only if people accept our way of understanding and using them. We act as gatekeepers, only allowing through those we think are worthy to be let near the remains. In the case of Stonehenge, the gates are very real. Access to the site is by paying for a ticket to take you through the barrier and along a path that goes by the site. Simply being able to go among the stones and visit the middle of the site is not allowed without special permission. This permission is not always given. A free music festival had been held at the site from 1972 to 1984. This was organised and attended by various anarchist, alternative lifestyle, pagan and New Age groups. Concerns about too many people visiting Stonehenge and damaging or eroding the site led to the festival being banned in 1985. Attempts to hold the festival were resisted violently by the police in what came to be known as the Battle of the Beanfield. The police were later convicted of wrongful arrest, assault and criminal damage. The whole episode made many archaeologists feel very uncomfortable.

Rather than being gatekeepers and high priests of the past, we should instead be the mediators between past and present. The past was lived by real people, now dead and gone. Archaeologists try to recover fragments of their lives by studying the remains they leave behind. People today have a fascination for the past, and use the remains of the past in many different ways. Archaeologists can communicate with people today to help them better understand the people of the past. We can help people get to know the facts about the past. We can give them ideas about the past they can use as they wish. We can enable them to visit sites and respect the sites at the same time. Part of our job as archaeologists is not only to study the past but to help people today get to know the people of the past, to shake hands with them across the generations.

The only way is ethics

As mediators, we have a responsibility to others for what we do and how we do it. Making sure we mediate in an acceptable way involves thinking about the ethics of archaeology. Ethics is the attempt to define what is right and wrong behaviour. A set of ethical principles is a set of guidelines that stimulate us to think about the complex issues and conflicts we face when practising archaeology. Creating a set of ethical principles is not easy. Different cultures, or people with different religious or political beliefs, will have different ideas about what is right and wrong.

Archaeologists have only recently been debating issues of ethics in any detail. Most would probably accept that we have a duty to seek after the truth about the past and do so in ways which are sincere and accurate. We try to create ideas about the past which are based on real evidence and do so for the common good. We do not tell lies about the past, nor do we create fiction. Nor should we pervert the evidence or only select the evidence we want to support our ideas (this is actually harder to do than it seems). If we work for the common good, then a major ethical dilemma for archaeologists is how to reconcile what is good for us with what is good for others. Not everyone shares the archaeologists' way of engaging with the past.

There are no generally agreed ethics for archaeology. The World Archaeological Congress has various codes of ethics which lay great stress on respecting the ways indigenous peoples engage with the past. The Archaeological Institute of America has its own code of ethics, and members of the Institute for Archaeologists in the UK are bound by its by-laws and standards which codify its understanding of professional ethics. The European Association of Archaeologists and the Museums Association also have their codes of ethics.

What follows are my personal ethical guidelines for being an archaeologist. Other archaeologists would come up with a different set of guidelines. These are based on some general principles:

- Accuracy: basing our work on the reality of the past;
- Sincerity: being true to acceptable standards of archaeological practice;
- Context: being responsible to the rest of society;
- Process: being mediators between people then and people now.

We must respect the original makers and users of the remains we study and manage. We should give meaning to the lives of the people who have gone before us. Artefacts are the last vestige of a human life and, if we destroy that through being careless or deliberately hiding evidence we don't like, then we are effectively erasing the memory of the person who made or used the artefact. People lived real lives and it is the reality of past lived experience that gives the remains of the past much of their force and relevance in the present. Without this sense of 'authenticity' the past can become the plaything of politicians, novelists and pseudo-historians to use as they please.

The role of the archaeologist depends on having specialist skills. We can validate the authenticity of the physical remains of the past as genuine remnants of past human action. We can also create convincing narratives of what happened in the past based on that evidence. It is this that gives us our authority: our handling of remains of the past. We need to follow proper archaeological methods and standards.

The past is easily misused by people for political, religious or other ends. Archaeologists have a duty to society to counter such misuse by pointing out the realities of what the evidence shows. Our understanding of human physical development, behaviour, variation in material culture and historical circumstances gives us unique insights into the shared humanity of all people.

As archaeologists, we are trained to be 'scientific' or scholarly in our approach, to respect the evidence and be objective. This can make it hard for us to understand the depth of emotion other people often have about heritage. We have to allow people to engage with the past through their emotions and understand why the past means different things to different people. Archaeologists can be enablers and facilitators, helping others to engage with the past and to debate with each other about the past.

Based on these principles, I can come up with six ethical guidelines for my own personal practice as an archaeologist. I must:

1 be true to the lives of the people who originally created the remains I investigate;
2 claim the authoritative voice that comes from how I study the remains of the past;
3 help to correct misuses of the past that violate its authenticity;
4 encourage debate about how the past is studied and used;
5 engage in dialogue with other people who have an interest in the past;
6 consider carefully the wishes of any living people whose material culture I study.

By following such guidelines, I hope I can practise an archaeology that has a real value for the world we live in today, as well as understanding more about the world of the past. Of course, other archaeologists may disagree with my list and create a different set of guidelines.

Archaeology has value because the remains we investigate have a part to play in the modern world. They are used by people for a range of purposes such as education, inspiration, enjoyment and commerce. Archaeology as the study of these remains cannot ignore the benefits of what we do for the rest of society. We deal with people's heritage and this places us in a powerful position. The relationship of archaeology to heritage is the subject of the next chapter.

10

Archaeology as part of heritage

The past does not just exist. What we see of its presence, and the uses we make of our ideas about it, are to a considerable extent contrived. . . . The past is a very powerful liberator of misunderstanding, strong emotions – and large bills.

Peter J Fowler (1992) *The past in contemporary society: Then, Now*, p. 81

Archaeology as a field of professional practice is linked closely with heritage management and interpretation, and increasingly academic archaeology is also engaging with the past as heritage. To understand the relationship between archaeology (the study of the past) and heritage (the use of the past) we need to understand why people are interested in the past. We explored this in Chapter 9 and saw that there was a range of reasons for interest in the past. For most archaeologists, their main motives are a fascination with other worlds in the past and the excitement of discovery. Some archaeologists also understand that the remains we study have to be treated as heritage, as objects for use in various ways in the present. It is perfectly possible to say that archaeology is part of the wider field of study and practice that is heritage studies.

However, heritage studies is only slowly being recognised as a legitimate academic subject with its own identity. It is as yet ill-defined, confused and lacking recognised identity. Only in 2009 was a book published claiming to draw together the disparate threads of heritage and try to establish its credentials as a subject in its own right. University subjects are regularly assessed for the amount and quality of research they produce in return for government funding. Heritage was not identified as a separate subject in the latest assessment. Instead, it was dispersed among 16 other subjects. Heritage is commonly taught in university courses with architecture, art and design, conservation, history, museums, tourism, and even sometimes with archaeology or on its own as heritage management or heritage studies. Heritage studies academics can be found in university departments of anthropology, architecture, art history, cultural studies, geography, history, leisure and tourism, museology and sociology as well as archaeology. When we investigate heritage as archaeologists we can have contact with all these other disciplines with their own ideas and theories and ways of looking at things; that can be very stimulating and exciting.

Heritage is usually seen as something to be managed, curated, conserved or exhibited, or something that is an object for tourism, for events and for visiting as an attraction. In fact, heritage is more of a state of mind. Being 'heritage' is not an inherent property of a site or an artefact or a place. We describe these things as heritage because we want to have a particular kind of relationship with them. They are heritage because we say they are heritage. Heritage is not a thing, it is a relationship where we use things from the past for various purposes in the present. Heritage is therefore a set of active processes that turn something into an object of heritage. Tangible cultural objects become heritage through processes of

- seeing;
- experiencing;
- understanding;
- using;

and are perpetuated through processes of

- communicating;
- handing on to those who come after us.

Heritage processes

Seeing heritage involves recognising something that is identifiably from the past but is more than simply recognising it as old. Heritage is old, but is also worthy of respect and needs conservation for future generations. What people think is worth conserving will differ. In the twentieth century, it was generally agreed by archaeologists that any building earlier than 1700 was in need of conservation. Should everything be conserved? Should only special things be conserved? But who decides what is special? Should a sample be conserved that represents all aspects of people's lives, but then who decides what goes into the sample? It is only in the past 40 years that archaeologists have taken seriously historic railways or twentieth-century military sites as heritage. Some heritage is very controversial, such as 1950s or 1960s modernist architecture. When the Park Hill flats building in Sheffield was listed as an important example of urban housing renewal, there were many former residents who felt it should have been demolished instead. It was built in 1957 as a radical piece of architecture, replacing bad housing, but ended up as an unpopular, poorly built and dangerous place to live. Just as controversial was the recent excavation of a 1991 Ford Transit van by archaeologists from Bristol University. Can an ordinary modern vehicle be an item of heritage?

The need to protect heritage can cause problems for archaeology, which sees the remains of the past as something to be investigated. All traces of an archaeological site are removed during excavation, effectively destroying it. This conflicts with the need to protect sites. Guidance on involving archaeology in the planning process was based on the principle that sites should only be excavated if they are already in danger of being destroyed by the proposed building work.

Experiencing heritage is both an intellectual and emotional experience. Being an archaeologist involves having an active relationship with the past. We handle the past. We discover remains no one else has noticed. We make connections and find understandings about the past. We think deeply about what life was like in the past and place ourselves in the minds of past people. For us, our relationship with the past is deeply personal and emotional, involving all our senses as well as our intellect. For others, their experience is different. We can describe many different groups of people who have different relationships to the past:

- The uninterested: there are many who have no focussed interest in the past. It forms no part of their lives and they do not seek it out. They may come across it by accident, and it will usually have some slight impact on them, but only very slight. They may recognise something that is old which looks perhaps attractive or intriguing but go no further than a superficial recognition of it. Some of them may actually be hostile towards it, seeing it as either irrelevant to their own lives, or as something that belongs to the rich and powerful.

- The casual: they do not usually, or habitually, engage with heritage. Their encounters with heritage will be casual and occasional, and may be incidental to other activities. They will enjoy their encounters and will accept that the past is important and even beautiful, but visits to heritage or watching of heritage television will be occasional activities only.

- The interested: these are people who willingly visit heritage sites, read magazines or watch TV programmes. They may even join the National Trust, the National Trust for Scotland, English Heritage, Historic Scotland or Cadw. The emotional and aesthetic experience of heritage is important to them. But it does not form part of their lives other than being something to see or visit. It brings enjoyment and a temporary experience they wish to repeat, but as visitors or sightseers.

- The involved: this group is purposefully and actively engaged in exploring the past. They join local heritage groups and societies, such as fieldwork groups, conservation groups, metal-detecting clubs, re-enactment groups, etc. (Figure 10.1). They do archaeology and other heritage-related

Figure 10.1 Active engagement in a Civil War re-enactment at Rowton Heath

activities in their spare time. It may be a leisure activity but it is seriously pursued. They have an active experience doing archaeology: the whole physical and intellectual experience, as well as emotional engagement with the past. Archaeology and heritage is part of their experience of life.

Professional archaeologists obviously have a lot in common with the involved, but more intensely as it is part of our paid profession, which we carry out every day of the week. We often elevate ourselves above the 'mere amateur' or voluntary sector, but this is wrong. Those who do archaeology for fun can be every bit as serious and skilled as professionals who do it as their job.

Religious views

Various religious groups have a special relationship with heritage. Their practices of worship occur in special places: churches, temples, synagogues, mosques, etc. Many of these are very old or have great significance in the history of the religion. They are sites that produce spiritual feelings in those who use them. Archaeologists have to respect this, no matter what their own personal beliefs are. Some modern pagans see a connection between their own beliefs and many ancient sites such as Neolithic and Bronze Age stone circles. There is no actual connection between these sites and modern pagan worship, but pagans have great respect for previous spiritual beliefs. Many pagans are members of ASLaN, the Ancient Sacred Landscape Network, and work with archaeologists to protect prehistoric sites.

Understanding involves assimilating new knowledge about the past or deriving insight from the past into the present. Archaeology is not only the study of the past. The task of archaeology is to better understand human behaviour. This is more interesting than simply discovering new sites or facts. Asking what happened when is easier but less important than asking why things happened. But understanding also involves more than learning *about* the past, it also involves learning *from* the past. If we understand why things happened, why people behaved in certain ways, then we can apply that understanding to people's behaviour today. All archaeologists know that there are limits to how far we can understand the past. Only scraps of evidence survive for us to find. We may use our imaginations to fill out the evidence and guess at things we don't have direct evidence for. But we always stay within the bounds of what is possible and use our imaginations incisively. When the remains of the past become heritage, for consumption by tourists or visitors, then filling out the evidence often goes beyond what most archaeologists would accept, to satisfy the curiosity of the visitor or viewer who wants as full a picture of the past as possible. There is usually a tension between presenting the remains of the past and presenting the insights of the archaeologist.

Using heritage covers a wide range of benefits for people. Perhaps the simplest use is for enjoyment. The past is fascinating, often exotic and can be aesthetically attractive. Visiting heritage sites or watching television programmes on history and archaeology bring pleasure to millions every year. There is a long history of using the past for creative inspiration. The development of Victorian architecture or pictorial and decorative arts by people such as Augustus Pugin and William Morris was based largely on a reverence for medieval Gothic architecture and craftsmanship. The Welshman Iolo Morgannwg set up the modern society of Druids, the Gorsedd Beirdd, in 1792 inspired by antiquarian speculations about the druids of the Iron Age. The Gorsedd has been closely involved in the festival of art and culture in Wales, the Eisteddfod, since 1819. The rituals of the Eisteddfod involve building a stone circle in imitation of Bronze Age circles supposedly (but falsely) associated with the ancient druids. The past, and archaeology, have also become a brand associated with particular features. Advertising often uses the past to convey a sense of authenticity and reliability. Age conveys stability and tradition, which elevates a product into something desirable. 'Traditional' is probably the most over-used word in describing products that companies wish us to buy. The idea of tradition, age and 'heritage' is an essential part of advertising anything from bread to houses to cars to watches to hotels to food to holidays and so on. Heritage itself is also a commodity that can be bought and sold, as we can see with the popularity of antiques. It can also be an economic asset. Heritage-led regeneration can help to bring visitors and businesses to run-down areas. The past is also highly political, subject to manipulation by politicians for non-historical and non-archaeological purposes. For the archaeologist, heritage is a form of cultural capital, enabling us to gain the respect of others through our specialist knowledge and skills. It is also there to be used by archaeologists to advance their careers by making new discoveries, developing new ideas, writing books, etc. The investigation of heritage through archaeology also provides intellectual fulfilment (the thrill of discovery and satisfaction of interpretation) and a social activity pursued with like-minded others, which brings great personal enjoyment. The key to using heritage is that it is consciously manipulated to produce a benefit. To enable sensible use, the heritage has to be managed. Heritage management is an important part of archaeology, but can bring archaeologists into conflict with others who demand uses for heritage that we deem to be inappropriate.

> ### Heritage-led regeneration
>
> Historic environments can often be the relics of former wealth, now long since gone. The historic centres of towns can become derelict, uncared for and shabby. In the 1950s and 1960s, the economic decline of an area would often be reversed by demolition and modernisation. The preferred option now is to renovate and keep the historic character of an area which makes it attractive to live in. The process of restoration itself can lead to the creation of local jobs. Carefully packaged as heritage, such regeneration can also attract visitors.
>
> Hartlepool was once the third largest port in England but more recently a by-word for dereliction and despair. The derelict docks have been restored as a marina and commercial centre, and are the home of HMS *Trincomalee*, a Royal Navy frigate of 1817. Restored by a volunteer trust, the ship's restoration took 11 years and provided skilled employment that returned £8 million to the local economy. The ship attracts 350,000 visitors a year and has led to the creation of shops, cafés and restaurants. Hartlepool is now a top tourist destination and the town has rediscovered a sense of pride that it had lost.

Communicating is the sharing of knowledge or experience of heritage with others. This is a necessary part of seeing something as heritage, without which heritage is only an individual experience and not something shared with the rest of society. The trouble is that we archaeologists are very bad at explaining what we do. We tend to keep our understandings to ourselves. We deliver talks at conferences of other archaeologists. We write articles in archaeological journals and books that only other archaeologists will read. When we do write popular books, or appear on television programmes, we are often accused by our colleagues of dumbing down archaeology for the masses and becoming inaccurate or misleading. There is a little bit of academic snobbery within archaeology. The conflict between getting across good archaeology and giving people what they want is starkest at heritage sites. Information panels at these sites will often have a site plan with different chronological phases marked on, and information about the physical structure of the site. They will be dry, intellectual presentations of facts. What they seldom do is bring the site to life by telling the stories of the people who once lived there. Some archaeologists though are good communicators and relish getting archaeology across to non-archaeological audiences, for example, through television, working with schools or as costumed re-enactors. They know how to create a narrative and a sense of emotional engagement with the past, as do the best museums. Museums are one of the most important places where the public get their stories of the past. Understanding how museums use material culture to communicate with their audiences is part of the discipline of museology. Traditional museums such as the British Museum, where artefacts are laid out in glass cases, can be contrasted with more inventive kinds of museum experience such as the Vasa ship museum in Stockholm with various interpretive spaces built around a seventeenth-century warship. There are increasing numbers of heritage visitor centres with inventive and attractive ways of communicating the past, such as Kilmartin House in Scotland or the Brú na Bóinne visitor centre in Ireland. Creating good displays and exhibitions, and attracting different kinds of audiences, is a fascinating and creative discipline in its own right, which more archaeologists ought to be aware of but which is seldom taught within archaeology degrees.

Heritage is something that is handed on to succeeding generations. The nature of the handing on will differ for different groups of people and different kinds of heritage experience. Not everyone wants to hand on remains of the past. For some people, the past is irrelevant and gets in the way of progress. Why should the remains of a medieval castle be preserved instead of building a new shopping centre on the site which will bring shops and jobs to local people? Fortunately, many people, not only archaeologists, agree that handing on the remains of the past to future generations is important. In an opinion poll in the UK in 2003, 94 per cent of people interviewed agreed that it was important to educate children about heritage. The process of handing down is a complex recreation of heritage from one generation to the next. This recreation may not be smooth. There may be disagreements about which elements of tangible culture need to be conserved and passed on. The remains of the past can be a reminder of distressing experiences and times. Key parts of the former Northern Ireland prison the Maze, where members of paramilitary groups were held during 'the Troubles', have been designated as listed buildings, to conserve them as historically significant. While applauded by members of Sinn Fein, this has been angrily opposed by some Unionists, who have attempted to delist the remains. Handing on heritage to future generations means not only caring for the remains of the past, but also of today. There are aspects of today's culture that we will wish to hand on to the future. Modern material culture is as much subject to becoming heritage as the remains of the past. Heritage conservation is so much more than simply treating the material fabric of remains and artefacts. There are deep debates about the merits of restoration or preservation of monuments, linked to the equally debated notion of authenticity. When visiting important prehistoric sites such as Knowth or Newgrange in Ireland, are you seeing a prehistoric site or a site recreated in the imaginations of the archaeologists? What is conserved, why and for whose benefit are questions to be endlessly argued about and which make conservation a fascinating topic of study.

Archaeologists as gatekeepers

Archaeologists claim a special status as guardians of archaeological heritage to the rest of the population through their work in heritage management. The earliest attempt at heritage management in the United Kingdom was the 1882 Ancient Monuments Protection Act. Under the Act, 68 monuments were placed on a schedule of sites to be protected. The schedule was kept by a government department, the Ministry of Works. The placing of monuments on the list was the work of an Inspector of Ancient Monuments. The schedule has grown in size since 1882. There are now nearly 35,000 scheduled monuments in the United Kingdom, and the lists are kept and maintained by English Heritage, Historic Scotland, Cadw (in Wales) and the Northern Ireland Environment Agency. A second category of protected site was created by the Planning Act of 1947 which listed buildings still in use as worthy of conservation. Around 500,000 buildings are graded 1, 2* or 2 (grades A, B and C in Scotland, A, B+ and B in Northern Ireland). It is a criminal offence to demolish, alter or extend a listed building without permission. Archaeologists in the relevant heritage agencies in each country in the United Kingdom have a key voice in deciding which buildings should be listed. All archaeological sites not visible on the surface were given protection after 1990 through the planning policies and guidelines laid down in the various nations of the United Kingdom. There are various other forms of protection given to heritage sites, all of which involve decisions made in consultation with archaeologists about whether particular sites are worth conserving. These include the protection of underwater wrecks, compiling registers of battlefields or of parks and gardens, designating World Heritage Sites, and creating conservation areas in towns and villages. There are also legally recognised Areas of Archaeological Importance (the historic centres of Canterbury, Chester, Exeter, Hereford and York). Protecting heritage is often controversial and archaeologists often

129

see themselves as battling against the commercial interests of builders and developers on behalf of a fragile historic environment.

Individual finds in the ground, or portable antiquities, are protected in a different way to monuments and structures. In Scotland, all lost or abandoned property with no clear owner is legally the property of the Crown. Any objects found by archaeologists, metal detectorists or others have to be declared and the Crown then decides whether to exercise its right to ownership or return the objects to the finder. The Crown's rights are exercised by the Scottish government through the Scottish Archaeological Finds Allocation Panel. In England and Wales, all finds in the ground belong to the owner of the land. Archaeologists will seek the agreement of the landowner that they can remove and own any finds they make, unless they are deemed to be treasure. This is a more narrowly defined category in England and Wales than in Scotland. The Treasure Act 1996 defines treasure as:

- any object over 300 years old that is at least 10 per cent gold or silver;
- any group of two or more prehistoric metal objects (all metals, not only gold or silver);
- groups of at least ten coins over 300 years old, or less than ten if made of gold or silver;
- all other objects found in association with any of the above;
- gold or silver objects less than 300 years old that were buried deliberately but whose owners failed to come back and recover them.

The Treasure Act was created through pressure from archaeologists concerned about the loss of information caused by irresponsible metal detecting. The Portable Antiquities Scheme (PAS) was set up to make the Act workable and increase cooperation between archaeologists and responsible metal detectorists. Anyone finding objects of any kind can report their finds to the PAS and have them recorded so that archaeological knowledge is not lost. Archaeologists working for the PAS as Finds Liaison Officers are the essential mediators between the public and archaeology. They act as a kind of gatekeeper.

The idea of gatekeepers comes from tourism. Gatekeepers are all the organisations and people that mediate between people and the remains of the past. These gatekeepers all have different messages to give to people about what they are seeing and shape their expectations of the past. Archaeologists can be seen as key gatekeepers of heritage. We produce the messages about the past that the public receive. We govern access to heritage directly through laws conserving the remains of the past. We also own and manage heritage sites that people will visit as tourists. As gatekeepers, we have a responsibility to tell people about the past and help them have an enjoyable experience of heritage. State organisations such as English Heritage, Historic Scotland, Cadw and the Northern Ireland Environment Agency own a great many heritage sites that people can visit. The entrance fees that visitors pay can be a significant source of income for these organisations. Around 15 per cent of English Heritage income is from admissions and sales at heritage sites, and this proportion will increase significantly as their government grant is cut over the next few years. This can produce a tension between the need to make money and the need to manage heritage for conservation and information. So, a visit to a medieval site may end in the site shop where your children could buy a range of historical souvenirs, including Viking helmets with horns, though we know that Viking helmets never actually had horns at all. The idea of horned helmets came from bad Victorian interpretation of archaeological evidence, long since disproved. As the gatekeepers, archaeologists have a role in making sure people have accurate information about the past.

Other organisations own heritage sites. The National Trust (which covers England, Wales and Northern Ireland) and the National Trust of Scotland own many historic buildings and landscapes containing archaeology. Not all owners of heritage have archaeologists to help them conserve and interpret sites to the public. There are private owners of historic buildings, many of whom can be found in the Historic Houses Association. There are also groups of volunteers in various societies and groups who care for or manage heritage. Many of these are part of the Heritage Alliance, a grouping of 90 organisations that exists to promote the role of voluntary heritage organisations. Archaeology, through the CBA and other bodies, is a full part of the Heritage Alliance. It is important for archaeology to make common cause with others who study and conserve all kinds of remains of the past. Many of these remains, such as theatres, cinemas and other public entertainment arenas, are seldom studied by archaeologists themselves. Yet, they are all part of the tangible cultural heritage alongside Neolithic long barrows, Roman forts or medieval castles. Archaeologists are realising that we are not the only gatekeepers.

The hierarchy of heritage

Being gatekeepers gives archaeologists and other heritage professionals great power. Keeping the gate allows you to close the gate as well as open it. But heritage as an idea is highly democratic. Everyone has a heritage; we all have ancestors and the places where we live all have a history. The remains of the past are not only of the rich and powerful. Archaeologists uncover evidence of everyday life of all sections of society.

The idea of what can be accepted as heritage has changed over time. Gradually, more and more relics of the past are accepted. But, it is usual for each extension of heritage to be championed by amateurs and others in the face of opposition from the professionals. In the nineteenth century, heritage was usually taken to be wealthy country houses and precious art objects. Then ancient monuments and buildings were accepted as heritage worth conserving. In the 1970s, work by devoted amateurs resulted in industrial heritage and transport (railways and canals) being accepted as proper objects of archaeological study. More recently, military heritage and twentieth-century architecture have been accepted. Everything remaining from the past is heritage, but not everything is yet accepted as a heritage that is worth conserving or investigating.

The authorised heritage discourse

In the nineteenth century there was a drive to conserve grand, beautiful cultural objects and buildings that were thought to have innate value. This was based on the idea that they were pleasing and of highly skilled manufacture, representing the best of human achievement. This idea of heritage was used to build a national identity and make everyone feel proud of the achievements of past generations. The problem with this was that it did not represent the identities of ordinary people. It represented the heritage of the upper classes and excluded working-class or other marginal heritages such as women, children, gay people and ethnic minorities. Laura-Jane Smith and Emma Waterton have described this idea of a national heritage as the 'authorised heritage discourse'. The discourse continues today in a view that heritage professionals must be the designators and guardians of heritage for future generations against what they see as the disinterest, ignorance and hostility of the mass of the general public.

Heritage arouses strong passions and deals with conflicting interests. Engaging with heritage is part of the fun of being an archaeologist. However, it does mean that there are often debates and disagreements in archaeology. Because we only have a partial and imperfect sample of the past surviving as remains, we often cannot give a straight answer to many of the questions we ask of the past. We also come into conflict with non-archaeologists who have different aims in engaging with the past than we do. Debate and controversy will always be a part of archaeology. In the next chapter we will take a look at some of these debates and see how they range from arcane and specialised arguments within archaeology to questions over issues that have a much wider importance.

11

Some key debates
in archaeology

The post-modern movement, and the fashions of deconstruction
that it embodies, is to an extent a game played by intellectuals
for their own incomprehensible concepts of amusement, just as
English persons of a certain type indulge in the incomprehensible
performances and cruelties of croquet.

Christopher Chippindale (1993) 'Ambition, deference,
discrepancy, consumption', p. 35

Archaeology has always been riven with disputes over interpretations
of the past, methodology or theory. Debate is a natural part of any academic subject. It is only through contesting ideas with others that we can
improve our understanding, reject obviously false ideas and make our
understanding of the past even remotely accurate. Sometimes a new theory
or new evidence can overturn what we thought we knew. At other times,
different people will see different things in the same evidence. For many
archaeologists, this is the fascination of the subject. The past is endlessly
fought over and debated. Different understandings can arise and our ideas of
the past can change.

Sometimes debate is less about the evidence and more about the political
or theoretical beliefs of the archaeologist. We often see what we want to
see in the past. Archaeologists can also come to feel a sense of personal
involvement in sites or ideas so that if they are challenged they feel personally
insulted. Academic debates can often be sharp tempered and highly personal!

Archaeologists can be especially defensive when they are challenged by outsiders, by non-archaeologists. The way archaeology is done, and the discoveries we make, can be highly important for political, non-archaeological reasons, and many people feel justified in engaging archaeologists in political debates and issues.

What follows are only a few examples of debates that have occurred in archaeology. There are many others that could have been included.

Debates within archaeology

Britain in the Roman Empire

Richard Reece proposed in the 1980s that Roman civilisation was only a thin layer on top of a society that stayed basically Iron Age and Celtic, imposed by the army and Imperial bureaucracy. When the Romans left in 410, the whole structure of Roman civilisation in Britain collapsed. Other archaeologists, such as Martin Henig, think that the native upper classes willingly and thoroughly embraced all the benefits of Roman civilisation, wanting to be part of an empire that brought wealth, position and power. Yet others, including Martin Millett, have emphasised the different experiences of Roman culture by different groups in society and in different regions. Greg Woolf sees the culture of the period not as bringing native peoples up to a level of an already existing Roman way of life but as something new, jointly created by native peoples and the Roman administration.

Anglo-Saxon conquest and migration

Historical documents tell us that various groups of Germanic-speaking peoples from northern Germany and southern Scandinavia migrated to Britain in the fifth and sixth centuries and conquered the south-east from the native Britons to create new Anglo-Saxon kingdoms. This was seen traditionally as a large-scale folk migration exterminating, displacing or subordinating the native Britons. In the 1980s, archaeologists such as Chris Arnold and Simon Esmonde Cleary began to argue that only a small elite of royal families and their followers came over and ruled kingdoms that were still mostly native British. Britain became Anglo-Saxon simply by the Britons copying high-status Anglo-Saxon fashions. Leslie Alcock and Ken Dark, Margaret Gelling, who is familiar with place-name evidence and early medieval language, and Heinrich Härke, who reads German and therefore knows the continental evidence for areas the Anglo-Saxons came from, would still argue for a large-scale movement of population, where the native Britons were simply swamped by incoming migrants. Advances in the analysis of DNA and of chemical traces in human bone are now allowing archaeologists to trace movements of people in the past. The results of these methods are as yet too few and hard to interpret, but are adding fuel to the debate about the extent and nature of ancient migration. DNA results have been used to argue both for and against large-scale migration of Anglo-Saxons.

Viking raiders and settlers in Britain

The Vikings have a bad reputation as fierce raiders killing, burning and looting. The traditional view of Vikings comes from medieval writers, who were mostly churchmen and hostile to the pagan Vikings, who attacked monasteries and churches. They wrote about large Viking fleets and armies, and the evidence of place-names, language and social organisation all supported large numbers of Viking settlers in Britain. Then in the 1960s, Peter Sawyer published his attack on this idea, claiming that Viking armies were small and their impact was limited. He was opposed by Nicholas Brooks who published a strong defence of the traditional view. Certainly the archaeological evidence for Vikings in Britain is very scarce. Yet, the evidence of Viking place-names is very common. DNA studies are also being used to trace Viking settlement, with some success. While Viking settlement in the west of Britain is easy to trace, Viking DNA is similar to that of the Anglo-Saxons and disentangling the two in eastern England is not so simple. We have to accept that archaeology is only one type of evidence for the past, and needs to be studied alongside other disciplines such as place-name studies, linguistics and history for a fuller picture of the past.

The Indo-European problem

We have seen that it was common for early archaeologists to think that an archaeological culture represented an ethnic group of people speaking the same language. It is equally common for modern archaeologists to dismiss the whole idea and think it impossible to identify cultures with ethnic groups. One common debate where this difference surfaces is over the identity of the Indo-Europeans. English is one of a group of Indo-European languages that are related to one another across Europe and Asia, from Portugal to Bangladesh.

These include German, Welsh, Spanish, Russian, Greek, Armenian, Kurdish, Persian, Hindi and many others. All these languages must have descended from a common language spoken at some time in the past and in a much smaller location than now. The location and date of the original Indo-European speakers are a matter of much dispute. Some nations for political reasons have claimed themselves to be the Indo-European homeland, while archaeologists and philologists (those who study the history of languages) cannot agree on where that homeland was. Lithuanian archaeologist Marija Gimbutas identified the middle Volga river in southern Russia as the homeland, identified with an Early Bronze Age culture she called the Kurgan people (named after their burial mounds, known as kurgans). British archaeologist Colin Renfrew claimed the Indo-Europeans began in modern Turkey and were responsible for spreading farming into Europe during the Neolithic. Others have identified a range of locations from northern Germany across to Kazakhstan and from the Baltic to the Balkans. The most recent overview of the debate by American anthropologist David Anthony places the original Indo-European speakers among a range of cultures from 4500 to 2500 BC in the Ukraine and southern Russia.

Mousterian mystery

The Mousterian is a name given to a Palaeolithic culture based on its types of stone tools made between 330,000 and 30,000 years ago. They were made mostly by *Homo neanderthalensis* and its ancestor *Homo heidelbergensis*. The debate about the culture was a three-way debate in the 1960s and 1970s between archaeologists from different countries with different academic traditions: Lewis Binford (USA), François Bordes (France) and Paul Mellars (UK). Finds of Mousterian tools in western Europe tend to cluster into five different groupings of types of tools. The traditional French culture history approach was to see these as made by five different tribes of Neanderthals. Processual archaeologists such as Binford used statistics to analyse the assemblages and saw each group as simply the result of different tasks (such as hunting, food processing, tool making) being performed at different sites by the same group of people. Paul Mellars offered the view that the different groups of assemblage were of different dates and that the nature of the Mousterian changed over time. So we have three completely different explanations of the same archaeological evidence, and there is still no agreement between them!

The first human settlers

Our species of modern human, *Homo sapiens*, developed in Africa and migrated to the rest of the world. When this migration happened has always been controversial, especially in Australia and America. In Australia, the debate has been about whether the Aboriginal inhabitants are even the same species as ourselves. Herman Klaatsch in 1908 argued that aborigines were descended directly from *Homo erectus* in South East Asia. Support for this view continued into the 1980s. Most archaeologists support the opposite view that aborigines are *Homo sapiens* who migrated early to Australia and developed their unique physiology and way of life separately from elsewhere. For most of the nineteenth and twentieth centuries, most white settlers in Australia looked on the aborigines as primitive 'savages' who could be treated with contempt and whose lands could be stolen. An origin for them as primitive *Homo erectus* descendants justified such racist views. Debate continues over the date of the first settlers, but is now agreed to be at least 50,000 years ago, earlier than the modern human colonisation of Europe.

The long-held view in America was that the earliest human settlement was represented by the North American Clovis Culture from 13,500 years ago, which came into America from Siberia when the ice sheets of the last ice age were retreating. However, finds made since the 1970s have revealed much earlier evidence for human occupation. For example, the site of Meadowcroft in Pennsylvania is at least 16,200 years old, Buttermilk Creek in Texas could be 15,500 years old, Monte Verde in Chile dates to 14,800 years ago and human faeces from Paisley in Oregon date to 14,300 years ago. A genetic study by Antonio Torroni and Ugo Perego has suggested that modern Native Americans belong to two different populations in America arriving 17–15,000 years ago, one along the coast and the other inland, both from Siberia. More controversially, there are claims for much older traces of human occupation, such as the site of Pedra Furada in Brazil from 48,000 years ago, and at the Topper Site in South Carolina at 50,300 years ago. These very early dates are highly contested and disputed. Even more disputed are the ideas of Walter Neves and Mark Hubbe that skulls from Lagoa Santa in Brazil are more like Australia and Melanesia than North America and Siberia, so represent an early and different migration to America from Asia. One controversial view, put forward by Dennis Stanford and Bruce Bradley, is that the Clovis culture was brought by Europeans from the French Solutrean culture. This has been opposed by most others who believe that America was populated only by migrants from Asia. Recent evidence, published in 2012, seems to support the Solutrean theory.

139

The great divide in archaeological theory

One of the foremost and most vocal exponents of New Archaeology in the 1960s was the American Lewis Binford. The main challenge to New Archaeology was led in the 1980s by the British archaeologist Ian Hodder. Binford had published his call for a new kind of archaeology in 1962, and Hodder had done the same in 1982 when New Archaeology had become the mainstream of archaeology in the UK and USA. New Archaeology was labelled as processual archaeology by its opponents who defined themselves as post-processual. In turn, the New Archaeologists labelled the post-processualists as 'coggies', short for cognitive archaeologists. The debates between the two sides were often fierce, blunt, challenging and personal. Post-processualists wanted to study aspects of past human behaviour different from those studied by the New Archaeologists. To do this they had to find new ways of thinking about the archaeological record and took their ideas from European sociology and philosophy. As in any debate, each side tends to characterise the other in simplistic and very broad terms that emphasise the extreme beliefs of the others. The complexities and subtleties of the other's position are usually ignored. The use of different philosophical approaches means there is no commonly agreed way of thinking about the issues and each side simply shouts its beliefs at the other without any meaningful exploration of key issues.

New Archaeologists saw themselves as scientific investigators of archaeological remains using objective, measurable and tested techniques. Good measurement and statistical analysis of data would reveal how the archaeological record had been formed. To understand the behaviour behind the record, we could look at how material culture is treated in modern societies and apply this to the past. We can most easily apply this to behaviour that is fairly predictable and has limits to the range of possibilities, such as how food is gathered or grown, how tools are made and used, or the impact of climate and environment on settlement and activity. Post-processualists saw that it was impossible to be objective, that we all bring cultural and personal biases to our study of the past. They saw that the archaeological record was made of remains created and used by individuals in the past, each of which had their own personalities and reasons for doing the things they did. They had choices and did not have to follow the rules. It would therefore be difficult to predict how people behaved and how that behaviour would be reflected in the archaeological record. This approach is more suited to studying past people's beliefs and social or political relationships, areas of behaviour that are hard to explore using archaeology alone, as pointed out in 1954 by Christopher Hawkes in his Ladder of Inference (see Chapter 5).

Hermeneutic relativism

Hermeneutics is the study of how we interpret things, how we give things meaning. Hermeneutic relativism means that all interpretations are judged relative to each other and not against any standard of right or wrong. All interpretations are therefore possibly true and we have no way to judge which are the most accurate.

The more extreme post-processualists denied that it was possible to know anything about the past from looking at remains. The past is gone, and we cannot avoid looking at it from our own, biased present-day points of view. This denies the possibility of doing archaeology at all if we cannot find out what really happened in the past. Instead, we use the remains of the past as a quarry of ideas and material for telling stories or for political and social uses in the present.

This is an extreme position that most archaeologists do not hold. It has been debated also in history as a discipline, and firmly rebutted by Richard Evans who pointed out that the past did actually happen and that there are things we can know for certain. No serious historian could claim that the Nazi Holocaust against the Jews did not happen, yet this is what relativism would allow historians to say.

Post-processualists defined themselves against the New Archaeologists, in a way typical of academic archaeology. They developed in Cambridge University as a group of postgraduate students and younger lecturers. In the British university system it is expected that scholars should have something new to say to make their mark. The way that Cambridge University is structured is different to most other universities. It is easier for lecturers to collect groups of students around them in a kind of guru and followers relationship, which is similar to the formation of religious sects. Each sect believes it has found the truth and that the other sects are the enemy. The reputation and relationships built up at university were the keys to getting jobs at a time when archaeology jobs were scarce. Which social or theoretical group you belonged to could matter for your future. There is also a lot of fascination and fun in thinking deeply about philosophical issues and methods. It is not surprising then that the debates between New Archaeologists and post-processualists have often been bad-tempered, confrontational and deeply personal. These confrontations have been through articles in print, and also in person at conferences and seminars. Thankfully, most archaeologists have moved on from these debates and either ignore them, have tried to reconcile the two sides, have proposed taking elements from both to study different aspects of the past, or have found other ways of thinking about archaeology. Modern versions of systems approaches have a post-processual twist, such as actor–network theory, while post-processual ideas seem to be more linked with archaeological data, for example using practice theory (as an interest in the social practices of individuals).

The whole debate could be summed up in the words of the philosopher Francis Bacon (Viscount St Albans, 1561–1626):

> this excess is of two kinds: the first being manifest in those who are ready in deciding, and render sciences dogmatic and magisterial; the other in those who deny that we can know anything, and so introduce a wandering kind of enquiry that leads to nothing.
>
> Francis Bacon (1905 [1620]), *Novum organum*

Stop Taking Our Past (STOP)!

The beginning of metal detecting as a popular pastime in the 1970s led to a highly negative reaction among most archaeologists, when they saw artefacts disappear into the antiquities market resulting in a loss of archaeological information and the degradation of ancient sites. Underlying this response by archaeologists was an element of elitist snobbery. Detectorists were mainly people of different backgrounds to university-educated archaeologists. They were obviously 'not one of us'. High-profile looting of sites by treasure hunters at night, as at Wanborough Roman Temple in 1983, led to a campaign by archaeologists, called STOP (Stop Taking Our Past), to try to get metal detecting outlawed (Figure 11.1). The use of the word 'Our' in the campaign title could be interpreted two ways. It was meant to refer to the past belonging to everyone, the whole public. But it could be taken to mean the past belonging to the archaeologists as their cultural capital. The campaign failed and relations between detectorists and archaeologists remained hostile for many years. Most detectorists were simply interested in the past, and did not have the qualifications, confidence or time to become archaeologists. Detecting was a cheap and easy way to find the past. It was only with the creation of the Portable Antiquities Scheme (PAS) in 1997 that relations between the two sides improved. This built on the work of one of the few archaeologists, Tony Gregory, who had been sympathetic to metal detecting

Figure 11.1 **Whose heritage is it? The STOP campaign against metal detecting**

and had encouraged detectorists to bring their finds to archaeologists to be identified and recorded. The archaeologists would then hand them back to the detectorist. Illegal detecting by treasure hunters still continues, however, now known as nighthawking, and archaeologists and detectorists together work with the police to try and stop this.

Debates between archaeologists and others

The effects of nationalism on archaeology

Nations need a sense of history as part of their identity. Their archaeological heritage is a visible reminder of that identity and can get caught up in the crossfire between nations. Archaeologists sometimes have to tread a fine line between conflicting claims on the past and standing up for the conservation of a past that may be politically unpopular. Excavations at Vergina in Greece revealed the burials of the ancient Greek Kings of Macedonia, the dynasty of Alexander the Great. Among the decorative symbols used on some of the artefacts was a sunburst (a disc at the middle of a number of rays exploding out from its surface), referred to as the Star of Vergina. This was adopted as a symbol by the modern Greek region of Macedonia. It was also adopted on the flag of the former Yugoslav Republic of Macedonia when it became

143

independent in 1991. This led to violent objections by the Greeks and the flag had to be changed to something a little less like the archaeological design. The World Heritage Site of the Preah Vihear temple was the subject of a simmering border dispute in 2011 between Cambodia and Thailand, each seeking to claim the site. Eighteen people were killed and thousands of villagers moved. The United Nations highest judicial court has now enforced a demilitarised zone around the temple. The break-up of Yugoslavia in 1991–5 involved a vicious war between Serbs, Croats and Bosnian Moslems. Symbols of cultural identity became military targets as each side sought to erase the others' identities from the region. The Serbian shelling of historic monuments in the Croatian port of Dubrovnik and the Bosnian town of Mostar were not isolated examples, and all sides did similar damage to the others' cultural heritage. Historic churches, mosques, libraries, archives and museums were all targeted and destroyed, in spite of the protests of archaeologists.

Looting of underwater wrecks

In United Kingdom waters, it is an offence to dive on, survey, excavate or interfere with a designated underwater wreck. These wrecks are designated for their archaeological, historical or artistic worth. Other wrecks may be designated as war graves under the protection of the Ministry of Defence. It is not only illegal to interfere with such graves, but obviously also immoral. The UNESCO Convention on the Protection of Underwater Cultural Heritage was adopted in 2001, but this has yet to be ratified by the United Kingdom, and the USA, Russia and China. There is a long-standing practice of commercial salvage of wrecks and looters often claim to be working within the law of salvage. The nature of wrecks is that they are highly vulnerable to erosion and decay. Salvagers and looters can also easily claim they are rescuing artefacts from destruction. Modern deep-sea diving technology allows any wreck to be visited, but it is highly expensive. Those salvaging such sites need to sell finds on the open market to recover their costs or to make a profit. The British government signed a deal in 2011 with Odyssey Marine Exploration to recover 200 tons of silver from the SS *Gairsoppa*, sunk during the Second World War, whereby the government will get 20 per cent of the silver with 80 per cent going to Odyssey. This follows the first agreement of this kind in 2002, between the British government and Odyssey, over the wreck of HMS *Sussex*. Naturally, archaeologists are very vocal in opposing the salvaging of sites without proper archaeological methodology and where the finds are sold for profit in the antiquities market. The government seeks to ensure that salvage is carried out using archaeologically acceptable methods, but many archaeologists still find these agreements, based on selling finds as treasure, to be unacceptable.

Repatriation of archaeological finds

The study of Middle Eastern and Mediterranean civilisations in the eighteenth and nineteenth centuries was dominated by Western European and American scholars and institutions. Many remains from Italy, Greece, Egypt, Turkey, Iraq, Persia, etc., found their way into other countries' museums. There developed an almost colonial attitude to the study of these ancient civilisations, where it was assumed that only the advanced Western nations had the scholarship and resources to be able to study them. Naturally, such an attitude causes some resentment today among nations whose scholarship is every bit as advanced as these other countries'. Having their ancestors' (or perceived ancestors') remains in foreign countries is often a source of dispute. The Greek demand for the return of the Parthenon marbles (also known as the Elgin marbles) from the British Museum is a good example of this. The marbles (a frieze, or strip, of figure sculptures running round the walls of the temple) were taken from Athens in 1801–5 by the British Ambassador to Turkey, which then ruled Athens. The Greek government has asked for the marbles to be returned. The marbles are today held by the British Museum, which claims that Lord Elgin had legal permission from Turkey to take them. The Greeks dispute this and say they were taken illegally. The British Museum claims they are part of the world's inheritance from ancient Athenian culture. The Greeks claim they are a symbol of Greek identity and that returning them would allow the marbles to be placed in their proper context on the temple. It seems there will be no resolution of this dispute.

Treatment of human remains

In our modern world, where people live relatively healthier and longer lives than in the past, we are no longer used to people dying around us. Death is something that happens seldom, and often happens in situations where the bodies are taken care of by professionals out of our sight. We have become therefore a lot more squeamish about death. Some people today feel that the physical remains of dead people should be treated with great respect as though the living person were somehow still inside their skeleton. They are unhappy about skeletons, even of the prehistoric past, being displayed in museums or

145

being handled and analysed. Some think that there is a religious basis for this, forgetting that in Christian theology there has never been anything sacred about the physical remains of the body. Skeletons were regularly dug up from cemeteries in medieval times to make room for more bodies. Others feel that we should try to respect the beliefs of the people whose skeletons we are uncovering. This though is almost impossible for prehistory when we have no records of what their beliefs were. Archaeologists who are happy excavating and displaying human remains all insist that they can do this in ways that are serious and respectful. The World Archaeological Congress adopted an accord on the display of human remains in 2005, which recognised the rights of communities to whom the remains belong having the final say on whether they can be displayed or not. Repatriation of remains is increasingly common. Maori remains have been returned to New Zealand from museums in various countries such as France, Sweden and the United Kingdom. It is accepted by many museums that any known living relatives should be consulted before displaying human remains, but this applies only to a small amount of material. Few studies have asked the public how they feel about human remains being on display. Those that have been done show high levels of public interest in human remains, and of support for museums in displaying the remains. Still, some archaeologists and museum curators seem a little bit over-protective. Museum of London guidelines suggest that human remains should be placed in displays in ways that give them some privacy. Why does an inert collection of bones with no living entity or consciousness need privacy?

Pseudo-archaeology

There is a fine line between coming up with ideas about the past that are different to those of others, but which are accepted as an interpretation archaeologists can argue about, and ideas about the past that can be dismissed as having no possible basis in fact. Good archaeologists always respect the evidence, even if that evidence goes against their own ideas about the past. If the evidence says our ideas are wrong then we have to change our ideas. Others are not always so rational in their interpretations of the past. Erich von Däniken became famous, and made a lot of money, in the 1970s by writing books that claimed the earth was visited by aliens from outer space who left behind evidence of their visits at various archaeological sites. Archaeologists have shown how he distorted and misrepresented evidence as part of his claims, but many people were willing to believe what he claimed. The stories developed by archaeologists are often too 'boring', too lacking in drama or excitement for many. There is a ready market for extreme claims and ideas of lost civilisations, or of aliens or secret societies. Other examples of pseudo-archaeological claims are:

- the idea by Robert Bauval that the pyramids and other monuments at Giza in Egypt copy the stars in the sky as they would have appeared 12,500 years ago, 8,000 years before the accepted date of their construction;
- a suggestion by Graham Hancock that there was a worldwide civilisation destroyed by catastrophic flooding at the end of the last Ice Age, which was the ancestor of all later civilisations some 9,000 years later;
- an original idea by Alfred Watkins in 1925 that ancient monuments in Britain occurred in straight lines (ley-lines) in the landscape and acted as prehistoric routeways, which has since been taken by others and turned into ley-lines as sources of psychic energy or power;
- a hoax by a local restaurant owner in the 1950s, which led to claims by Henry Lincoln in 1969 that a local priest had found the marriage certificate of Jesus Christ and Mary Magdalene at Rennes le Château in France, and which was further embellished by Dan Brown in his book *The Da Vinci Code* in 2003.

Although we archaeologists now accept that others have an interest in the past and that we have to engage with this, we still have the attitude that we know best what should be conserved as heritage and how the past should be investigated. Archaeologists definitely have a role as gatekeepers between the past and the public. Taking part in debates about the past should mean listening to what people say about heritage and enabling everyone to feel that heritage is something they can relate to themselves. Archaeologists may also have a more active role than this. We can help people to see, experience, understand and use their own heritage for their own advantage. This is what we will explore in the next chapter.

12

Activist archaeology

men have entered into a desire of learning and knowledge, sometimes upon a natural curiosity, inquisitive appetite; sometimes to entertain their minds with variety and delight, sometimes for ornament and reputation; and sometimes to enable them to victory of wit and contradiction; and most times for lucre and profession; and seldom sincerely to give a true account of their gift of reason, to the benefit and use of man.

Francis Bacon, *Novum organum*, 1620

Politics and archaeology

Archaeology is a discipline carried out by people in the present. That may seem a statement of the obvious. But there are important consequences that follow from this that archaeologists tend to ignore. People in the present have many non-archaeological concerns. These can affect archaeology. In turn, archaeology can affect present-day issues. Archaeologists are not simply people investigating the past for its own sake, for fun and excitement. They have relevant things to say to the present, and have a duty towards people today to help them benefit from archaeology. An ethical archaeology takes into account the context of archaeology: its responsibilities to the rest of society. It also understands archaeology as a process of mediation between people today and in the past.

How does archaeology, and knowledge of the past, help us today? Here are a few ways put forward by archaeologists over the past 40 years:

- past experience can guide future action by applying the lessons of the past to solve today's problems (some archaeologists have said that archaeology provides information essential for the future survival of humankind);
- we can look to the past for a better understanding of what makes us human and our common humanity;
- we can use archaeology to study the origins and nature of issues important to people today;
- we can help the public to interact with the past in their own ways and to their own benefit;
- we can better understand how people can benefit economically or socially from good heritage management.

The use of archaeology in the present is not always simple or easy. It can be misused for politically dangerous purposes. The selective and inaccurate use of archaeology by Nazi Germany in the 1930s and 1940s is one of the most famous examples of misuse. It is not the only example, as I showed with the events at Ayodhya in India (Chapter 7). Archaeology is always liable to be used by politicians for their own ends. In divided societies or in regions with hostile neighbours, this is especially true. The Middle East, with the disputes between Israel and its neighbours and between Jews and Palestinian Arabs, is one area where archaeology cannot be politically neutral.

In countries with settled democratic politics, it is easier for archaeology to ignore the present day and concentrate on understanding the past. It has been pointed out that archaeology in the United Kingdom is largely divorced from politics, rarely applies archaeological understanding to the present and even when lobbying for itself is politically weak. Even worse, non-archaeologists very rarely come to us to ask us to contribute our knowledge and perspective to the solution of present-day problems. Others do not see us as having anything of value to contribute. It is worrying that some see archaeology as a subject concerned with excavation and finding remains of a dead past, simply for its own sake and with no actual purpose. Unfortunately, the one question people usually ask an archaeologist is 'what have you found?', when finding things is only the starting point of archaeology, not its end.

Das Ahnenerbe

Ahnenerbe can be translated from German as ancestral heritage. It was the name given to a research institute founded in Nazi Germany in 1935 by Heinrich Himmler, the head of the SS (the Nazi police and security organisation). The aim of the institute was to research the culture and anthropology of the Aryan race. Respected academics Herman Wirth and later Walter Wüst would serve as its Presidents, but the man who actually ran it was its secretary, Wolfram Sievers. It was formally incorporated into the SS in 1939. While it included folklore and musicology among its activities, most of its research was archaeological.

Das Ahnenerbe financed or ran various research expeditions abroad, such as to Sweden to study ancient rock carvings, to Finland to find evidence of ancient myths and pagan beliefs, to the Crimea to find evidence of Gothic settlements, and to Tibet to explore possible early Aryan influence on Tibetan culture. They were able to make an astonishing claim that Hitler's Nazi ideology was essentially the same as Buddhism! Inside Germany, das Ahnenerbe carried out various excavations, for example at Palaeolithic sites in the Mauern caves and the Iron Age hill fort at Heuneberg.

After the war, Sievers was executed for his part in human medical experiments and the murder of Jews for their skulls to be used in physical anthropology research. Walter Wüst returned to teaching at the University of Munich.

One area where archaeology could be more obvious in current affairs would be in environmental issues. But, there is a long-standing and unfortunate way of thinking that there is something called nature that is separate from human culture, that there must be a natural environment distinct from the historic environment. As a result, the management of the environment is partitioned between nature and culture agencies, for example Natural England and English Heritage or Scottish Natural Heritage and Historic Scotland. Likewise, there is a long-standing and deep-seated division between 'nature' and 'culture' studies within universities and academic life. This is completely at odds with the archaeological understanding that there is no such thing as a natural landscape free from human intervention in western and central Europe. Archaeology is educationally and administratively divorced from the natural sciences and therefore has failed to make itself heard as part of the 'natural' environment sector.

There are also other reasons for archaeologists' reluctance to become involved in current affairs. Archaeology is a profession and a discipline, and all such professions and disciplines are naturally cautious and conservative, fearing changes to the way that they work. Higher education funding does not reward work in applying archaeology to current issues, and academia usually elevates pure research as higher in worth than applied research. Many archaeologists see the subject as a science and try to keep to scientific notions of being objective towards their evidence and fear that working on political issues will move them away from that. There is a natural revulsion at Nazi and other misuse of archaeology that makes archaeologists wary of getting involved in political issues, or using archaeology for the present. Many people became archaeologists because of a deep interest in the past, and have a focus which is wholly in the past itself, not the links between past and present. Some have become archaeologists as a conscious escape from the present and have no interest in returning to it. Archaeologists have also accepted the professional role of heritage managers where the past has become an object kept in a sealed bubble called 'heritage' to be conserved and kept safe from erosion or damage by the present rather than used.

Cross-disciplinary initiatives

Archaeology has occasionally played a key role in some cross-disciplinary research projects, for example ARCHAEOMEDES, which looks at the causes of environmental degradation in the Mediterranean, and CAPLTER, which looks at the ecology of desert areas in Arizona, USA. Yet few archaeologists have followed the path of Charles Redman, who in 2007 set up and runs the School of Sustainability at Arizona State University, USA. This is a university department with a focus on finding real-world solutions to environmental, economic and social challenges in the present. It is not an archaeology department but merges archaeology with other disciplines in the service of the people living today.

Happily, more archaeologists are now becoming dissatisfied with being passive and are debating the contemporary role of archaeology. We are slowly overcoming our lack of nerve and attitude. Many archaeologists now realise that, if we are to receive funding and support from government, then we should surely show that what we do benefits taxpayers. An active, or activist, archaeology is beginning to be created. But there are different forms of active archaeology. Here I will describe four types of activism: utilitarian, democratic, dogmatic and methodological. These are not hard and fast categories, and projects can overlap more than one category.

Utilitarian activism

We can use our knowledge of the past for the benefit of the present, and we have already seen that there are various kinds of instrumental value in archaeology. The archaeologist has the role of expert, contributing to public debate and the formation of political policies.

For example, archaeology helps us to accept that all human beings have a common origin; we share a common humanity. We can therefore accept that the differences in religion, language, skin colour, etc., are all part of the wonderful variety of human groups and are part of a long tradition of cultural differences going back many years. To persecute someone for being different from ourselves is deeply illogical. We can also see how different ways of life have different kinds of social organisation behind them and how differences in wealth and power have arisen. We can have a greater understanding of why societies go to war, or of the relationship between levels of population and exploitation of resources.

Many countries are nervous about the effects of migration today. Using our knowledge of material culture and using DNA evidence we are now beginning to understand patterns of migration in the past much more clearly. We can show that societies are the result of both native development, migration of people and contact with other societies. The idea of a single, homogeneous nation with one identity, shared by everyone and unchanging over time, is nonsense. Yet the idea of nations based on a single ethnic group has been the basis for most of the European countries created in the twentieth and twenty-first centuries, often with forced exchanges of population to 'purify' the nation and make it more ethnically homogeneous. The tragedy of the violent dissolution of Yugoslavia under hostile Serb, Croat and Bosnian nationalist groups, each claiming an ethnic identity supposedly based on history, brought needless suffering to thousands. In more stable countries such as the United Kingdom, both right-wing and nationalist groups try to appeal to notions of Britishness, Englishness, Scottishness or Welshness that any archaeologist (or historian) could easily challenge.

One of the big themes of modern times is climate change. Archaeology studies human culture over long timescales. We are the one discipline that can understand how human behaviour changes in response to both sudden and long-term changes in climate. We can also see the evidence for human over-exploitation of resources and the degradation of the environment that results. Work by archaeologists has already led to changing policies on the disposal of waste in the United States. Some archaeologists have begun to

153

look at evidence for old farming practices in Bolivia, Mexico and Peru to see if they can be revived to help modern-day farmers. Likewise, archaeologists are looking at prehistoric settlement of the Negev Desert in Israel as part of creating modern sustainable settlements in the same area.

Archaeological evidence for human effects on past environments and climate can be of great help to scientists modelling climate. We can show that increases in global CO_2 (carbon dioxide) since the last Ice Age began with humans beginning to clear woodland for farming on a large scale around 8,000 years ago. We can also show that increases in CH_4 (methane) in the atmosphere began with rice farming around 5,000 years ago. More specific examples of environmental evidence would include studies of ancient fish bones in prehistoric middens (rubbish dumps) that tell us the natural background level of mercury in the environment in the northern USA, which challenged the levels that scientists had previously assumed to be safe.

Recent research in the United Kingdom about the archaeology under the North Sea has revealed evidence for the former land that was flooded in the global warming after the end of the last Ice Age, with clear and explicitly drawn lessons for current global warming. The Council for British Archaeology and English Heritage organised a session at the Institute for Archaeologists conference in 2008 on climate change and the historic environment. This explored how archaeological research can bring new understanding of the processes and outcomes of climate change. On television, Channel 4 showed a series in 2009, *Man on Earth*, devoted to looking at how changes in climate have influenced humans throughout history, asking what we can learn from this. The series was presented by Tony Robinson, also the presenter of the long-running archaeology series *Time Team*, and well known as the public face of archaeology on TV.

Democratic activism

Archaeologists can help people to engage directly with their own past and to benefit from their own heritage. Giving people pride in their past is not only the work of nationalism but can be a way of empowering disadvantaged or minority groups.

Some American archaeologists have worked on evidence for the lives of African slaves in the USA, for example at Wye House plantation in Maryland, in Manhattan and in Oakland, California. This work often involves modern black communities and can highlight the history of communities previously ignored in the histories of these places. Native American groups have also sometimes benefited from archaeology, such as the Narragansett in Rhode Island, who use archaeology to help revive their cultural identity. In the Colorado coalfield, it is working-class communities that have been studied and brought back to life through archaeological excavation. In Britain, there are now some excavations of working-class housing, such as Shoreditch in London, which brought back together communities disrupted by the bombing of the Second World War and later redevelopment of the area. In Africa, where global commercial interests interact with the needs and rights of local people, archaeologists are playing a part in helping those people find a heritage and avoid being helpless victims of Western economic interests (Figure 12.1).

There are examples of archaeology being used directly to help descendant groups engage in political action. Black South African soldiers died during the First World War, when the steamship SS *Mendi* sank off the British coast. The investigation of the wreck by Wessex Archaeology has been used in reconciliation between black and white South Africans after the ending of Apartheid in South Africa. The Pueblo Indians and others in the United States have used archaeological evidence to help them in claims to land. Archaeological evidence has also helped native Aleuts in Alaska hold on to their salmon fishing traditions in the face of government attempts to regulate them.

Figure 12.1 Archaeologists working with local people in Sierra Leone

155

More than simply having pride in the past, we can help people do archaeology themselves by including them in our research and fieldwork. Some people now have jobs as community archaeologists, working with local societies and other groups of people to run projects that they can take part in. This can help people who would not otherwise be able to do archaeology to gain new skills, self-confidence and self-esteem. This can benefit especially disabled groups or people from disadvantaged backgrounds. The University of Manchester Archaeology Unit undertook a project, Dig Manchester, excavating three sites around the city for local people to join as volunteers. One of the goals of Dig Manchester was to get children from inner city areas to aspire to higher education at their local university. One of the few organisations to have a permanent community archaeologist is the York Archaeological Trust. Jon Kenny offers advice on how to set up a local interest group or project, provides training on how to identify and understand the historic environment, lends fieldwork equipment to help with projects, puts local groups in touch with heritage specialists and gives talks to schools, evening classes and interest groups about a variety of subjects relating to archaeology. He also runs a monthly archaeology and history club for York People First, a self-advocacy group for people with learning difficulties. After taking the group to a major city excavation and the local archives and library, the group approached a local theatre company to suggest a theatre production based on their research. The result was a play entitled *Number 4 Haver Lane* (one of the sites excavated by the Trust). The play was performed by people with learning difficulties at the Theatre Royal studio, mostly members of the archaeology and history group.

This top-down community archaeology where we provide the opportunities for others can be contrasted with a bottom-up approach where the communities themselves run their own projects and call in the professional archaeologists as and when they are needed. The democratisation of archaeology is a process of enabling everyone who wishes to do archaeology for themselves. Archaeology becomes no longer the preserve of a professional elite. For example, in the drought of 1995, residents of Mellor village, Ann and John Hearle, noticed crop marks in and around their garden. They set up the Mellor Archaeological Trust to investigate them, and called in the University of Manchester Archaeology Unit to help them with advice and expertise. The crop marks proved to be the deep ditch of a remarkable and pre-viously unsuspected Iron Age hilltop settlement. The Trust has since gone on to study the whole 10,000-year history of the Mellor Parish. The Friends of Judy Woods in Bradford are a group of local people who have come together to maintain and research the history of a local woodland. As well as clearing rubbish, getting rid of invasive non-native vegetation and creating woodland trails, they have invited Bradford University to carry out geophysical surveys as part of the group's research into the industrial history of the woods. Some local archaeology groups are very large and successful. The Sussex Archaeological Society, founded in 1846, is one of the largest. It owns and manages its own heritage sites, which are open to the public, including Fishbourne Roman Palace, as well as carrying out its own field research.

A more controversial approach to involving local people in archaeology was tried by the *Time Team* television series in 2003. They organised and filmed ordinary families excavating one-metre-square test pits in their own gardens across the nation. Over 1,000 people took part and there was a great deal of criticism from the professional archaeological community to the whole project. They were concerned that 'ordinary people' (that is non-archaeologists) would be damaging possible evidence of the past. Some of the criticism was elitist, from archaeologists who felt that only they were qualified to dig proper holes in the ground. The approach has, however, become accepted. Access Cambridge Archaeology, run by Cambridge University under Carenza Lewis (formerly part of *Time Team*), successfully organises two projects – Archaeological Field Academies and Dig on Your Doorstep – which involve local communities and young people excavating their own test pits with professional supervision and support. The recent (2010) BBC television series *Story of England*, created and presented by Michael Wood, involved the inhabitants of one English village, Kibworth in Leicestershire, in carrying out their own archaeological and historical research, including excavation. These initiatives are important for helping people carry out archaeological processes for themselves rather than relying on the professionals to do it for them. The people themselves feel empowered and more connected with their own heritage.

A special form of democratic activism involves the way in which we practise archaeology itself. The Sedgeford Historical and Archaeological Research Project in Norfolk is an overt exercise in democratic archaeology, believing that all those who participate in the project have an equal say in how the project is run. They have a constitution with a team of directors, supervisors and committee members. The committee runs the project and is elected by the members, who are everyone who has directly and actively participated in the work of the project. Such direct democracy is rare in archaeology.

Dogmatic activism

Archaeology can be used in the service of political and other ideological agendas, either to support dogmas or to challenge the dogmas of others. Archaeology becomes a servant of other non-archaeological purposes. There are as many kinds of dogmatic archaeology as there are ideologies.

Archaeology has often been done in the service of nationalism. This is dangerous when it is in the service of an aggressive and antagonistic nationalism. Dogmatic assertions of connections with ancient monuments or sites of events in a nation's history can lead to an unbalanced view of the past. We could perhaps call this the *Braveheart* syndrome. The 1995 Hollywood film *Braveheart* was a historically inaccurate fable based on legends surrounding William Wallace's fight against the English occupation of Scotland in the early fourteenth century. It was accused of stoking hatred of the English among some nationalist Scots, and was overtly used by the Scottish National Party to increase its support and membership. The mythical past had become stronger than the reality of pro- and anti-English factions among the medieval Scottish nobility. Likewise, the Battle of Culloden in 1746 has sometimes been portrayed as the defeat of Scots Jacobites by the English Hanoverian army. In reality the Jacobite army was made up of Scots, French, Irish and English, and the Hanoverian forces were English, Scots, Irish and German. Most Scots were opposed to the Jacobites, and most modern Scots are aware of the historical reality. Nevertheless Culloden is still seen by some as a symbol of unthinking, romanticised nationalism. On the other hand, archaeology was used in a more benign way in Scandinavia to give a sense of identity and pride to nations such as Denmark, Sweden and Norway as part of their nation-building and rivalries since the seventeenth century.

Religious dogma can be a powerful force directing archaeology. Some fundamentalist positions in religion are sharply opposed to rational scientific method, and archaeology can be misused to support particular religious viewpoints or beliefs. American amateur archaeologist Ron Wyatt claimed a whole list of discoveries in the Middle East linked to the Bible, all of which were dismissed by reputable archaeologists and scientists, and by many Christian groups and Biblical scholars. One of his most famous claims was that he had found the remains of Noah's Ark high up in mountains in Iran; it was really a natural rock formation. The most extreme version of religious dogma misusing archaeology is creationism. Creationism is a key argument of fundamentalist Christians who believe that the Bible is a literal truth, and put forward the view, against all scientific evidence, that the world was created 6,000 years ago. There are also Islamic, Jewish and Hindu creationists who put forward their view of the origins of the world against those of science. Christian creationism has been rebranded as 'intelligent design', in which the complexity of the world is said to be impossible without an intelligent designer, that is, a god. Many creationists are US Protestant Christians and there are also US creationist museums with displays which misuse archaeological evidence. This involves claims that humans and dinosaurs lived at the same time in spite of the scientific evidence that the dinosaurs died out 63 million years before humans evolved. However, not all religiously motivated archaeology is wrong. Using archaeology to shed light on the conditions in which religious groups began and developed is well practised, and can lead to archaeology of a high standard. Biblical archaeology is a well-established part of mainstream archaeology, seeking to uncover ways of life in the Middle East during the prehistoric and Roman periods.

There are all kinds of political motivations for using archaeology. Some ideologies have a particular view of human behaviour and how it developed. Marxists see the past as a succession of stages in human development marked by economic exploitation and class conflict. They will inevitably interpret the evidence to support that view. The Soviet Union's Academy for Material Culture directed all archaeology after 1924 as a search to prove the Marxist development of society from communal hunters to slave-owning farmers, to feudal landlords and to capitalist industry. Any evidence of change brought about by migration of people was ignored. A more recent ideology within archaeology is feminism. Feminists will seek to correct what they say are biases of male archaeologists, who assume gender roles in the past were the same as gender roles today. They have provided a much-needed reminder that the role of gender cannot be assumed, and that the lives of women and children in the past are less well studied than the lives of men. Feminists have sought to challenge the male domination of society and achieve respect and equality. Archaeological evidence for gender roles and the lives of women in the past can help in this.

Methodological activism

Archaeology does not only deal with the remote past. It can be applied to the present and very recent past. Using archaeological methods to study modern material culture can shed light on aspects of the modern world that we would not normally think about, and can have a practical application to present-day problems or issues.

A study of twentieth-century British and Swedish beer cans showed how the visual symbolism of their design and advertising was being deliberately manipulated. The weaker the alcoholic strength of the beer, the stronger the masculine imagery, while stronger beers were associated with images promoting a safe, traditional and wholesome image. Other studies have included looking at the portable radio and how changes in its design reflect changes in society in twentieth-century America.

One of the most famous examples of using archaeology to study the present is the Tucson garbage project of William Rathje in the United States, begun in 1973. The project analysed the rubbish thrown out by modern households and excavated modern rubbish land-fill sites. The archaeologists were able to show that we cannot trust what people tell us about what they eat and drink, or about how much. The excavations were also able to correct mistaken ideas about how rubbish behaves when breaking down in land-fill sites. The project's results have been used by politicians to change their management of rubbish disposal.

More recently, English Heritage has supported an archaeology of homelessness in Bristol, understanding the material culture and landscapes of homeless people, as well as understanding the material conditions that make homelessness possible. There is an overlap between this and democratic activism. Some of the homeless people themselves have been full partners of the archaeologists, and have presented the project at archaeology conferences. This has helped to give them a greater self-confidence as well as giving archaeologists insights into places they would not otherwise have seen, such as how to identify safe places to sleep at night. Work by archaeologists who study the present is slowly gaining greater acceptance within archaeology in the UK. The Contemporary and Historical Archaeology in Theory (CHAT) conferences held since 2003 have helped to raise its profile.

A special case of archaeology in the service of the present is its use in forensic studies, where archaeologists play a role in unearthing evidence of criminal activity, in routine police investigations, investigations into war crimes in former Yugoslavia or helping with the search for victims of the Northern Ireland Troubles. In the United Kingdom, archaeological sciences has been merged with forensic sciences into one category by UCAS, the national service for entry into higher education degrees. An interesting cross-over between forensic and traditional archaeology is the excavation of First World War battlefield graves in Europe. Archaeological excavation of

250 British and Australian war dead at Fromelles in France led to the reburial of identified remains and 'closure' for the families of the deceased.

Conclusion

An activist archaeology is based on the idea that archaeology deals with everyone's heritage, and we have a duty towards the people whose heritage we are studying. We can help people to recognise their own heritage and that their own past is worthy of study or conservation. We can help people to experience archaeology for themselves and to make the same emotional connections with the past as we do – through doing archaeology. It would also help if we thought more about how we practise archaeology and improve the experience for everyone involved, including professional and voluntary archaeologists. We need to constantly remind everyone (including other archaeologists) that archaeology is all about understanding human behaviour, not about the mechanical collection of past relics. Archaeologists have long had an obsession with improving their methods and the technologies that they use. But we should never confuse *how* we do archaeology with *why* we do it. We can then apply archaeological knowledge to real-world current affairs and help people solve particular problems. Not all archaeological research has to be directed to this end but we need to be more aware of the possible uses of what we do.

In addition to the worthy reasons for doing archaeology outlined in this and earlier chapters, there is one more reason that I have not yet looked at. The personal satisfaction you can get from archaeology is immense. That should always be your main reason for doing it. Now that we know why we do archaeology, we can turn to look at archaeological methods, which will be subject of the next chapter.

PART III

DO IT, STUDY IT, ENJOY IT

13

How to do archaeology

Rakka	Fallen blossoms
eda ni kaerazu,	do not return to branches,
hakyou futatabi terasazu.	a broken mirror does not again reflect.
	Japanese proverb

Archaeologists try to re-assemble past life from the broken remains it leaves behind. There is a wide range of methods used in archaeology for finding sites and artefacts, recording earthworks and buildings, remote sensing of unseen remains, field collecting, excavation, post-excavation analysis of finds, environmental sampling, dating of materials, writing up reports, interpreting sites to the public, arranging museum displays and so forth. Archaeology is more than only excavation. Whole books are written about archaeological methods. All I have room for here is a short summary. More details can be found from books in the reading list at the end of this book.

I describe archaeology as a set of processes:

- finding sites;
- recovering and recording evidence;
- analysing remains;
- dating remains;
- interpreting the evidence and debating understandings of the past;
- storing finds;
- caring for and protecting remains;

- interpreting the remains to others;
- teaching about the past and archaeology;
- engaging with the public;
- publication of results.

Finding sites

Sometimes we don't have to find sites. Historic buildings exist in all our villages, towns and cities. Other remains survive as ruins or earthworks, obvious and highly visible. Some sites do have to be found, though, since they have long since been ruined, worn away or deliberately removed. Even very recent sites, such as Second World War defences, can leave no obvious trace to see.

Aerial photography can reveal many sites that are invisible on the ground. Low earthworks can show up as shadows cast by the sun or by a light dusting of snow. Dark earth of ancient ditches can show up in the soil when fields are ploughed. Stone walls under the soil stunt the growth of crops, while ditches can have a richer soil which helps crops grow tall; both are often seen in dry summers.

Geophysical methods such as resistivity or magnetometry can help us find underground remains. A ditch with wetter soil than the compact ground around it will pass an electric current more easily than a stone wall which will resist the current being passed. Areas of burning such as a hearth, or areas where rubbish has been dumped, will often have a high magnetic reading. Ground-penetrating radar can see features much deeper than the other two methods. A relatively new method is light detection and ranging, known as LIDAR. A laser is fired at the ground and the time it takes to be reflected back to an aircraft or ground station is measured. It can record earthworks in very fine detail, and can even reveal features underneath woodland that cannot be seen at all by eye from an aircraft.

Systematically walking ploughed fields is a good way to find sites where artefacts are being brought up to the surface by the plough. A method that yields similar results is test-pitting. This involves digging a grid of one metre square pits at regular distances apart on the field, excavating downwards until finds (or no finds) are made.

Archaeologists also look at written evidence for anything that is known about an area they are researching. This may be the historic environment record held by the local planning authority, medieval or later documents held in archives, or the published works of other archaeologists. Using old maps can reveal buildings that no longer exist, while evidence of early place-names can reveal activities once carried out or structures once standing in a place.

Recovering and recording evidence

Whatever fieldwork is done, it is essential to record what currently exists at the surface. Surveying is the process of recording upstanding remains, including buildings. Building survey involves making very accurate line drawings of the outside of the building, and an accurate record of its floor-plan. Photogrammetry involves taking accurate, high-definition stereoscopic photographs of the outside of the building. Photographic cameras can be replaced by lasers for highly accurate laser scans to pick out the finest of details.

Features in the landscape can be recorded by a total station, which accurately measures the position and height of any point on the feature, and places the data directly into a computer database. This can then be used by a Geographical Information System (GIS) to produce maps of the landscape. More traditional methods are far cheaper and more suitable for use by volunteer community groups. Tape measures can be used to plot the position of remains from known points and these positions are then drawn by hand onto a plan. The plane table is a horizontal drawing board placed on a fixed point of known location. Distances are then plotted along the line of sight from the board to the feature. This is usually done with an instrument called an alidade (a small telescope attached to a ruler) to take a distance reading off a surveyor's staff. The result of these simple survey methods is a pencil drawing which can then be gone over in ink or scanned into a computer.

Excavation is a methodical removal of archaeological evidence that effectively destroys the remains of the past. Excavation must be done for good reasons: to rescue information that is going to be destroyed by modern building work or erosion, or for sound research reasons to answer specific questions. Everything excavated has to be recorded. Many sites were excavated in the eighteenth and nineteenth centuries without proper recording and much information about the past has been lost as a result. In some countries all sites are protected by law against unlicensed excavation. In Britain, only sites placed on a list (the schedule) are given legal protection. Permission to excavate these sites is given by the government on the advice of English Heritage, Historic Scotland, Cadw or the Northern Ireland Environment Agency. Some sites may be in Sites of Special Scientific Interest, where permission has to be granted by Natural England, Scottish

Natural Heritage, the Countryside Council for Wales or the Northern Ireland Environment Agency. Most archaeological sites are on private land and, whether scheduled or not, the archaeologist must have the permission of the landowner and, in England and Wales, have agreed with them the ownership of any finds.

The basics of any excavation are simple. Everything on site, and the site itself, must be located precisely. This usually involves creating an imaginary site grid with a baseline. The imaginary grid allows locations to be plotted from east to west and north to south, just as on a modern ordnance survey map. The excavation itself involves the removal of layers of soil or stone to reveal features and earlier layers. To do this well enough to be able to see everything involves being methodical, neat and tidy (Figure 13.1). The soil may be sieved to recover finds too small to be easily seen by the excavator. All finds made on site have their position and depth on site plotted, and context listed. The excavator's most precious possession and their most useful excavation tool is their trowel. A three- or four-inch pointing trowel with a solid cast blade and tang is best. Most archaeologists keep their trowel until it wears down very small. The inverse size rule is that the smaller your trowel, the more digging you have done, and the more respect you are owed as a long-standing field archaeologist. There are two other major 'rules' of excavation. One is that, no matter how long the excavation, the most important find will not occur

Figure 13.1   Careful excavation of a prehistoric site at Chapel House Wood, Yorkshire

until the last or last-but-one day. The other is that the spoil heap will always be placed over a key part of the site that will need to be excavated and so the spoil heap has to be moved!

Archaeological sites are a complex layering of deposits and features cut into these layers. This is the site stratigraphy. Excavation of each layer and feature has to be done and recorded accurately. Modern archaeology owes a great debt to pioneers such as Sir Mortimer Wheeler and Dame Kathleen Kenyon for their advances in stratigraphic excavation. The end result on modern excavations is the Harris matrix, which is a diagram showing how each context is related to the others. On urban sites these matrices can be very complex.

Underwater sites face specific challenges not found on land. Sediments are often being actively eroded or deposited on sites, visibility may be very poor and the weather or the tide may make it impossible to dive except for short periods of time. Archaeologists must be skilled divers, and there is a limit to the depth people can dive and work. Underwater archaeology covers not only the excavation or survey of shipwrecks, but also sites now underwater because of changes in sea level or coastal erosion, or sites that were deliberately sited in water (e.g. crannogs or lake dwellings). The position of a site is usually fixed by GPS (which is also often used on land sites). The site can be surveyed by sonar, or by divers using tapes and depth gauges. When excavating the silts or other sediments, these are often removed and carried away by a water- or air-powered hose. Conservation of the artefacts recovered is a major consideration in underwater archaeology.

A special kind of environment, with its own challenges, is the coast, with its intertidal areas. Some coastlines can be hazardous, with active erosion or steep cliffs, while intertidal zones may include quicksands and will only allow short periods of work at low tide. Working in these areas can be challenging, but it is usually rewarding as remains may be well preserved but actively being worn away by the wind and sea.

Photography is an important part of archaeology, recording accurately a site, its features and artefacts. There is skill in making sure that a photograph accurately captures differences in colour and texture. Recording a site can be done using photographs shot vertically above the site, but these must be backed up by hand-drawn plans and written records. Plans are drawings made of a feature or part of the site as seen from above. Other drawings made on site are section drawings (Figure 13.2). Each drawing is done accurately by measurement using tape measures, and never freehand by eye alone. For making detailed plans, a one-metre-square planning frame with strings

Figure 13.2 **Drawing a profile of a wall in Upper Wharfedale, Yorkshire**

forming 20 centimetre squares can be placed over the site to help make the drawing more accurate. The heights of the plans and sections, and their precise location on the site, will be plotted using a total station.

Analysis

The finds from an excavation will be taken away from site for analysis and description as part of the post-excavation phase (which includes publication of the results); known simply to most archaeologists as post-x. Finds analysis is usually a job for specialists in a particular type of find, such as lithics (stone tools), ceramics (pottery), metalwork, glass, animal and human bone, and botanical remains, such as small seeds, pollen or charcoal. Specialists have developed their own methods for studying these types of finds, and have their networks of conferences and publications to share ideas and expertise. Many have become finds specialists through studying for a Masters degree or through their postgraduate research.

The analysis of finds is much more than simply identifying the date of the find and its use. Good finds analysis can add to the interpretation of human behaviour at a site and can shed light on activities such as cooking, feasting, hunting and how people in the past thought. Making a stone tool involves a complex process of trying to reproduce a mental template through skilled mechanical activity. A knapper will have in their mind the shape of the tool they create from the nodule of flint. The use of that tool in different ways will leave traces we can study. How and why it was lost, thrown away or deliberately buried will be questions that need answering. An artefact such as a flint arrowhead or a pot has a life history. The specialist's job is to recover as much of that history as possible.

Artefacts made from animal or plant products such as wood, leather and textiles seldom survive well on archaeological sites. They survive best in either very dry conditions such as deserts or sub-arctic frozen environments, or in permanently waterlogged conditions. They need very careful treatment and conservation, and easily decay when removed from the environment that preserved them. We forget that most of material culture in the past was made of organic materials because they so rarely survive. Finds such as Ötzi, the Copper Age man found in the Alps, frozen and preserved with his clothing and gear intact, are priceless for what they tell us about past life.

Analysis of finds can be done by experimental copying and use of the artefacts, by studying their form and manufacture by eye, microscope, chemical means and techniques such as spectrometry or X-ray or computer-aided tomography. Few projects, however, will have enough funding to afford the full battery of possible techniques. One of the most exciting advances in our ability to study people in the archaeological record has come from the analysis of DNA. The DNA molecule is contained in structures called chromosomes in all the cells of our body. When we reproduce, our children inherit a mix of both parents' DNA in new combinations, except that Y-chromosomes are only inherited from the father, while the DNA in the cell's mitochondrion is inherited only from the mother. The Y-chromosome DNA can therefore be used to trace our ancestry back through successive mutations in generations of males, while mitochondrial DNA allows the same trace-back through females.

Experimental archaeology involves the making and use of tools or sites to test how they might have been made or used in the past. Good experimental activities are highly structured and systematically recorded, and aim to answer specific questions about artefacts from sites. They are also good fun. Using stone tools to butcher an animal carcass or building a prehistoric round house teaches us to have a great deal of respect for the abilities of people in the past. The earliest experimental archaeology centre in the UK was founded in 1972 at Butser Ancient Farm in Hampshire and became a working Iron Age farm. The longest experimental project is the Experimental Earthwork Project, which was begun in 1960 to test how ancient earthworks decay over time and is designed to run for 128 years!

Dating

How to describe the passing of time is a problem. One solution, popularised by an English monk nearly 1,300 years ago, was to count the years for any event since the birth of Christ. Since Christian nations became dominant in much of the world in the nineteenth century, this dating became accepted by convention as 'normal' for much of the rest of the world. However, not all nations are Christian. The Jewish calendar begins in a year that Christians would describe as 3760 BC, the Moslem era begins in AD 622. The Hindu calendar begins in AD 78, and the calendar of Buddhist Thailand begins in 543 BC. Sensitivity to non-Christian viewpoints has led some in the West to redefine BC and AD as BCE and CE, meaning before the Common Era and from the start of the Common Era. This may make sensitive souls feel less guilty about the past dominance of their own Christian culture, but does little to establish a neutral non-culturally defined method of dating. The Common Era is still based on the notional date of the birth of Jesus Christ.

A common basis for describing dates in archaeology is to date events BP, 'before present', where the present is the date of the first scientific radio-carbon date published in archaeology. This was AD 1950, so BP represents dates before that year. While this is useful for archaeologists, it is hardly sensible for historians, who need to describe events by years in historical documents. We would find it odd to say that Henry VIII ruled England from 441 to 403 BP, or that Columbus's first voyage to North America was in 458 BP. In practice, European and American archaeologists use a mix of BP and BC/AD dates. For dating events in later prehistory we use BC while early hominid remains and events before the end of the last Ice Age are usually dated BP. This can be confusing!

There are various scientific dating methods used in archaeology. Dendro-chronology measures the thickness of the yearly growth rings of trees. The pattern of rings on ancient wood samples can be compared with patterns of known date. Radio-carbon dating is the most important of the methods used by archaeologists. All plants and animals breathe in carbon dioxide from the air. They break this down and fix the carbon (C) into their bodies. Carbon has different forms. Mostly, it is C^{12} but there is also some C^{14}, which is radioactive and breaks down into nitrogen (N^{14}). While the plant or animal lives, it can keep up the amount of C^{14} by breathing. As soon as it dies, it can no longer do this and the amount of C^{14} will begin to diminish. Measuring the amount of C^{14} relative to the amount of C^{12} will give us the length of time since the organism died. We can use this method to date remains such as bone and charcoal. Thermoluminescence (TL) and optically stimulated luminescence (OSL) depend on minerals that have tiny imperfections in their crystal structures which act as traps for electrons absorbed from radioactive elements in the environment. These electrons can be released by light or by heat and the trap reset to zero. Measuring the amount of electrons trapped can give an idea of the age since the mineral last saw daylight (i.e. since it was buried) or was last heated. This is useful for dating layers of sediment, rock surfaces or pottery. Molten lavas when they solidify begin to accumulate argon (A) from the radioactive decay of potassium (K). Measuring the amount of argon relative to potassium gives the age of the lava. Finds of fossil hominids are often dated by their position above or below lavas of known date. Rehydroxylation is a very new method which measures the amount of water absorbed by pottery after leaving the kiln.

Residual and intrusive finds

Features are usually dated by the finds they contain. This can be dangerous. A pit dug into an earlier feature may disturb ancient artefacts which can then be deposited in the pit. These earlier artefacts are described as *residual* finds. The pit itself is *intrusive* into the earlier feature. Intrusive finds will give a date far later than the true date of the feature, while residual finds will be far earlier than the feature. Only careful excavation can identify these kinds of finds.

As well as trying to find specific dates for remains, we also divide the past into periods of time. The original three-age system of a Stone Age followed by a Bronze Age and in turn followed by an Iron Age has long since given way to an early, middle and later Palaeolithic (Old Stone Age), an Epipalaeolithic in the Mediterranean and Mesolithic (Middle Stone Age) in northern Europe, an early, middle and later Neolithic (New Stone Age), a Chalcolithic or Copper Age, an early, middle and later Bronze Age and various Iron Ages. These are all useful ways of referring to different kinds of evidence found at different times in the past. Not all parts of the world went through all the periods, and different parts of the world went through their periods at different dates. While ancient Egypt was going through its Bronze Age, Britain was still in its later Neolithic.

> ### *Terminus post quem* and *terminus ante quem*
>
> Basic sequences of events or features on an archaeological site are often referred to by the Latin phrase *terminus post/ante quem*. A layer containing pottery of a certain known date may overlie the posthole of an earlier building. The pottery provides a *terminus ante quem* for the posthole, which must have been created some time before the date of the pot. The same pot may provide a *terminus post quem* for a wall built above the layer, which must have been built after the date of the pot.

Interpretation (1)

The word 'interpretation' unfortunately has two quite different meanings in archaeology. In this paragraph, it refers to the identification of past human behaviour derived by the archaeologist from the remains of the past. The remains may be a prehistoric round building, but the interpretation is that it was a house or a religious site or a workshop for producing goods. A pattern of fields revealed by low walls or lynchets (terraces of soil created by cultivation) does not tell us very much about the past. We have to interpret the fields as fields for growing crops or grazing livestock, and how the fields relate to settlements to assess patterns of ownership. The nature of sites and features is that they are seldom clear-cut, and archaeologists will often disagree about their interpretations.

We cannot simply 'read' archaeological sites to reveal the past behaviour they represent. The American archaeologist Michael Schiffer did a lot of work in the 1970s on what he called C-transforms and N-transforms. These are simply the cultural (C) and natural (N) processes that intervene between an element of human behaviour and its representation in the archaeological record. A simple find of a flint tool tells us little. We have to decide whether it was lost or deliberately placed there. We also have to decide whether the place we found it was its original site of deposition or whether it had been brought there by natural processes such as by a river in flood, by creep of soil downhill, or by earthworms sorting the soil and moving it deeper into the ground. Even then we have to untangle a whole set of cultural processes between its original manufacture, its use and possible reuse as something else, and the reasons for its deliberate deposition. What we see is only the end of the life of an artefact or structure. We excavate buildings that have been abandoned and left to decay or have been deliberately destroyed or recycled. We have in some way to unwind the past to get back to the living behaviour represented by the artefact or structure. This is the single most awkward feature of archaeology and the one that causes most argument and discussion between archaeologists.

Storing finds

There is a crisis in British archaeology at the moment. Archaeologists are simply excavating too much stuff. This stuff consists of boxes of pot sherds, floor tiles, iron nails, stone tools, animal bones, etc., that all have to be stored somewhere. This is usually the role of museums. Storing finds is not simply placing them in a box on a shelf. The finds have to be kept in good condition (e.g. in acid-free cardboard boxes, or in controlled, dry environments). They also must be recorded and described, that is, properly catalogued. However, museums are rapidly running out of space and some are refusing to accept any more archaeological finds. Many finds are now stuck in temporary storage with the field unit which excavated them. There can be thousands of boxes of finds without a permanent home. Without proper storage, the finds cannot be made accessible to future researchers, or put on display for the public. Archaeologists are now beginning to question the assumption that we must keep everything we find. Just how many boxes of rusty iron nails or sherds of Roman pottery do we need to keep? Can we not simply return many of our finds to the site? But how do we decide which finds to keep and which to return? A lot of work is being done on this issue by the Society of Museum Archaeologists.

It is not only finds that need to be stored and looked after. The record of fieldwork, site notebooks, plans, section drawings, photographs, etc., all need long-term storage. Only then can they be available for others to study. A paper archive has to be stored in the right environmental conditions to stop paper degrading or drawings fading over time. Modern digital data has to be stored in a way that will allow the data to be used when computer technology changes. Site data on $5^{1}/_{4}$ inch or $3^{1}/_{2}$ inch floppy discs from the 1970s can no longer be read by modern computers. The Archaeology Data Service at York University is the only service in the United Kingdom specialising in long-term storage of digital records.

Caring for and protecting remains

Heritage management makes sure that sites are conserved for the future. Conservation of sites and finds involves more than only preventing their destruction. Finds conservation can be a highly specialist job. Waterlogged

175

finds and organic materials need very careful treatment, as can metalwork and glass. Caring for sites can involve preventing natural erosion or human activity that might harm the site, such as ploughing or the extraction of peat for use in gardens.

Legislation and guidelines now make sure that archaeologists are involved in recovering remains in advance of activities such as building, quarrying, etc. But even sites above ground need careful protection. Normal forces of nature such as wind, rain and frost can damage remains, as can the growth of plants and trees in or near remains. Burrowing animals like rabbits or badgers can cause a great deal of damage to sites. The popularity of walking as a pastime is eroding trackways in upland areas, some of which are on or near archaeological sites such as hill forts or stone circles. Ruined abbeys and castles and other sites open to the public need to manage the flow of people around the site and their behaviour in order to minimise erosion and damage. There is often a conflict between protecting sites and allowing them to be visited by the public. Occasionally, people even deliberately damage, deface or rob material from sites.

Interpretation (2)

'Interpretation' is also used in heritage management to signify the means of communication of our ideas about a site or landscape to an audience. A museum display or placing information panels on a historic site are media of interpretation. Archaeological digs can themselves be interpreted to the public, through open days and being open to public view. As well as booklets, leaflets and information panels, there are audio-guides, downloadable apps or hand-held digital trails, live re-enactors and guides, activity days and so on. Displays at sites and in museums are sometimes more interesting than simply placing objects in glass cases with a label. Recreated rooms, use of models, sounds, visual displays, etc., can all help create an engaging and informative experience. The key to good interpretation is understanding the audiences who come to the site. Organisations carry out surveys of their visitors and classify them into particular groups with different expectations and needs (this is called audience segmentation). They then try to make sure that these groups have what they need through a variety of products and media. The National Trust, for example, has identified these key groups among its visitors:

- out and about, people who like spontaneity and like being sociable;
- explorer families, who are active, educated and enthusiastic;

- curious minds, who like to piece together information and will ask questions about the site;
- home and family, liking safe, familiar activities for the whole family;
- kids first families, who first and foremost want their children to be entertained and happy;
- live life to the full, busy intellectuals on a quest for escapist relaxation;
- young experience seekers, who like physical activity, challenges and excitement.

Some of these groups will seek out the site shop, the café or places to sit, while others will want to actively explore the site. Some will accept the audio-guide, while others are happier with a map and their sense of curiosity. There is no single method of interpretation that works for everyone.

One of the most influential advocates of good interpretation was the American Freeman Tilden, who published his principles of interpretation in 1957 (Tilden, 1957). The most important of his principles are that interpretation should relate what is being displayed or described to something within the personality or experience of the visitor, that interpretation is more than simply giving information but should lead to new understanding by the visitor, and that the chief aim of interpretation should be provocation, to provoke the visitor by challenging their assumptions or making them think in a new way. Not many heritage sites or museums make as much use of Tilden's principles as they should.

Teaching

Teaching people about how we do archaeology is important. Archaeology appeals to people who like to think, and to people who prefer to learn by doing, such as surveying or making and using replica tools. It also appeals to the emotions by giving people today a sense of being in contact with people in the past. Good teaching balances the emotional, the intellectual and the physical appeal of the subject. Archaeologists work as lecturers in universities and teach undergraduate and postgraduate degrees. But some archaeologists now find careers in teaching in schools and colleges or as educators within field units or museums. As well as working with schools, archaeologists can work with their local branch of the Young Archaeologists' Club. This can be immensely satisfying work. Some archaeologists think that the subject is too difficult to be taught to children. They are wrong. Even difficult ideas such as radiocarbon dating can be taught successfully to children if taught in the right

177

way and using the right language. It is a common mistake to think that young children are not intelligent. They are intelligent, but their intelligence has less knowledge behind it and often works in different ways to older children and adults. Good archaeology educators are passionate about communicating archaeology and passing on their own love of the subject to others.

Public engagement

An increasingly important part of modern archaeology is reaching out to the public. This is sometimes known as public archaeology or community archaeology, although archaeologists seldom agree on what these terms actually mean. Some field units, universities or museums run projects in which the public are invited to take part and be trained in how to do survey, excavation or recording. Some open up their projects or sites to be visited and give public lectures. Others are happy to publicise their work in local newspapers or on local radio and television. Archaeologists can work closely with local people on long-term or permanent sites. The local community feels involved in the work and takes pride in the site or project. Arbeia Roman fort at South Shields, for example, is a heritage site in the middle of a housing estate where archaeologists work well with local people; it has no problems with vandalism, theft or graffiti.

There are national schemes which make archaeology or heritage available to the public. The Festival of British Archaeology is organised by the Council for British Archaeology every July. Archaeology Scotland organises Scottish Archaeology Month every September. Any archaeological organisation can take part in these and put on events for the public. Heritage Open Days in September involve owners of historic buildings opening their doors to the public for free admission to sites that are normally closed or which charge for entry. Museums at Night involves one weekend in May when museums are invited to put on special events in the evenings when they would normally be closed. Local festivals and events are held in many places. For example, York Archaeological Trust organises the Jorvik Viking Festival every February, while Norwich has a special organisation, HEART (Heritage Economic and Regeneration Trust), which runs various projects to increase public interest in local heritage.

Publication

The final word on how archaeology is practised must be about publication. No amount of research about the past is worth anything unless the results are publicised. You may have the most fantastic site in the world, have worked on it for 20 years and worked out that it provides a new insight into the past that no one else has discovered. But if you do not tell people about it then all that work is pointless. When you die, your work will be unknown and the site might just as well never have been excavated. Excavation without publication is as bad as simply driving a bulldozer through the site and deliberately destroying it. All archaeologists know this and proclaim it, yet it is surprising how many archaeologists fail to publish or to publish properly (in detail, with full references to the site records and archive). Some of the famous sites not properly published include the tomb of Tutankhamun and the excavations at Stonehenge in the 1950s and 1960s. Lack of publication is not always the result of negligence. Pulling together the results of a large excavation is time consuming and lengthy work. Professional excavators can afford to pay for this to be done as a specialist task without distraction. Many early archaeologists had to fit in writing up their projects around the heavy demands of their daytime jobs. However, there are archaeologists who find writing up the results of fieldwork far less exciting and fun than doing the fieldwork itself. Now, with ready access to computers and the Internet, it is easier to publish than ever before, and to make available the site archive for others to study as well as publish regular reports and newsletters. A good example of this would be the website of the excavation of Çatalhöyük in Turkey, being led by Ian Hodder (http://www.catalhoyuk.com). Some excavations have had daily blogs or live podcasts, or invite comments on Internet forums. All these are ways of publicising archaeology, but are not a substitute for the full publication of the site.

14

Studying archaeology

> Archaeology – the knowledge of how man has acquired his present position and powers – is one of the widest studies, best fitted to open the mind, and to produce that type of wide interests and toleration which is the highest result of education.
>
> Sir Flinders Petrie (1904) *Methods and aims in archaeology*

Archaeology is a wonderful subject to study. It covers a wide range of topics and has links with many other subjects. It mixes practical activity with thoughtful analysis. It allows people to make new discoveries and understandings. It helps us to make sense of the present-day world we live in. Archaeology is a subject that can change lives and bring a fulfilment to students that is both fun and rewarding. There is something in the subject for everyone, from grappling with the big issues in human history to the detailed analysis of one particular type of artefact. There is intensely physical work, work that demands great patience and attention to detail, work involving intellectual puzzles, and technical and computer-based work.

Archaeology is not a subject generally taught within schools in the United Kingdom. A few schools may have an after-school archaeology club, but it is not a subject within the school curriculum. Where archaeology is used, it is usually within history, and usually to support teaching about the Romans or the early medieval period, which is a pity. Archaeology involves using mathematics, science and English, and can provide good evidence for use in art, technology, all periods of history, geography, religious education and can even support aspects of physical education (e.g. looking at Greek vase painting or ancient Egyptian wall paintings for evidence of early dance). The first opportunity for studying archaeology itself is through GCE Archaeology (AS and A Level). There is one specification (syllabus) offered by the AQA Awarding Body. This provides a good introduction to archaeology.

A-level Archaeology

The full A-level consists of 4 units. The first two can be taken on their own as the AS-level Archaeology.

Unit 1: the archaeology of religion and ritual

Students are expected to be familiar with the specialist terminology associated with religion and ritual, such as inhumation, liminal and propitiation. They will have to focus on the study of named sites from one particular topic out of a choice of prehistoric Europe 30,000 BC to AD 43, ancient Egypt 3,000 BC to 50 BC, and Roman Europe 753 BC to AD 410. They will also have to answer two questions on any aspect of religion or ritual from their period of focus or one of the other cultures.

Unit 2: archaeological skills and methods

The question paper will have an extract from a real site report, as well as general questions on method. Students will have to cover how sites are formed, the discovery and recording of sites and landscapes, excavation, dating of sites and how sites are interpreted through analysis and experimentation. They will be expected to understand drawn plans and sections, and diagrams.

Unit 3: world archaeology

Students must study at least two out of three possible themes. People and society in the past includes human populations, social and political organisation, social differentiation, power and social control, and social change. Sites and people in the landscape includes the physical environment, sites, structures, territories and boundaries. Economics and material culture covers the exploitation of plants and animals, extraction and production, economic strategies, economic change, the relationship between economics, material culture and society. Students must also study contemporary issues in world archaeology, which includes cultural resource management, debates about archaeology and between archaeologists, the relationship between archaeology and society, between archaeology and ethnic identity, relations with indigenous peoples, and issues relating to human evolution.

Unit 4: an archaeological investigation

Students must undertake their own investigation of an archaeological topic and write this up in a 4,000-word report. The topic must include archaeological sites or artefacts, either in the field or in museums.

A-level Archaeology is a good qualification for delivering a broad knowledge of archaeological methods and understandings of the past. The fact that it includes a personal study in Unit 4 means that students have a chance to use archaeological methods on real evidence, a valuable taster of real archaeology. Unfortunately, it is not widely available in schools or colleges. There are not enough teachers with a background in archaeology to be able to teach it. But it is always worth asking whether there is a school or college nearby where it can be studied. You can study for A-level without being taught at a school or college. This is known as being a 'private candidate'. You will have to tutor yourself and find a school or college willing to provide the facilities to take the exams. You must consult the AQA awarding body for advice on taking archaeology this way.

Archaeology at university

It is not essential to have A-level Archaeology in order to study archaeology at university, although it will provide a very good basis for this. Most people will study archaeology for the first time as part of a university undergraduate degree. You may want to do this because you want to become a professional archaeologist. You will find that many study it out of interest and will move on from university to other careers. It is not often understood that archaeology provides an excellent general degree that makes its graduates highly sought after by employers. Archaeology is a broad subject and therefore a degree in archaeology can provide you with a very good basis for a career in business, politics, science, the arts and many other areas. The advantages of studying archaeology are:

- the use of logical thinking and problem solving;
- attention to detail and methodical working;

- the use of maths and statistics;
- being able to analyse numerical data;
- critical assessment of evidence and weighing up arguments against data;
- good literacy skills such as writing clear reports;
- the use of computers and digital technology;
- being able to work on your own but also as part of a team;
- the wide range of other subjects touched upon from, for example, science to geography to sociology.

These are all skills that are highly sought after by a variety of employers outside archaeology. Employers have noted the flexibility of archaeologists who are willing to have a go at almost anything.

University undergraduate degrees in archaeology can be either a Bachelor of Arts (BA) or a Bachelor of Science (BSc). In Scotland, the undergraduate arts degree is a Master of Arts (MA), not to be confused with the MA in the rest of the United Kingdom, where it is a postgraduate degree. There are degrees that are simply titled BA, MA or BSc Archaeology, but archaeology is also offered in degrees with other titles, such as archaeological practice or field archaeology, bioarchaeology or biological anthropology, conservation, Egyptology, environment and heritage, forensic archaeology, geoarchaeology, heritage studies or heritage conservation, historical archaeology, marine or nautical archaeology, medieval archaeology. Archaeology can also be studied in combination with other subjects as a joint or combined degree. Common combinations with other subjects include ancient history, history, geography, classics and anthropology. Titles of courses can change from year to year, so you must always go through the UCAS website to find the current archaeology courses.

The Quality Assurance Agency for Higher Education has issued a benchmark for archaeology. This is a statement of what an undergraduate degree with over 50 per cent archaeology should aim to cover. Most degrees will include elements relating to humanities, sciences and professional practice. Students will be expected to have first-hand experience of doing archaeology through the department's own research. The benchmark can be summarised under three headings of knowledge, archaeological skills and generic skills.

Knowledge includes:

- the origins and development of archaeology as a discipline;
- archaeological theory, debates over interpretation and archaeology's relationship with other disciplines;

- the historical, social, cultural, ethical and political contexts of archaeology;
- diverse sources of evidence (excavated, documentary, representational, observational, artefactual, environmental and scientific);
- concepts such as assemblage, culture and style, typology, taxonomy, context, temporality and landscape;
- the reliability of different evidence, caused by taphonomy; cultural and non-cultural transformations; depositional processes; and recovery procedures;
- the institutional context of how archaeology is practised;
- the legal and ethical frameworks for research and professional practice;
- recovery of primary data through practical experience in the field, collections-based, records-based, or artefact-based study;
- methodologies for quantifying, analysing and interpreting primary data;
- scientific methods used in collecting, analysing and interpreting archaeological data;
- interpret scientific information;
- the use of analogy and experiment in archaeological analysis;
- broad and comparative knowledge of a number of geographical regions;
- broad and comparative knowledge of a number of chronological periods;
- deep understanding of one or more distinct classes of archaeological material;
- the fragile nature of the archaeological resource and the need for sustainable use and conservation.

Archaeological skills include:

- apply appropriate scholarly, theoretical and scientific principles and concepts to archaeological problems;
- practise core fieldwork techniques of identification, surveying, recording, excavation and sampling;
- practise core post-excavation/post-survey techniques such as stratigraphic analysis of field records, phasing and data archiving;
- practise core laboratory techniques of recording, measurement, analysis and interpretation;
- discover and recognise the archaeological significance of material remains and landscapes;
- interpret spatial data, traces surviving in present-day landscapes and excavation data;
- observe and describe different classes of primary archaeological data;

- select and apply appropriate statistical and numerical techniques to process archaeological data.

Generic skills include:

- assemble coherent research/project designs;
- marshal and critically appraise other people's arguments;
- produce logical and structured arguments supported by relevant evidence;
- present effective oral presentations for different kinds of audiences;
- prepare effective written communications for different readerships;
- make effective and appropriate use of relevant IT;
- make critical and effective use of information retrieval skills using paper-based and electronic resources;
- make effective and appropriate forms of visual presentation;
- plan, design, execute and document a programme of primary research, working independently;
- collaborate effectively in a team via experience of working in a group, for example through fieldwork, laboratory and/or project work;
- appreciate the importance of health and safety procedures and responsibilities in the field and the laboratory;
- appreciate and be sensitive to different cultures, and deal with unfamiliar situations;
- to evaluate critically one's own and others' opinions;
- engage with global perspectives, employability, enterprise and creativity.

Entrance requirements for degrees vary a great deal. Always check with the admissions tutor of the archaeology department for their requirements. It is a good idea also to go to the university's open days where you can visit the department and ask questions. There are usually no specific subjects you will need at A-level for admission to archaeology. An AS- or A-level in history, geography, geology, classical civilisations or archaeology is useful. A science A-level will be needed for entry to an archaeological science degree. Admissions tutors are far more interested in applicants who are enthusiastic about archaeology and can show evidence of previous interest than only in looking at their exam results. Being a member of the Young Archaeologists' Club would be an advantage, as could experience on an excavation, or volunteering with local groups or museums. Looking at the Council for British Archaeology website is a good place to begin finding opportunities (http://www.britarch.ac.uk/getinvolved). Subscribing to magazines such as

British Archaeology or *Current Archaeology* is a good way to find out about and keep up to date with archaeology within Britain.

It can be hard to decide which university to apply to. Always take a look at the archaeology department website. Look at what range of courses they include in the degree. Also look at the academic staff and the range of their research interests. Find a department which has strength in the area of archaeology you are interested in, or if wanting simply to study archaeology in general then find a department with a wide range of topics on offer. There will be opportunities to go on fieldwork with lecturers and others during the summer (Figure 14.1), so their research interests will give a good idea of where they might be working. The precise requirements for fieldwork as part of the degree will vary a lot from university to university. The size of department can make a difference. Big departments will have a lot of topics they can offer, yet teaching may be fairly anonymous. In a smaller department, you may get more chance to get to know and talk with the lecturers and postgraduates. Some universities are based on a separate campus outside the town while others have their departments dispersed within the town. Some are in small historic towns, some in modern new towns, others in big cities and a few are very rural. All these differences can affect how you feel living at

Figure 14.1 **Archaeology undergraduate students in the field at Chapel House Wood, Yorkshire**

the university for three years. Choose somewhere you feel happy in and you will get more out of your time at university.

One option for people who may find it hard to apply for a full degree, is to study for a foundation degree (FdA or FdSc). There are a few of these for archaeology, offered through further education colleges that have an affiliation to a university. They are intended as vocationally related qualifications, and so usually include a lot of practical experience. Students can often carry on to a full-time undergraduate degree from these foundation degree courses.

Many people who want to become professional archaeologists now stay on after their BA, Scottish MA or BSc to study for a postgraduate degree. A Masters degree (usually studied over one year, occasionally over two) offers the chance to specialise in a particular area of archaeology and develop more employable skills. There are both taught Masters degrees, where students attend lectures, and pure research Masters degrees, where students do a research project. Taught degrees are usually either an MA or MSc, while some universities offer an MLitt, an MPhil, an MRes or an MSt. Continuing on to do research for a Doctorate (usually a three-year PhD degree) is the normal route for someone who wants to become a university lecturer. There are many more postgraduate degrees than there are undergraduate degrees, and some are highly specialised. There are generic MA Archaeology degrees, often designed as 'conversion MAs' for people with an undergraduate degree in another subject who wish to 'convert' to archaeology. Most Masters degrees can be classified as dealing with archaeological methods or the time, place and people dimensions of archaeology.

Examples of methodology Masters topics would be archaeological surveying, artefact studies, biomolecular archaeology, buildings archaeology, conservation, field archaeology, forensic archaeology, GIS, heritage management, maritime archaeology, materials studies and museum studies. Masters dealing in particular periods of the past include Celtic studies, classical archaeology, Egyptology, historical archaeology, industrial archaeology, medieval archaeology and prehistory. Those that cover places include specific places such as Africa, Europe, the Mediterranean and places in general such as environmental archaeology and landscape archaeology. The archaeology of people is covered by the archaeology of food or health, biological anthropology, early hominid studies and osteoarchaeology (human bone studies). Other kinds of degree topics include archaeology in film and television, heritage interpretation and presentation or public archaeology.

Taught postgraduate courses change constantly with new courses being developed or existing courses closing. A good way to find what postgraduate courses are available is to search on the Internet. There are three good websites to use: www.postgrad.com, www.prospects.ac.uk, and www.ukpass.ac.uk.

Other ways to study

Full-time attendance at university is not the only way to study archaeology. Some people can only attend part-time or study from home. Home study, usually called distance learning, is rarely offered. The Open University now offers archaeology courses, although not as part of a full archaeology degree. Leicester University has a long tradition of offering distance learning in archaeology, and other universities have also offered such courses. Studying archaeology by distance can be fraught with problems. There are bogus colleges and universities, and it can be hard to decide which are genuine. The Internet-based College-on-the-Net is a proper provider of archaeology courses and can be trusted.

There are still opportunities for studying archaeology courses in the evenings, at weekends, at day schools or other kinds of part-time course. These may be offered by a university as part of its continuing education or lifelong learning provision. The number of universities offering such courses has shrunk alarmingly over the past 10 years, but it is still worth enquiring whether a nearby university does run such courses. Similar courses are often offered by the WEA (Workers' Educational Association), an organisation that runs part-time courses for anyone to enrol on. There are local branches of the WEA and the local library will usually have information about them. Courses are sometimes advertised through the Council for British Archaeology (CBA). Local archaeology societies will often have a programme of evening lectures or field visits and will usually welcome non-members. The CBA has information about where local societies exist.

Archaeology on TV

For many people, their main knowledge of archaeology comes from television. There are various kinds of programme on archaeology. The very first archaeology programme on television was entertainment, an archaeology quiz show called *Animal, Vegetable, Mineral?* from 1952 to 1960. The most traditional, and still the commonest kind is the documentary presentation of archaeological discoveries. The long-running series *Chronicle* ran from 1966 to 1991 and was, for many current archaeologists, their first taste of archaeology. The demands of television formats will often impose a narrative

189

on the discovery involving a puzzle to be solved or a mystery to be revealed. But these programmes are really showing what archaeologists have uncovered about a particular topic. One of the most popular topics to be covered is ancient Egypt, followed by ancient Rome. Some programmes are made to present a particular point of view and have a strong presenter claiming new knowledge, revealing new ideas or with a particular point to make such as the need for better conservation of remains. The viewer has to be careful in judging these kinds of programme. There are some pseudo-archaeologists who are highly skilled communicators and can create TV programmes that are very persuasive. Popular programmes include magazine-style formats, where a range of topics is covered in one programme which need not all be archaeology. One of the most successful of these is *Coast*, on screen since 2005. Dramatisation of the past as fact-based fiction within a documentary setting has been very successful. *Pompeii: the last day*, shown in 2003, was a dramatisation with commentary of the destruction of the Roman town of Pompeii by the eruption of Mount Vesuvius in AD 79, attracting 10-million viewers (the largest ever audience for archaeology on television). Other kinds of programme focus on the processes involved in doing archaeology. This has been the great success of *Time Team* (on screen since 1994) with its focus on geophysical and landscape survey, and excavation. The series *Meet the Ancestors* (from 1998 to 2003) focused on reconstructing the lives and appearances of particular bodies excavated by archaeologists. Experimental archaeology is also a good topic for television, especially in its modern form of placing people back into the past to try and live as people did then. *Tales from the Green Valley* (2005) and *The Victorian Farm* (2009) are good examples of this. Television programmes or series can sometimes lead to genuine archaeological research being done. The combination of history and archaeology in the recent series *The Story of Britain* (2010) involved local people digging their own test pits under archaeological supervision as part of research into the history of their village.

Other sources of information about archaeology

Magazines are a good source of information about archaeology. *British Archaeology* is published by the Council for British Archaeology and appears every two months. It contains the latest news stories and debates within archaeology along with regular articles on archaeology on television, archaeology on the Internet, articles by Mick Aston about different parts of Britain, book reviews and lists of fieldwork, courses and conferences.

Current Archaeology is an independent magazine which covers some of the latest discoveries as well as news about archaeology and information about courses and fieldwork. Both magazines together will keep a reader fully up to date with archaeology. *Current World Archaeology* is a partner magazine to *Current Archaeology* and obviously covers news about archaeology elsewhere in the world.

Many people will of course search the Internet for information about archaeology. Some websites are developed by archaeological organisations, others by enthusiastic individuals, and not all websites are accurate. It can be hard knowing which websites to trust. The website of the CBA is a good place to begin. *Current Archaeology* also has a useful website. The BBC history website has some good information about archaeology, as does the *Time Team* website and the British Archaeological Jobs Resource (BAJR), a website about far more than only jobs in archaeology. The same team behind BAJR also run the web-based magazine *Past Horizons*. Details of these and other websites are given in Resources (pp. 209–16).

There are some useful sites that enable people to find information about archaeological sites and the historic environment. The Pastscape website of English Heritage gives access to the 400,000 records in the National Monuments Record. The equivalent National Monuments Record in Scotland is maintained by the Royal Commission on the Ancient and Historical Monuments of Scotland, made available through the Canmore website. Wales has the Coflein website for the records of its Royal Commission. For Northern Ireland, the equivalent website is Rascal. Local historic environment records are held by local authorities and are available for England through the Heritage Gateway website. For Scotland, they can be found through the Pastmap website.

Archaeological societies

Joining a society can be a good way of getting in touch with other enthusiasts and learning more about the subject. There is a wide range of groups and organisations to join. The most wide-ranging and useful organisation to join is the Council for British Archaeology, which also has its Young Archaeologists' Club for those aged 8 to 16. There are various national societies that cover specific aspects of archaeology and produce academic journals, such as the Prehistoric Society, the Society for the Promotion of Roman Studies, the Association for Roman Archaeology, the Society for Medieval Archaeology, the Society for Post-Medieval Archaeology and the

Association for Industrial Archaeology. Other societies cover geographical areas. The most well established, usually with their own journals, are the county archaeology societies. More local societies also exist and have events that can be easier to attend. Some will run their own fieldwork projects and getting involved in these can be a good way of getting experience. The TORC and *Current Archaeology* websites have details about where to find societies. Local libraries should also have information about local groups and societies.

Studying archaeology is only the first step. It can lead to a lifetime career in the subject or enjoying the subject as a part-time hobby. Reading about it, watching it on TV or being taught about it is no substitute for doing it. Doing archaeology, especially if part of a team with others, is enormous fun and very rewarding.

15

Archaeology is fun

Wow!! . . . [followed by 10 minutes of stunned silence, unable to speak].

Don Henson, 1993, on seeing the
1625 ship the *Vasa* in a Stockholm museum

There is no standard career for an archaeologist, and every archaeologist has a different tale to tell. Rather than try to tell you what a usual archaeologist's career might be, I will illustrate one possible range of experiences from my own career in the subject. The first thing to say is that archaeology is fun! It can also be incredibly surreal. You will get to do things that people would not normally get to do. You will also be surrounded by like-minded people and be part of a very comforting world.

Doing a degree

I can begin my story on 30 September 1975 as I boarded a train to Sheffield University to study in the Department of Prehistory and Archaeology. I had no idea what to expect. My ideas about universities were of Oxford- or Cambridge-style institutions, venerable and ancient, and my ideas of students came from watching *University Challenge* on television. Likewise, my only idea about archaeology had come from watching the long-running TV series *Chronicle*, and voraciously reading any books I could find in the local library. What a shock Sheffield was! My home was to be a 1960s' concrete hall of residence (Sorby Hall), the archaeology department was on the 9th floor of a glass and steel tower, and the students on my course looked like they had raided the nearest charity shops or army surplus for their clothing. I soon settled in to courses about topics I had never heard of and cultures whose names I couldn't pronounce, and began having a lot of student fun. My lecturers were clearly important people who knew a lot but were surprisingly approachable, very un-stuffy and some were hard to tell apart from the students.

The second shock was my first dig. At last, archaeological fieldwork, doing it for real! I found myself camping in a field in Devon with a load of other students and – a big culture shock – some Americans. We were working under Andrew Fleming looking at prehistoric settlement on the top of Dartmoor. It was Easter time, so we had hot sunshine, heavy rain and snow. I had my own trowel, which easily broke, so I was given a proper trowel instead and was soon on my hands and knees scraping away at soil. In my head, I was still dreaming of exotic civilisations in far away (and hot and sunny) places. Surprisingly, it was great fun. My great find was seeing stripes in the soil that were left by ancient ploughing. Being away from home, not having to bother too much about washing and shaving, spending every night in the pub (beware of the local scrumpy!) definitely had its attractions. Dartmoor was also beautiful. That first experience left me in love with upland landscapes for life.

Another student dig was on Oronsay in the Hebrides with Paul Mellars. The site was a Mesolithic shell midden by the shore, made up of thousands upon thousands of broken limpet shells. After the first day we were fairly bored with trowelling through limpets. We still had another 4 weeks to go! The wonderful Scottish scenery was spoiled only by the famous midges. Little black biting flies that would only go away when we could persuade Paul to come over to where we were trowelling as they seemed not to like his cigar smoke. At least we weren't camping. We were staying in a farm. This was fine except that our rooms were next to the silage store and the smell was not what we faint-hearted city folk were used to. It didn't help that the only pub on the island was an hour and a half walk away. But we did get invited by the locals to their regular ceilidh, which was superb fun and taught me how lacking in dancing skills I really was.

Doing the degree was three years of sheer joy. I loved being a student, living an independent life for the first time, the social life and above all the intellectual fun of new knowledge and new ways of thinking and seeing the world. Sorby Hall brought me a circle of good friends outside archaeology, as well as involvement in the Film Society showing feature films every week. My course took me in directions I could not predict. Why did I find the Neolithic so interesting? Was I a little odd for enjoying the statistics course so much? I found what I was good at (applying systems theory to Anglo-Saxon England), and what I was less suited for (remembering details of the chronology and typology of Mediterranean cultures). I even loved writing the essays and doing the exams. The hard things were writing the extended projects – a seminar paper on prehistoric trade and exchange, and a dissertation on the uses of plants in the past. School had not prepared me at all for this kind of work, and I felt a little bit lost. But doing the research for both was fun and I ploughed on regardless. Doing a degree is being given the freedom to research and to study, to develop in new ways and explore possible futures for yourself. It is the greatest gift education can give.

Doing research

After my degree, I spent a year working at a visitor centre at Creswell Crags, but I realised I needed to develop my archaeological education some more. I went back to Sheffield to do research for an MPhil degree. I could choose for myself what I wanted to do and decided to look at the sources of flint in northern England and how they were exploited to make stone tools in the prehistory of the region. This allowed me to mix my love of geology with archaeology. I enjoyed it so much it ended up taking two years.

I developed a lifelong love of stone tools. Some people think I am mad to find stone tools so interesting. But, then, they find potsherds equally interesting, which I find hard to understand! To truly understand stone tools, you must learn how to make them. I lived in a one-room flat and took nodules of flint home and tried my hand at flint knapping. This involves striking the flint nodules with stone or antler to take off flat flakes of flint and then shaping the flakes to make tools. Flint is sharp! I soon learnt to keep plenty of plasters nearby and get used to the sight of my hands bleeding from lots of tiny cuts. I also found when going to bed afterwards that splinters of flint would lie hidden in the carpet waiting for me to step on them.

After my MPhil, I stayed on to do a PhD on how flint tools were being made and used in the Neolithic of Yorkshire and the East Midlands. I continued knapping of course. Being a postgraduate research student is a precious time. You have the independence to decide for yourself how to spend your time and have the time to think deeply about your own data and what it means. You are debating with fellow students and really feel at the forefront of new ideas. Life is intense and exciting. My own research involved looking at publications of other people's excavations or their finds stored in museums. I spent hours measuring the length, width and thickness of thousands of flint flakes, recording the measurements on large paper record sheets and then having them inputed into the main university computer for analysis. This was the days before personal computers. My supervisor was Pat Phillips, a lecturer who was genuinely concerned about the welfare of her students. She was kind, thoughtful and always there to help. I owe her a great deal.

While doing my own research, I also got involved helping others. This could sometimes be exciting. I have been arrested by the Spanish police, chased off a field by a farmer with a shotgun and done fieldwork surrounded by soldiers attacking an RAF base. Less adventurous, but just as fun, was helping a friend who was researching how to identify how stone tools were used. This involved using tools in various ways and looking at microscopic traces of wear on their edges. It is not often you get to skin dead animals with flint flakes.

I spent a few years helping with a project near Waterford in south-east Ireland jointly run by lecturers from Sheffield and South Carolina. The beauty of the the red sandstone cliffs against a clear turquoise sea was enchanting. The fact that the local pubs stayed open for much of the night was an added attraction. Most of the project was walking ploughed fields to pick up stone tools to find evidence of prehistoric settlement. One memorable field had been sprayed with pig slurry fertiliser by the farmer! One of the leaders of the project was Marek Zvelebil, a refugee Czech lecturer at Sheffield, who sadly died in 2011. Marek was a larger than life character of great passions and hotly expressed views, but who thought deeply about archaeology and had a great love of life. He was also a very kind man with a wicked sense of humour. We would spend a hard day out in the field to come back and find that Marek had given up work for the day to put together an enormous buffet of the finest food and drink he could make and find. It was a great way of cheering up a tired field crew.

Working in archaeology

My early jobs in archaeology were all to do with investigating the past: doing field work and working in a heritage centre. Excavating at Sheffield Manor taught me how wet clay gets when it rains and how like concrete it is when the sun shines! Being the finds specialist at the excavation of a Bronze Age barrow (burial mound) at Hognaston was fun. The team planted some North African flints on site to fool me one day. And I was fooled, for about

30 seconds. We spent six weeks digging to find the burial only on the last but one day; but I did get physically very fit. For a year, I worked at Creswell Crags Visitor Centre, a fabulous set of caves with remains from the Palaeolithic in a beautiful limestone gorge. My job was to make a catalogue of all the animal bones excavated from the caves over the past 100 years on a card index system (this was the days before computers!). It taught me how to classify every land animal and bird in Britain and beyond. It also taught me never again to get a job in a building only 400 yards away from a sewage farm (the sewage farm has since been removed).

Later, I had six years at Wakefield working as an education officer in their museums and art galleries. Here I was covering an art gallery when art was the one school subject I had failed with the lowest possible grade! But, I could use my archaeology and treat the paintings and sculptures as artefacts, which was very interesting to do. I had great fun and a huge amount of satisfaction working with school parties of all ages from 4 up to 16. I also worked with adult groups, including people in the local prison and patients with head injuries in the local hospital. Having access to the whole collections in the storerooms was an incredible privilege and like having your own big box of toys. My work with school pupils at the museum or art gallery is still among the most rewarding and enjoyable work I have ever done. It taught me that the importance of archaeology lies not in remains and artefacts but in the relationship people have with them. I also learned that my skills as an archaeologist were just as easy to apply to artefacts from the Second World War as they are to artefacts from Roman Castleford. Working in the museum brought me into contact with the art world for the first time and I learnt to appreciate the importance of creativity and the world of the imagination. It made me realise that simply recording artefacts and sites was not enough. If we are to truly understand past lives, we have to accept the creative side of human experience, not only the struggle for survival.

I worked for the Council for British Archaeology for 17 years. My role was very varied and involved advising teachers and students about archaeology, advising archaeologists about education, organising conferences, editing publications, being the advocate for archaeology education within national initiatives and to politicians, organising campaigns, helping to vet A-level Archaeology question papers, compiling databases of courses and sitting on far too many committees. I seemed to spend whole weeks travelling on trains to and from London, Birmingham, Manchester, Bristol, Newcastle and other places. My work brought me into contact with historians, heritage groups, teachers, politicians and other kinds of people. All shared a passion for the

197

past and for teaching that past to others. Working with them was always a pleasure.

When I joined the CBA in 1994, the offices were in a medieval timber-framed house in York. Working in such historic surroundings was a real bonus. I would have enjoyed it more had I not been 6 feet 2 inches tall, as I regularly hit my head on the low wooden roof beams. Some of the most enjoyable times at the CBA were working with their Young Archaeologists' Club (YAC). The Club held residential holidays for members aged 8 to 16. A favourite venue was Trewortha Farm, deep inside Bodmin Moor in Cornwall. The holiday leader, Tony Blackman, was a very kind man who was tireless in communicating his passion for archaeology to young people. He was highly respected and valued by all who knew him. The local farmers, too, Graham and his wife Lizzie, were very welcoming and friendly. Lizzie's cooking in particular made a deep impression on me. The beauty of the moor was enhanced by the night sky. A truly black night sky is no longer possible in our cities, towns and villages. Only in the remote countryside can the full glory of the Milky Way be seen. Breathtaking is the only word for it. The archaeology was also superb. The farm had the remains of Bronze Age houses in one of its fields and the local YAC members had built their own excellent replica round houses to one side of them.

YAC relies heavily on its adult volunteers to run the local branches of the Club. Training these volunteers is taken very seriously. I was lucky in helping to run one training weekend at Bolton Castle in Yorkshire. We ran a programme of activities training the volunteers in all kinds of experimental archaeology, being taught by various very talented re-enactors and experimenters. The sun shone, everyone was enthusiastic and enjoyed getting stuck into physical activities. The medieval feast created by the re-enactors was superb and the evening afterwards was spent in the kitchens with them singing songs into the early hours of the morning. It was a memorable weekend when everything worked to perfection (aided by the meticulous and detailed planning of the YAC Coordinator, Wendi Terry).

Teaching

There are many areas of archaeology that I know I am hopeless at. Drawing good plans of features on an excavation is a skill I really do not have. I really would not have much of a clue about how to analyse pottery. Using GIS software to analyse site data is something I have never done. But one of the things that I recognise I am good at is teaching adults and university students.

It is also one of the most rewarding things I have done now for more than 30 years. This is something of a mystery to me. I do not find it easy talking to people I don't know, and find it hard to circulate and chat to strangers at parties or events. The idea of giving a talk in front of an audience used to fill me with sheer terror when I was younger.

I taught my first evening class when I was working at Creswell Crags back in 1979. I would get a lift from work into Worksop and be dropped off to have my tea at a local café before going to the library to teach the class. There are many in British archaeology who think that one of my key skills is to eat large quantities of food at any time of day or night, and who will find it hard to believe that I was so nervous that I could never finish my meal at the café. Going back to Sheffield on the bus after the class, I would be in an agony of nerves about whether what I had just taught made any sense and berating myself for all the things I had forgotten to say. Yet the class stayed with me and I slowly realised that I enjoyed getting across what I knew to an audience eager to learn. I can even enjoy teaching when it goes wrong. Teaching an MA class at Newcastle University one year, the computer attached to the projector simply would not read my data stick with the presentation on it. So I had no presentation and no printed notes to work from, and a two-hour class to teach. I grabbed a flipchart, a marker pen and simply made up the lecture out of my head, covering the main points that I knew had to be covered. The round of applause I got from the students at the end was more than satisfying. I knew I had not let them down.

Teaching children, as a museum education officer or in the Young Archaeologists' Club, is different in many ways to teaching adults, and is even more rewarding. The delight in a child's eyes as you hand him or her a real Roman leather shoe to handle is priceless. The child can touch what people in the past also touched and their imagination fires in ways not possible in many classrooms. Children on a school trip are taken into a new environment and challenged to learn in a different way from what they are used to. They can blossom in this different environment and the class teacher's eyes can often be opened by seeing a child willing to learn, but whom they often see as disinterested or a problem when in school. Finding the key artefacts or other evidence that will unlock the child's interest is a wonderfully enjoyable challenge.

Sometimes I have gone into a school with artefacts. One secondary school arranged with me one year to go and teach technology to a class. I got to the school with my carefully chosen artefacts from the museum collection to find they had decided this was too good an opportunity to miss and had the whole year group of 120 pupils waiting for me in the main hall, instead of the 30 that I was expecting. By then I was confident about what I was doing and simply arranged them in groups and got to work. We all had a great time and I think they may even have learned something.

I often found that adults can be too dismissive or protective of children. Knapping flint and using flint flakes with their razor-sharp edges seems like a recipe for disaster with children. Yet the only people I know who have cut themselves and bled have always been the adults, never the children themselves. I have been with YAC members casting molten copper without any accident. I have also had a class of six-year-old school pupils correctly distinguishing between Neolithic and Bronze Age stone tools, a feat beyond most undergraduates.

Fieldwork

While working for the CBA, I would often be asked by others what I did. I would say that I was an archaeologist, but learned very quickly to follow this by saying that I didn't actually do any archaeology as part of my job. What I meant by that was that I didn't do any field archaeology. Most people assume that all archaeology is excavation and that if you say you are an archaeologist then you must be out in the field digging up sites. By now, having read the previous chapters, you will of course know that archaeology is much more than this. My work at the CBA was just as much archaeology as being out in the field, but would not be recognised as such by others.

However, fieldwork is still something special that many archaeologists look forward to every year. For me, my fieldwork since 1993 has mostly been helping out as part of my holidays in a project in Upper Wharfedale in Yorkshire (Figure 15.1). This has involved survey and excavation of a multi-period landscape with field systems and settlements from prehistory to the present day. I have worked with students, a local heritage group and Americans through an organisation called Earthwatch, and got to know the local farmers and villagers. Our workforce has included all ages from 16 to 85, and from all kinds of background. Most of them have been great fun to work with. Some have struggled to climb the steep hillsides, but all have enjoyed the Yorkshire Dales landscape. The main difficulty has been the weather. I learned never to trust the weather forecast. Wake up in the morning and see a blue sky? Immediately pack your waterproofs for the day ahead. We have had heavy rain, glorious sun, snow, hail, lightning and high winds. One day can be summer, the next day winter and at any time of year.

Figure 15.1 **The author, happy with trowel in hand**

We have had tents on site blown down and trenches waterlogged with rain. None of this is really irritating compared with the midges! On one site, a barn provided shelter from the rain but also a host for fleas and ticks. I counted 16 big, red and heavily itching bites on my body afterwards. Sheep become a constant hazard. Trying to survey when the whole flock decide you are their farmer come to feed them and crowd round the survey equipment is not easy. But the reward is understanding in detail how a landscape has unfolded and developed over 3,000 years.

The project is still going on, run by the Yorkshire Dales Landscape Research Trust. After 18 years, we have only scratched the surface. The more fieldwork you do, the more you realise how rich is the historic environment. To fully understand just one small area takes more than one archaeologist's lifetime.

The surreal, the weird and the frightening

Archaeology can be very weird. Fortunately, many archaeologists find so-called normal life rather boring. The very act of excavation itself is somewhat strange. Kneeling on the ground scraping away at the soil or stone with a trowel is rather odd, as is jumping up and down on turf placed back on site at the end of an excavation to get it to fit back in the trench.

To protect the site at Oronsay from rain we had a large metal and polythene tunnel over the site and a smaller tunnel used as our tool shed. One day, the wind began to get up and a storm came in from the Atlantic. Sitting at lunchtime eating our sandwiches, we suddenly saw the tool shed blown across the island and the big tunnel over the site begin to rise into the air. After a quick dash by some twenty of us, we caught the edges of the tunnel and spent 15 minutes trying to pull it back to the ground and sandbag it down to stop it too blowing away.

My first dig on Dartmoor was fun but physically punishing. As well as the students, there were some experienced diggers on site. The Director needed to clean the site for photographing. This called for speed trowelling: cleaning up the site as fast as possible before the soil dried out to allow a good photograph to capture the different soil colours. For some reason, I was put with the two experienced diggers. They were very fast. I tried hard to keep up, and just managed it, but I felt as though my hand was going to fall off at the wrist by the end. Experienced diggers looked different to us students. We met up with a group of diggers from another project in the pub one evening. In hushed tones, it was explained that they were the Central Excavation Unit of the Department of the Environment. This was somewhat like being the SAS of archaeology. We went to the pub to see these grizzled, bearded, physically very fit and imposing archaeologists and suddenly felt very small and insignificant.

Occasionally, archaeology has given real cause for fear. For example, finding a hand grenade while field-walking in Lincolnshire. Nothing though has been as frightening as giving my first talk at a conference. I was a postgraduate student and some of us organised a poster session at TAG (the Theoretical Archaeology Group, the main academic archaeology conference) in Durham. A poster session is easy. You make posters showing people your research and pin them to a display board. On the second day of the conference the organisers came to say that there was a lot of interest in our posters, and asked us whether we would mind giving talks about them in a hastily arranged session the next day. I was immediately terrified. To calm my nerves, I spent the rest of the day looking at how other people delivered their conference papers. I soon realised that many of them were awful, mumbling, stumbling over their words, hard to hear or just boring. I began to feel more confident. After all, they had delivered awful papers and not been lynched or pelted with rotten fruit. What was I afraid of? Just before my talk, one of my lecturers gave me a good piece of advice. Go up to the podium and slowly pour yourself a drink of water. A simple technique, one that slowed me down, helped calm me and gave me the psychological upper hand over the audience. They were waiting for me, and I was not rushing to speak to them. Making eye contact and speaking slowly, I got through it and realised that actually public speaking is not really something to be frightened of (although the nerves never really go away).

The rewards

The rewards of doing archaeology are many. I only have space here for a few highlights. I have met an extremely wide mix of people in archaeology, from royalty to labourers with criminal records. All have been charming, enthusiastic, interesting and fun. Prince Charles visited the CBA offices in his role as the CBA's patron one year and went out of his way to speak for a long time with the members of the Young Archaeologists' Club. I have met with politicians and ministers, not something most archaeologists get to do. I gave evidence to a committee of inquiry in the House of Lords set up by the All-Party Parliamentary Archaeology Group. Fortunately, I had by then overcome my fear of speaking in public as it was quite a daunting occasion.

A major perk is being invited to speak at conferences abroad. Countries I have visited include Belgium (Ghent), Ireland (Dublin), Italy (Lake Garda), Japan (Osaka and Gunma), the Netherlands (The Hague) and Spain (Barcelona). Being invited twice to Japan was the most wonderful experience, a world so similar and yet so unlike our own (with great food!). Likewise, I can never tire of being invited to Barcelona. Lake Garda in Italy was stunningly beautiful. All these places I would never have gone to without archaeology.

Archaeology has taken me to many beautiful ancient landscapes and sites. The beauty of the Yorkshire Dales is matched by the coast of south-east Ireland. The Bronze Age landscapes on Dartmoor are matched by the amazing prehistory on Orkney. I have been fortunate to stand at Neolithic houses in Skara Brae, in Newgrange Neolithic Passage Grave, the chapel of Bede's seventh-century monastery at Jarrow, the Roman streets under Barcelona and to see the seventeenth-century ship the *Vasa* in Stockholm. To be able to touch the past and make a link with people long dead is a priceless benefit of archaeology. The sense of wonder and awe inspired by the past, that heart-stopping, jaw-dropping moment of coming face to face with the people from another age, exemplified for me by the *Vasa*, is something that inspires all historians and archaeologists (the great historian A J P Taylor once gave it as the main reason for studying the past).

Archaeology has stimulated my mind, given me a mix of physical and intellectual challenges, and broadened my horizons. It has not given great wealth, but I am richer in better ways than having money. Archaeology has given me an understanding of human life and behaviour that makes sense of the world I live in. It throws up endless challenges and is a never-ending quest for knowledge and understanding. I have met many wonderful people whether as professionals or volunteers who all share a passion for the past. There is absolutely nothing else I would rather be. I do not work as an archaeologist. It is not a job, it is a state of being. I *am* an archaeologist.

Conclusion

Archaeology is the study of how people in different places in the past have behaved through the physical evidence that they have left behind. It covers every aspect of human existence, and all times from the prehistoric to the present. The basic methodologies of archaeology were developed between the 1640s and 1760s: believing that remains can be studied in their own right, using analogy to identify artefacts and sites, understanding stratigraphy, developing a chronology for the past, classifying artefacts (taxonomy), and arranging artefact types in a chronological sequence (typology). Over the past 250 years we have discovered ever more remains of the past, and have developed new ways of studying and thinking about them. We now know we cannot fully recover the past as it was, but only come up with partial ideas of what we think it was. We also know that it is the debate between the different ideas we have of the past that is the beating heart of archaeology.

The three dimensions of archaeology are time, place and people. Through studying time we understand processes of change, the development of different cultures over time and the evolution of human society and behaviour. We seek to understand why cultures and behaviours change. We study places at different scales from the global to the local. We understand the relationship we have with our environment and how fragile this is. We understand the relationships that cultures have with each other and how human communities do not exist in isolation but depend on others. Our study of people helps us to understand the complexities of human behaviour, the agency of individuals and issues surrounding identity such as defining ethnicity and the role of gender. Archaeology reveals the connections which make us who we are and our dependency on all aspects of our lives.

Archaeologists can be found in all kinds of organisations, carrying out various roles. A key area of work for most archaeologists is heritage management. Being an archaeologist is not just a matter of having a job as an archaeologist. There are many archaeologists working in their spare time as volunteers where archaeology is their hobby. Archaeology studies all periods from human origins and prehistory to post-medieval and industrial periods. Each period has its own characteristics and the archaeology of each period also differs from other archaeologies. Yet all archaeologists have in common a kind of nonconformist attitude and independence of mind, and a sceptical point of view on the present where our current behaviours and fashions are seen as only a temporary phase in the long sequence of human culture.

Understanding what archaeology is, where it is practised and who practises it is only a partial understanding of archaeology. Archaeology is important, has great value and is intimately connected with the management and use of heritage. Archaeology is an active intervention in the uses of the past in the present.

Archaeology as practised in Britain is part of an international discipline with various conventions and charters, and yet is different to how archaeology is practised in many other countries. We not only study the past of our own country. We have a long tradition of working overseas, especially in the Mediterranean and Near East. British archaeologists have often been at the forefront of developing a world archaeology, rather than tying archaeology to the history of one nation. We see our topic as the history of all humanity.

People value the past. It gives them a sense of antiquity and the status that age confers. It provides a sense of continuity and gives us a sense of rootedness. The past provides a sense of unchanging stability at a time of disorienting change. We also feel comforted by knowing our place in the sequence of human existence. The remains of the past have an intrinsic value as objects of beauty or of mystery, or have emotional associations or meanings for our lives. What we do as archaeologists has instrumental value. We help to provide a sense of place and identity. Our insights into the past can help us make choices for the future. Our work can unlock the economic potential of the past in tourism and economic regeneration. Archaeology also has value for the archaeologist. Archaeology is our cultural capital, where our expertise allows us to pose as the expert guardians of the past with an elevated status above the non-archaeologist general public. This means we have ethical responsibilities: to be true to the original lives of past people, to use our authoritative voice responsibly to correct misuses of the past, to encourage debate about how the past is used and engage in dialogue with other people who have an interest in the past. We also have to consider carefully the wishes of any living people whose material culture we study.

The past as a valued set of objects is the heritage of people living today. This heritage is itself the result of various processes which we are only slowly beginning to recognise and deal with as part of archaeology. Objects and sites have to be seen or recognised as 'heritage'. This heritage has to be experienced, understood and then used. It is perpetuated through communicating and handing on to succeeding generations. Archaeology has a role to play in all these processes and we can easily see ourselves in the role of gatekeepers. This is a position of power and we must guard ourselves against the arrogance that often comes with power. We often come into conflict with people who have a different view of the past. Archaeologists also themselves like to argue. There are numerous debates within archaeology and between archaeologists and others. Debate is good. It sharpens our own thoughts and tests our ideas against those of others. It is only human nature, though, that some archaeologists do not like to have their ideas challenged, and debate can become personal, but debate should always be welcome. Disputes within archaeology are due to the imperfect nature of our evidence for the past and the different beliefs that archaeologists have about the past and about human behaviour. Disputes between archaeologists and others are about the role of tangible heritage and who has the right to use and manage it.

The best way to avoid the arrogance that can come from being a gatekeeper is to accept a role as activists, enabling archaeology to play its part in the lives of people today. There are various kinds of active archaeology. A utilitarian activism uses our knowledge of the past for public benefit. Archaeologists should be active in public debate, even in highly political debate about issues such as migration and climate change. A democratic activism enables others to engage with the past on their own terms and develop archaeological skills for themselves. Archaeologists can use archaeology to empower others and give voices to marginalised groups. Dogmatic activism is placing archaeology in the service of ideological agendas. Archaeologists need to be aware of the agendas that seek to use what we do. Methodological activism is using archaeological methods to understand the material culture of the present. Archaeologists have long debated how we do archaeology, but have only recently begun to ask why we do it. An active archaeology is the natural outcome of asking why do archaeology at all.

There are many methods involved in archaeology. We have to recognise and find remains of the past. We have to methodically recover and record those remains. We have to analyse and date our finds. We eventually come up with an interpretation of those remains based on what we think people were doing in the past. The remains have to be stored, cared for and protected. They can then be made available and interpreted to the public. We communicate our understandings of the past, we teach others about archaeology and we involve the public in our activities as much as we can. Finally, we may find the time to publish the results of our work so that what we have done is revealed to others. Archaeology without publication is simply a form of vandalism.

There are many places where you can study archaeology, and many different kinds of archaeology to be studied. To study the subject is to embark on a lifelong love affair. Archaeology will change how you see yourself and the world around you. It will give you an insatiable curiosity about material culture and the past. It will enable you to enjoy a fascinating subject, meet wonderful people and share in an intellectual and physical adventure. Above all archaeolog   y is fun.

Archaeology is nothing less than the study of humanity; the whole history of humanity. It covers every aspect of human behaviour and sees how human life has developed since its origins over 2 million years ago. It is an important subject. This has long been realised and, yet, archaeology lacks self-confidence. Archaeology is highly enjoyable. Because of this, we often fail to take it seriously enough. Because we spend so much of our time studying the past, we often forget that it has things worth saying in the present.

I hope that you have seen in the previous chapters that archaeology is an important subject, as well as being great fun. Study it. Better still, do it. You can help archaeology achieve its rightful place as a subject. You will also be better able to understand yourself and the world you live in!

Resources

There are many organisations that cover archaeology. Some of them are for specialist areas of work or interest. Some cover particular periods in the past, or specific geographical areas. There are literally thousands of local archaeology and heritage societies and groups. Some campaign for the conservation or management of remains or sites. Some organise regular lectures and trips to sites. Some engage in their own fieldwork, including excavation. Information about them may be held in your local library. Good places on the Internet to search for organisations are the TORC and *Current Archaeology* websites.

There are also hundreds of websites dealing with archaeology in the UK and world-wide. The magazine *British Archaeology*, published by the Council for British Archaeology (CBA), has carried reviews of archaeological websites since May/June 2005. Back copies of the magazine can be looked at for free online at the CBA's website.

Key organisations

AQA

Devas Street, Manchester M15 6EX
http://www.aqa.org.uk

The awarding body for AS- and A-level Archaeology. The specification for archaeology, and support for tutors, is available on their website.

Archaeology Scotland

Suite 1a, Stuart House, Station Road, Eskmills, Musselburgh EH21 7PB
http://www.scottisharchaeology.org.uk/

The association for all those interested in archaeology in Scotland. They work to secure the archaeological heritage of Scotland for its people through education, promotion and support, and bring together those for whom archaeology is an interest, an active pastime or a career, support local archaeological action and initiatives, and provide a comprehensive information service to all.

Council for British Archaeology

St Mary's House, 66 Bootham, York YO30 7BZ
http://www.britarch.ac.uk

The UK-wide association for all archaeological organisations and individuals interested in archaeology, acting as the national voice for archaeology to government and the media. The CBA publishes the magazine *British Archaeology* every 2 months. Their website has details of fieldwork opportunities, conferences and courses, as well as advice about practising and studying archaeology. Every year in July, the CBA runs the Festival of British Archaeology with hundreds of public events. The CBA also publishes a range of books on archaeology. The CBA runs an email discussion list, Britarch, which is a useful place to post questions about archaeology.

Institute for Archaeologists

SHES, Whiteknights, University of Reading, PO Box 227, Reading RG6 6AB
http://www.archaeologists.net/about

The association that sets standards for archaeological fieldwork and practices. It is open to both professional and volunteer archaeologists through various grades of membership: student, affiliate, practitioner, associate and member.

Young Archaeologists' Club

St Mary's House, 66 Bootham, York YO30 7BZ
http://www.britarch.ac.uk/yac

The association for young people aged between 8 and 16 interested in archaeology, run by the CBA. There is a national magazine and a network of local branches running monthly activities.

Organisations outside the United Kingdom

The main archaeological organisations for the USA are the Archaeological Institute of America, the Society for American Archaeology and the Society for Historical Archaeology.

Useful websites

Archaeological Box

http://thearchaeologicalbox.com

An international social networking and reference website for archaeology (based in Canada), covering news stories from around the world, details of field projects etc.

Archaeological tools

http://www.archtools.eu/
http://www.pasthorizons.com/shop/

Most tools used by archaeologists can be found in good ironmongers or artists' materials shops. But there are a few companies that specialise in selling tools directly to archaeologists. As a student or new entrant to archaeology you will not be expected to have a wide range of tools as most will be provided by any field project. On the other hand, you should at least have your own trowel, the basic tool for all archaeologists.

Archaeology: an introduction

http://cw.routledge.com/textbooks/greene/

This is the on-line back up for the book by Kevin Greene and Tom Moore, *Archaeology: an introduction*. There are links to various resources that go into more detail about particular topics than was possible in the book.

Archaeology coursebook

http://cw.routledge.com/textbooks/9780415462860/

The on-line support website for the AS- and A-level Archaeology textbook, with a wealth of links to useful websites.

Archnews

http://www.archnews.co.uk

A good site for up-to-date news stories about archaeology from the UK, with links to the rest of the world.

Bad archaeology

http://www.badarchaeology.com

Archaeology has long been prone to hoaxes and mischievous or downright malicious misuse and falsification. This is a good website that explores these issues, debunking many examples.

BAJR (The British Archaeological Jobs Resource)

http://www.bajr.org/

This is so much more than simply a website advertising jobs in archaeology. There are links to a discussion forum, web resources, publications, sellers of tools, courses and volunteering opportunities.

BBC

http://www.bbc.co.uk/history/ancient/archaeology

An interesting website with a variety of articles on selected topics about archaeology, often linked to television programmes broadcast by the BBC. There are also some interactive archaeological 'games'.

Chronicle

http://www.bbc.co.uk/archive/chronicle/

The BBC have made available some programmes from their archive of the television series *Chronicle* which ran from 1966 to 1991, a major and important part of communicating archaeology to the public.

Current Archaeology

http://www.archaeology.co.uk

A website that aims to be more than simply a version of the *Current Archaeology* magazine. There is a wide range of information about archaeology and opportunities to take part in it or study it.

Digital Digging

http://digitaldigging.co.uk

An attractively laid out website that focuses on archaeology in the south west of England, covering sites of major importance, including Stonehenge.

Explorator

http://tech.groups.yahoo.com/group/Explorator/

This is a service for receiving news of latest discoveries and developments in archaeology worldwide delivered to you once a week by email.

Fieldwork opportunities

http://www.britarch.ac.uk/briefing
http://digs.archaeology.co.uk/
http://www.pasthorizons.com/worldprojects

Details of fieldwork available to volunteers can be found through the CBA and *Current Archaeology* websites. Most projects will charge a fee for taking part. Always contact the project for further details of what they are offering. For opportunities abroad, you need to subscribe to *Archaeology Abroad*. See the CBA website for further details.

Heritage Daily

http://www.heritagedaily.com

An international news website for archaeology, that also covers palaeontology (fossils).

Local societies

http://www.torc.org.uk

The TORC website is a directory of archaeological organisations, and is one of the best ways to find details of local societies or archaeological services.

Megalithic Portal

http://www.megalithic.co.uk

The portal is devoted to the documenting and publicising of prehistoric sites in Britain and elsewhere. It can be a good source of images and information about sites.

Past Horizons

http://www.pasthorizonspr.com

An on-line magazine about archaeology, including video sharing as well as written articles, news, opinion and information about field projects for volunteers.

Postgraduate courses

http://www.postgrad.com
http://www.prospects.ac.uk
http://www.ukpass.ac.uk

Finding details of taught postgraduate masters courses can be daunting. These three sites together will cover most of the courses. Be inventive in searching for courses. Don't rely only on the word 'archaeology' to throw up all the relevant courses.

Time Team

http://www.channel4.com/programmes/time-team
http://www.channel4.com/history/microsites/T/timeteam

The *Time Team* television programme has two separate websites. The first is simply about the TV series, the second is more about archaeology.

Undergraduate courses

http://www.ucas.com/students/coursesearch/

The national service for finding and applying for undergraduate degree courses.

Other UK websites

Websites of various archaeological organisations are listed on the CBA webpages at http://www.britarch.ac.uk/archonline. There are some useful sites that enable people to find information about archaeological sites and the historic environment. The Pastscape website of English Heritage (www.pastscape.org.uk) gives access to the 400,000 records in the National Monuments Record. The equivalent database for Scotland is the record of the Royal Commission on the Ancient and Historical Monuments of Scotland, made available through the Canmore website (www.rcahms.gov.uk/canmore.html). Wales has the Coflein website (www. coflein.gov.uk) for the records of its Royal Commission. For Northern Ireland, the equivalent website is Rascal (www.rascal.ac.uk). Local historic environment records are held by local authorities and are available for England through the Heritage Gateway website (www.heritagegateway.org. uk). For Scotland, they can be found through the Pastmap website (www. pastmap.org.uk).

Some websites from other countries

The USA obviously has many websites in English. Here is a selection that might be of interest: http://archaeology.about.com (an encyclopedia of archaeology), http://archaeologica.org (a source of daily news about archaeology) and http://archaeologychannel.org (carries streaming audio-visual media about archaeology). The Archaeology in Europe website, http://archeurope.com, has a blog of the latest archaeological news from the continent and the UK.

Social media

Facebook and Twitter are good places to engage with archaeologists, with a variety of facebook pages and twitter accounts to choose to follow. You should check the authority and status of the pages or people you choose to follow by searching their profiles or for further information about them on the Internet.

A final word

Beware of simply searching for archaeology on Google or another search engine. There are lots of sites dealing with the past. Some are by people who are not trained archaeologists, and may have an alternative perspective on the past that cannot be supported by real evidence. If you are unsure about any website then ask a question on a discussion list such as Britarch or a forum on one of the other websites noted above.

Mobile device apps

Archaeological apps for mobile phones are still quite rare. One fun app is MEanderthal that turns a photograph of you or a friend into a Neanderthal. You can see how you might have looked as a different species! The iMibac Voyager app allows you to take a virtual tour of famous archaeological sites such as the Forum in Rome and if you are there to impose augmented reality over what you see. Similar augmented reality apps have been produced by the Museum of London: Streetmuseum and Streetmuseum Londinium. Streetmuseum allows you to impose old photographs over the street you can see while walking around London. Streetmuseum Londinium brings to life the buildings and scenes of Roman times, and lets you digitally excavate artefacts found at the site.

Selected reading

There are many, many books about archaeology. There are far fewer books written for those who are new to the subject or as general introductions. What follows is a highly selective and personal choice of books which might be useful. Not all are written for the general reader. Some are written for specialist audiences or for practising archaeologists. Nevertheless, those with a deep interest in the subject will find them worth reading, and they cover most of the topics raised in this book.

General guides

Bintliff, J (2004) *A companion to archaeology*, Oxford: Blackwell

Fagan, B (1995) *Time detectives: how archaeologists use archaeology to recapture the past*, New York: Simon & Schuster

Flatman, J (2011) *Becoming an archaeologist: a guide to professional pathways*, Cambridge: Cambridge University Press

Grant, J, S Gorin and N Fleming (2008) (3rd edn), *The archaeology coursebook,* London: Routledge

Greene, K and T Moore (2010) *Archaeology: an introduction* (5th edn), London: Routledge

McIntosh, J (1999) *The practical archaeologist: how we know what we know about the past*, London: Thames & Hudson

Renfrew, C and P Bahn (2008) *Archaeology: theories, methods and practice*, London: Thames & Hudson

Scarre, C (2010) *The human past*, London: Thames & Hudson

Wheeler, Sir M (1954) *Archaeology from the earth*, Harmondsworth: Penguin Books

What is archaeology?

Bahn, P (1996) *Archaeology: a very short introduction*, Oxford: Oxford University Press
— (2004) *The bluffer's guide to archaeology*, London: Oval Books
Courbin, P (1988) *What is archaeology?*, trans. P G Bahn, Chicago, IL: Chicago University Press
Gamble, C (2008) *Archaeology: the basics*, London: Routledge
Gosden, C (1999) *Archaeology and anthropology*, London: Routledge

How did archaeology begin?

Aubrey, J (1980 [1665–93]) *Monumenta Britannica,* Wincanton: Dorset Publishing Company
Bahn, P G (1999) *The Cambridge illustrated history of archaeology*, Cambridge: Cambridge University Press
Fagan, B M (2005) *A brief history of archaeology*, Upper Saddle River, NJ: Pearson Prentice Hall
Kennedy, M (2002) *The history of archaeology*, New York: Barnes & Noble
Schnapp, A (1996) *The discovery of the past*, trans. I Kinnes and G Varndell, London: British Museum Press
Stiebing, W H (1994) *Uncovering the past: a history of archaeology*, Oxford: Oxford University Press
Trigger, B G (2006) *A history of archaeological thought*, Cambridge: Cambridge University Press

Understanding time

Childe, V G (1942) *What happened in history*, Harmondsworth: Penguin Books
— (1957 [1925]) *The dawn of European civilisation*, London: Routledge & Kegan Paul
Diamond, J (1997) *Guns, germs and steel*, London: Random House
Lucas, G (2005) *The archaeology of time*, London: Routledge
Murray, T (1999) *Time and archaeology*, London: Routledge
Rius, T E (1990) *Marx for beginners*, New York: Pantheon Books
Service, E R (1962) *Primitive social organisation*, New York: Random House
Singer, P (1990) *Marx: a very short introduction*, Oxford: Oxford University Press

Understanding place

Aston, M (1985) *Interpreting the landscape*, London: Routledge
Butzer, K W (1982) *Archaeology as human ecology*, Cambridge: Cambridge University Press

Clark, G (1952) *Prehistoric Europe: the economic basis*, London: Methuen & Co. Ltd

Clarke, D L (1977) *Spatial archaeology*, London: Academic Press

Evans, J G (2003) *Environmental archaeology and the social order*, London: Routledge

Goldberg, P and R I Macphail (2006) *Practical and theoretical geoarchaeology*, Oxford: Blackwell

Hoskins, W G (1955) *The making of the English landscape*, London: Hodder & Stoughton

Rapp, G R and C L Hill (2006) *Geoarchaeology*, New Haven, CT: Yale University Press

Understanding people

Binford, L and S Binford (eds) (1968) *New perspectives in archaeology*, Chicago, IL: Aldine Publishing

Clarke, D L (1968) *Analytical archaeology*, London: Methuen

Diaz-Andreu, M, S Lucy, S Babić and D N Edwards (2005) *The archaeology of identity*, London: Routledge

Fowler, C (2004) *The archaeology of personhood*, London: Routledge

Gilchrist, R (1999) *Gender and archaeology: contesting the past*, London: Routledge

Hodder, I (1986) *Reading the past*, Cambridge: Cambridge University Press

Johnson, M (2010) *Archaeological theory: an introduction*, Chichester: Wiley-Blackwell

Jones, S (1997) *The archaeology of ethnicity*, London: Routledge

Sahlins, M D (1972) *Stone age economics*, Chicago, IL: Aldine-Atherton

Smith, A D (1986) *The ethnic origins of nations*, Oxford: Blackwell

Wheeler, M (1954) *Archaeology from the earth*, Harmondsworth: Penguin Books

Where archaeologists work

Aitchison, K and R Edwards (2008) *Archaeology labour market intelligence*, Reading: Institute of Field Archaeologists

Flatman, J (2011) *Becoming an archaeologist: a guide to professional pathways*, Cambridge: Cambridge University Press

Hudson, K (1981) *A social history of archaeology*, Basingstoke: Palgrave Macmillan

Hunter, J and I Ralston (2006) *Archaeological resource management in the UK*, Stroud: Alan Sutton

Schofield, J, J Carman and P Belford (2011) *Archaeological practice in Great Britain: a heritage handbook*, New York: Springer

Swain, H (2007) *An introduction to museum archaeology*, Cambridge: Cambridge University Press

Thomas, S and P G Stone (2009) *Metal detecting and archaeology*, Woodbridge: Boydell Press

Wass, S (1992) *The amateur archaeologist*, London: Batsford

Which pasts do we study?

Alcock, S E and R Osborne (2007) *Classical archaeology*, Oxford: Blackwell

Andren, A (1998) *Between artifacts and texts: historical archaeology in global perspective*, New York: Springer

Crossley, D W (1990) *Post-medieval archaeology in Britain*, Leicester: Leicester University Press

Gerrard, C (2003) *Medieval archaeology*, London: Routledge

Gosden, C (2003) *Prehistory: a very short introduction*, Oxford: Oxford University Press

Hunter, J and I Ralston (1999) *The archaeology of Britain: an introduction from the palaeolithic to the industrial revolution*, London: Routledge

Orser, C E (2004) *Historical archaeology*, Upper Saddle River, NJ: Pearson Prentice Hall

Palmer, M and P Neaverson (1998) *Industrial archaeology: principles and practice*, London: Routledge

Renfrew, C (2009) *Prehistory: the making of the human mind*, New York: Random House

Wood, B A (2005) *Human evolution: a very short introduction*, Oxford: Oxford University Press

World archaeology

Cleere, H (2000) *Archaeological heritage management in the modern world*, London: Routledge

Council of Europe (2005) 'Framework Convention on the Value of Cultural Heritage for Society', available at http://conventions.coe.int/Treaty/EN/Treaties/Html/199.htm (accessed 27 February 2012)

Cunliffe, B, W Davies and C Renfrew (2002) *Archaeology: the widening debate*, Oxford: Oxford University Press

Layton, R, S Shennan and P Stone (2006) *A future for archaeology*, London: UCL Press

Nicholas, G (2010) *Being and becoming indigenous archaeologists*, Walnut Creek, CA: Left Coast Press

Pickard, R (2002) *European cultural heritage: a review of policies and practice*, Strasbourg: Council of Europe

UNESCO (2009) *World heritage sites*, Richmond Hill, Ontario: Firefly Books

Archaeology's value

Darvill, T (1993) *Valuing Britain's archaeological resource*, Bournemouth: Bournemouth University Press

Evans, J (1975) *Archaeology as education and profession: an inaugural lecture*, London: Institute of Archaeology

Fowler, P J (1992) *The past in contemporary society*, London: Routledge

Lowenthal, D (1985) *The past is a foreign country*, Cambridge: Cambridge University Press

Mathers, C, T Darvill and B J Little (2005) *Heritage of value, archaeology of renown*, Gainesville, FL: Florida University Press

Pluciennik, M (2001) *The responsibilities of archaeologists: archaeology and ethics*, British Archaeological Reports International Series 981, Oxford: Archaeopress

Priestley, J (1803) 'Lectures on history and general policy', in J T Rutt (ed.) (1817–31) *The Theological and Miscellaneous Works of Joseph Priestley*, Vol. 23, London

Scarre, C and G Scarre (2006) *The ethics of archaeology*, Cambridge: Cambridge University Press

Vitelli, K D and C Colwell-Chanthaphonh (2006) *Archaeological ethics*, Lanham, MD: AltaMira Press

Archaeology as part of heritage

Carman, J (2002) *Archaeology and heritage: an introduction*, London: Continuum

Fairclough, G, R Harrison, J H Jameson and J Schofield (2008) *The heritage reader*, London: Routledge

Harrison, R (2010) *Understanding the politics of heritage*, Manchester: Manchester University Press

Howard, P (2003) *Heritage: management, interpretation, identity*, New York: Continuum

McKercher, B and H du Cros (2002) *Cultural tourism*, New York: Haworth Hospitality Press

Skeates, R (2000) *Debating the archaeological heritage*, London: Duckworth

Smith, L (2004) *Archaeological theory and the politics of cultural heritage*, London: Routledge

Stig Sørenson, M L Carman and J Carman (2009) *Heritage studies: methods and approaches*, London: Routledge

Some key debates in archaeology

Bacon, F (1905 [1620]) *Novum organum*, trans. R Ellis and J Spedding, London: George Routledge

Binford, L (1962) 'Archaeology as anthropology', *American Antiquity* 28: 217–25

— (2009) *Debating archaeology*, Walnut Creek, CA: Left Coast Press

Bintliff, J and M Pearce (2011) *The death of archaeological theory?*, Oxford: Oxbow Books

Bradley, B and D Stanford (2004) 'The North Atlantic ice-edge corridor: a possible Palaeolithic route to the New World', *World Archaeology* 36(4): 459–78

Chippindale, C (1993) 'Ambition, deference, discrepancy, consumption: the intellectual background to a post-processual archaeology', in N Yoffee and A Sherratt, *Archaeological theory: who sets the agenda?*, Cambridge: Cambridge University Press

Evans, R (1997) *In defence of history*, London: Granta Books

Fagan, B M (2004) *People of the earth: an introduction to world prehistory*, Upper Saddle River, NJ: Pearson Prentice Hall

Fagan, G G (2006) *Archaeological fantasies*, London: Routledge

Harrold, F B and R A Eve (1995) *Cult archaeology and creationism*, Iowa City, IA: University of Iowa Press

Hodder, I (1982a) *Symbols in action*, Cambridge: Cambridge University Press

— (1982b) *The present past*, London: Batsford

Killion, T W (2008) *Opening archaeology: repatriation's impact of contemporary research and practice*, Santa Fe, NM: School for Advanced Research Press

Kohl, P L and C Fawcett (1995) *Nationalism, politics, and the practice of archaeology*, Cambridge: Cambridge University Press

Lohman, J and K Goodnow (2006) *Human remains and museum practice*, London: Museum of London

Lucassen, J, L Lucassen and P Manning (2010) *Migration history in world history*, Leiden: Brill

Mallory, J P (1989) *In search of the Indo-Europeans: language, archaeology and myth*, London: Thames & Hudson

Merryman, J H (2009) *Thinking about the Elgin marbles*, Alphen aan den Rijn: Kluwer Law International

Neves, W A, M Hubbe, M Mercedes, M Okumura, R Gonzalez-Jose, L Figuti, S Eggers and P A Dantas De Blasis (2005) 'A new early Holocene human skeleton from Brazil: implications for the settlement of the New World', *Journal of Human Evolution* 48: 403–14

Richards, J D (2002) *Blood of the Vikings*, London: Hodder & Stoughton

Shanks, M and C Tilley (1987) *Social theory and archaeology*, Cambridge: Polity Press

Urbach, P and J Gibson (1994) *Francis Bacon: Novum Organum with other parts of the great instauration*, Chicago, IL: Open Court

Activist archaeology

Little, B J (2002) *Public benefits of archaeology*, Gainesville, FL: Florida University Press

— and P A Shackel (2007) *Archaeology as a tool of civic engagement*, Lanham, MD: AltaMira Press

McGuire, R H (2008) *Archaeology as political action*, Los Angeles, CA: University of California Press

Merriman, N (2004) *Public archaeology*, London: Routledge

Sabloff, J A (2008) *Archaeology matters: action archaeology in the modern world*, Walnut Creek, CA: Left Coast Press

Stottman, M J (2010) *Archaeologists as activists*, Tuscaloosa, AL: Alabama University Press

How to do archaeology

Balme, J and A Paterson (2006) *Archaeology in practice: a student guide to archaeological analyses*, Oxford: Blackwell

Beavis, J and A Hunt (1999) *Communicating archaeology*, Oxford: Oxbow Books

Bender, S J and G S Smith (2000) *Teaching archaeology in the twenty-first century*, Washington, DC: Society for American Archaeology

Burke, H and C Smith (2007) *Archaeology to delight and instruct*, Walnut Creek, CA: Left Coast Press

Catsambis, A, B Ford and D L Hamilton (2011) *The Oxford handbook of maritime archaeology*, Oxford: Oxford University Press

Collis, J (2001) *Digging up the past: an introduction to archaeological excavation*, Stroud: Sutton Publishing

Connah, G (2010) *Writing about archaeology*, Cambridge: Cambridge University Press

Drewett, P L (1999) *Field archaeology: an introduction*, London: UCL Press

Fagan, B (2006) *Writing archaeology: telling stories about the past*, Walnut Creek, CA: Left Coast Press

Hems, A and M Blockley (2006) *Heritage interpretation*, London: Routledge

Henson, D, P G Stone and M Corbishley (2004) *Education and the historic environment*, London: Routledge

Hodder, I and S Hutson (2003) *Reading the past: current approaches to interpretation in archaeology*, Cambridge: Cambridge University Press

Howard, P (2007) *Archaeological surveying and mapping*, London: Routledge

Hunter, J and M Cox (2005) *Forensic archaeology*, London: Routledge

Hurcombe, L (2007) *Archaeological artefacts as material culture*, London: Routledge

Jameson, J H (1997) *Presenting archaeology to the public*, Walnut Creek, CA: AltaMira Press

— (2004) *The reconstructed past*, Walnut Creek, CA: AltaMira Press

Maschner, H D G and C Chippindale (2005) *Handbook of archaeological methods*, Lanham, MD: AltaMira Press

May, E and M Jones (2006) *Conservation science: heritage materials*, London: Royal Society of Chemistry

Oswin, J (2009) *A field guide to geophysics in archaeology*, New York: Springer

Pearson, V (2001) *Teaching the past: a practical guide for archaeologists*, York: Council for British Archaeology

Riley, D N and R Bewley (1996) *Aerial archaeology in Britain*, Princes Risborough: Shire Books

Rodgers, B A (2004) *The archaeologist's manual for conservation*, New York: Springer

Ruppé, C V and J F Barstad (2002) *International handbook of underwater archaeology*, New York: Kluwer

Schiffer, M B (1976) *Behavioral archaeology*, New York: Academic Press

Stone, P G and R MacKenzie (1990) *The excluded past: archaeology in education*, London: Unwin Hyman

Stone, P G and B L Molyneaux (1994) *The presented past: heritage, museums and education*, London: Routledge

Tilden, F (1957) *Interpreting our heritage*, Chapel Hill, NC: University of North Carolina Press

Uzzell, D L (1993) *Heritage interpretation: the natural and built environment*, Chichester: John Wiley & Sons

Studying archaeology

Clack, T and M Brittain (2007) *Archaeology and the media*, Walnut Creek, CA: Left Coast Press

Curtis, E and N Curtis (eds) (1996) *Touching the past: archaeology 5–14*, Dalkeith: Scottish Children's Press

Grant, J, S Gorin and N Fleming (2008) *The archaeology coursebook*, London: Routledge

Henson, D (1997) *Archaeology in the English national curriculum*, York: Council for British Archaeology

Howell, R (ed.) (1994) *Archaeology and the national curriculum in Wales*, National Museums and Galleries of Wales

Petrie, W M F (1904) *Methods and aims in archaeology*, London: Macmillan

Rainbird, P and Y Hamilakis (eds) (2001) *Interrogating pedagogies: archaeology in higher education*, BAR International Series 948, Oxford: Archaeopress

Index